The '45

to gather an image whole

edited by

LESLEY SCOTT-MONCRIEFF

1988

 THE MERCAT PRESS

EDINBURGH

JAMES THIN
The Mercat Press
53–59 South Bridge

Edinburgh

First published 1988

© As on Contents list

Design, typography, lay-outs and Jacket
by T. L. Jenkins, Edinburgh

ISBN 0901824 87 9

Printed in Great Britain by Billing & Sons Ltd., Worcester

CONTENTS

PHOTOGRAPHIC PLATES

These plates will be found between pages 104 and 105.

FOR PETER

ACKNOWLEDGEMENTS

I WISH TO THANK Dr John Lorne Campbell and his wife Dr Margaret Faye Shaw, also Dr Rosalind Marshall and Dr Donald Meek, for their assistance and encouragement.

The Scottish National Portrait Gallery gave permission to reproduce portraits of James VIII, Prince Charles and Lord Loudoun: His Grace the Duke of Atholl allowed the reproduction of portraits of Lord George Murray and President Forbes: the Royal Commission on the Ancient and Historic Monuments of Scotland provided the engraving of Dundee and the British Museum gave permission to use the MacIan print of Cluny MacPherson. It is a pity D.C. Thomson & Company could not have afforded us a glimpse of Wild Young Dirky.

For their longanimity I am grateful to my husband and members of my family.

Above all I am indebted to the men and women who have contributed to this Symposium in the midst of all other claims made upon them. *Mor an tainge.*

LESLEY SCOTT-MONCRIEFF

INTRODUCTION

THE RISING OF 1745 was enacted in almost all corners of Scotland and affected most families. Somehow this ubiquity has travelled through time as well, and after two hundred and forty years many of the questions raised by the campaign are still with us. The fourteen essays in this book go some way to exploring why this should be so.

Perhaps more than elsewhere people in the Highlands do still appreciate that sense in which, as Sorley MacLean says: 'Once a thing has been it always is.'

My own interest was woken as a child by our neighbour Hugh MacKinnon, crofter and bard in Eigg, whose oral memory went back for nine generations in Eigg and included of course the awful descent and predations made upon Canna and Eigg in 1745 and 1746 by Captain Ferguson and crew from the ship *Dreadnought*: thirty-eight of the men from Eigg were tricked and shipped for transportation, though twenty-two seem to have died in the hulks at Tilbury.

In later years Nan Fraser, teacher at Inverinate, who was a MacKenzie from Achiltibuie, and Duncan her husband, a stone-mason from Glen Urquhart, also inspired me with their traditional memories from those parts. These people are now alas no longer with us.

Of course socially, culturally and geo-physically, in the Highlands the '45 is inescapable, from the ruined houses and empty glens, relics of the Clearances, to land-ownership by ever-richer and less-comprehending land-lords, with all the difficulties and frustrations that imposes. The ubiquitous occupying armies of Sitka spruces, the Crofting Act, the teaching of Gaelic in schools, the question of a Scottish Assembly, or of Land Use in the Highlands, these daily disputations are still the unsolved legacy of an 18th-century battle and its aftermath.

More deliberately, and impressively, since the last war books on the '45 campaign by such scholars as John Lorne Campbell, Evelyn Cruikshanks, John S. Gibson, Ian Grimble, Bruce Lenman, F.J. MacLynn, Alasdair Maclean, Duncan MacNeill, Annette Smith, Katherine Tomasson, Colin Youngson and others have appeared, including that remarkable book *The Christian Watt Papers*; erudite and fascinating works which have greatly unravelled the story and enlightened the scene. (How much of this percolates through to the school class-room is another matter).

Scotland and England during the first half of the 18th century had gradually found themselves at the mercy of a powerful, over-centralised, autocratic and corrupt government. At the same time their resources of manpower and money were being drained to a vast extent by a seemingly endless series of bloody continental wars, of primary interest to the House of Hanover.

So if questions about the '45 are fraught for us today, consider part of a letter written by Lord George Murray in September 1745 to his Whig brother Duke James, on his own decision to fight for the Prince.

> 'I never did say to any person in Life that I would not ingage in the cause I always in my heart thought just & right, as well as for the Interest, good & Liberty of my country.
>
> My Life, my Fortune, my expectations, the Happyness of my wife & children are all at stake (& the chances are against me), & yet a principle of (what seems to me) Honour, & my Duty to King & Country, outweighs evry thing.
>
> If I er, it is only with respect to you. I ow obligations to no body else (I mean the Court of London) & if you find you cannot forgive me, yet sure you will pitty me.

Think what a weght there is upon my spirets, . . .

I will not venture to recommend my wife & my children to your protection. All that I shall say on that head is, that a man of worth never repented of doing good natur'd offices. After what I have said, you may believe that I have weighted what I am going about with all the deliberation I am capable off, & suppose I were sure of dieing in the atempt, it would neither deter nor prevent me.

. . . I forgot to tell you that I never spoke or interfeared with any of the Atholl Men, but now they are up (as I hear) you will excuse my doing my best, both with them & others.'

Even today no-one, John Simpson maintains, can write about the Rising of 1745 dispassionately. Yet he manages with a light but caring touch to out-line many of the causes and amusingly compare, demolish, or uphold some of the assumptions of his fellow-labourers in the historical vineyard: finally laying an accolade at the feet of the Gaelic poet Alasdair MacMaighster Alasdair.

Lord Hugh Douglas-Hamilton, archivist and himself a kinsman to Lord George Murray, gives an exposition of the relationship between the Scots and the Stewart monarchy prior to the Union of the Crowns. He extends the same large charity to the Prince as Lord George once showed in his writings during the years of exile, but brings a modern insight on Charles's later predicament.

Cross-fire is provided by the Reverend G.V.R. Grant, maintaining that the rising of 1745 was a 'rash, feckless, foolhardy enterprise.' The reasons given for his view are far from those of conventional Whigs or their spiritual successors. His perspicacity has been gleaned in a long life as a Highland parish minister and as an active member of the Kirk and Nation Committee of the Church of Scotland. He also traces the persecution of the Episcopal Church as a result of the rising.

Donald Fraser, the Gameliel of Strontian, writes from that peninsula where he labours in the vineyard of teaching Gaelic to the young. He is in a position to feel most keenly that Culloden was a watershed from which the Highlands may never have recovered. But his concern here is with the Highlanders before the rising, a people acutely aware of the European, Irish, and British political situations. He quotes among other sources the Fernaig manuscript, most of which is unknown in English.

It is fashionable today to paint Prince Charles as the enemy of the people who sacrificed all to his personal ambition. But William Gillies's paper on the Gaelic songs of the '45 shows that if ever anyone was 'willed' over the water it was Prince Charles. Professor Gillies deals particularly with the work of the bards and shennachies who composed so much to rouse people to the cause and then to contain their trauma after Culloden; also the more direct marches and laments of the *vox populi*.

Although the Irish contribution to the rising included brave exploits in Sutherland and the heroic rearguard action fought by the Irish Picquets at Culloden to protect the retreating Highlanders, Owen Dudley Edwards has had the temerity to deal with less competent souls: namely George Kelly, Sir Thomas Sheridan, Captain O'Sullivan, and John MacDonnell. In doing this he reveals a scene in Ireland which was to be slowly, though with major deviations, transferred to the Highlands. At that time a rising to restore the Stuarts seemed to the Irish a chance to alleviate the religious and political persecution in their own country. It was indeed a desolate field from which the 'wild geese' had flown, and to which they could in no way return.

We turn to the Lowlands and the Continental scene with Alice Wemyss's vivid account of the part taken by her kinsman Lord Elcho in the Rising. Here we have all the complexities in human terms of parents, brothers, and friends ranged on different sides, and of Elcho's own friendship and indignation with the Prince. Elcho was the only Wemyss to join Charles, raising for him the famous Elcho Lifeguards. One Gordon brother-in-law joined Cumberland though somewhat slowly, whilst another was busy raising the Gordons for the Prince.

Nor surprisingly, in a country where almost everybody is either acquent or related, if not consanguiniously then at least co-laterally, *Houses Divided* is an ever-recurring phenomenon in the Jacobite story. Ian Grimble explores this in the cases of two great families, the MacLeods of the North West and the Forbeses in the North-East. Of the Forbes family Dr Grimble notes that in their devotion to almost every shade of belief they repeatedly risked losing everything. Included in his account is that patriotic/politick Whig, President Forbes, to whom perhaps more than to any one man the Havoverians owed their success, and who was a cousin of the unrepentantly Jacobite 4th Lord Pitsligo.

One wonders over Forbes's dying comment to his nephew in 1747: 'Were I to live longer Willie, I could but mourn with you over my country.' What were his regrets, and on what account? Or was he no more repentant than was the beloved Pitsligo?

Ten thousand Dundonians on the other hand kept a remarkably low profile during 1745 and '46. In her erudite and amusing contribution Annette Smith points out that, Dundee being ostensibly a Lowland town but situated on the Highland border and the approach to the Jacobite North-East, the discretion of the Town Councillors was 'excusable, if extreme.' She describes how most of the doucer citizens eschewed heroism and got on with the nitty gritty of life.

The Highlands were divided as well. Alasdair Maclean has here traced for the first time the marches of the Independent Companies of Militia raised for the Hanoverians, particularly Loudon's and MacLeod's. This saga, so much in keeping with Scotland's story, has been largely gleaned by Dr MacLean from unpublished sources. From the government's point of view Loudon seems to have been wonderfully inept as a general, and his reputation as such has sunk in oblivion.

Yet is is only fair to quote the Jacobite John Cameron, Presbyterian Chaplain at Fort William, on how Loudon conducted himself and his men in the aftermath in contrast to many of the other commanders. In Lochaber 'he met with no opposition, received a great number of arms, and gave protections. . . . The Earl, though as an officer he with exactness discharged his duty, yet behaved with great humanity to the unfortunate.'

This account of course comes in *The Lyon in Mourning*, those extra-ordinary volumes of memorabilia of the '45 collected by Bishop Robert Forbes. John S. Gibson traces the story of their discovery, the pursuit of evidence and the emergence even today of documentary sources on 1745. In *The Summer's Hunting* he shows how the 'too familiar tale . . . becomes something much more subtle, truer to the heights and depths of human nature; something much more highland.' The tale also raises an eternal question.

Though much of Bishop Forbes's collection is related to the Prince's Highland adventure, it also contains stark tragedy in the accounts of the atrocities after Culloden.

In the last volume can be found an extremely apprehensive letter to the Dutch Ambassador in England from the Marquis d'Argenson, French Minister of State for Foreign Affairs, dated May 26th, 1746. It is evident that he considers the revenge being carried out after Culloden 'against persons of every age and sex' to be very ominous indeed, and fears that this sort of 'animosity and fury' may spread to the Continental wars.

> 'It is easy to foresee . . . the fatal consequence of such rigour; and how many innocent persons may perhaps on one side or other during the present war fall victims to that violence which must necessarily irritate and increase the evil, and certainly will not be edifying in Europe.'

Perhaps Europe had to wait until the Spanish Civil War, and in the Second World War the behaviour of some of the German S.S. Units, as at Ocadour sur Glanes, and of the Japanese Army, to find parallel atrocities.

Neil Usher, for many years a working hill farmer, is now in his eighties. Long acquaintance with high hills and lonely places and the men and women of Badenoch and Lochaber, among whom history was still a collective possession, have fitted him to write an account of the Parish of Laggan since 1745. It is both extremely funny and very sad and adds an essential dimension to this Symposium.

But is our concern not better spent on the present and the future? Should we consider past wrongs at all? Why should we still stand on windy doorsteps discussing the decision taken at Derby or indeed, at Invergarry? Is the pursuit of new evidence and understanding of the '45 still a valid chase?

In the final chapter Christopher Small grasps the moral nettles such questions raise. We talk of our responsibility to the future, 'and it is obviously true that, since we are in a position to abort any future, we had better act responsibly'. But he insists that our first responsibility is to the past, for unless we acknowledge what is valuable in the past we can assign no value to the future. In this spirit he explores the position of the defeated of the '45.

We are left, as he shows, not with a romance but a debt and an obligation.

LESLEY SCOTT-MONCRIEFF

Newmains,
Stenton,
East Lothian.

1

THE CAUSES
OF THE '45
by
John Simpson

John Simpson was educated at Daniel Stewart's College in
Edinburgh, and at the University of St Andrews. His awareness
of Scottish history owes much to outstanding teachers in both
places — John Thompson and Ronald Cant. He is a senior
lecturer in Scottish history at the University of Edinburgh,
where he has taught since 1964. He also teaches a course in
Scandinavian history. He is the author of numerous articles in
historical journals, and of the article 'United Kingdom:
Scotland: History' in the 1985 printing of the *Encyclopaedia
Britannica*. He is married, with three children, who like him
take pride in the continuity of Scottish history.

SIXTY ODD YEARS may seem a long time in politics, yet everything is relative. In the summer of 1745, Charles Edward Stewart began
what was to prove the final military attempt to restore his family to the
British thrones. His grandfather, James VII of Scots and II of England, had
been forced out of Britain in the winter of 1689. We are in danger, with the
excessive use of hindsight, of supposing that the Stewarts should, in the
interim, have adjusted gracefully to exile as a permanent state. The world of
the 1980s, after all, contains quite a few deposed and deported rulers.

But most people in Charles Edward's world subscribed to the idea of
hereditary and indefeasible kingship. James VII and II, while heir presump-
tive to his brother Charles II, had represented Charles as his commissioner to

the Scots Parliament. That Parliament was dominated by the Scottish landowners, and they took particular satisfaction in James's appearance in their midst. It represented the bond between king and land, a bond that Covenants and Cromwell had failed to break, and a bond regarded as immemorial. Thus, in February 1680, the Scots Privy Council wrote to Charles II:

> 'The remembrance of having been under the protection of your Royal Family above two thousand years . . . of having received from their bounty the lands wee possess; Hath been very much refresh'd and renew'd by having your Royall Brother among us. . . '

Quite soon thereafter, most of the landowners of Scotland and of England were to adjust themselves to a rather different state of affairs though how readily and completely they adjusted themselves, even by 1745, is something that we shall have to consider below. That the Stewarts could adjust is, I believe, not to be expected. Even if we were to conclude that the '45 was a rash or forlorn adventure, it was for Charles Edward a necessary one, the reclaiming for his family of what was rightfully theirs. In March 1744, at the start of his initiative, he wrote to his father James Edward:

> '. . . the little difficulties and small dangers I may have run are nothing when for the service and glory of a Father which is so tender and kind for me . . . '

He may have protested too much, but these were not the affairs of a *private* family that he was discussing. He was an actor on a very public stage. The continuing claims of the royal house of Stewart are the obvious first cause of the '45 and not to be left unstated merely because they are so obvious.

Detailed consideration of international politics in 1745 is beyond the scope of this essay. But it should be emphasised how much France had to gain and how much Britain, at least in the short term, to lose by a Stewart restoration in the mid-1740s. The War of the Austrian Succession began in 1740. It has been seen as a series of overlapping struggles between Austria and Prussia for Silesia, the Sardinian bid for expansion in northern Italy, a maritime contest between Britain and Spain, an almost world-wide contest between Britain and France. It is impossible, in judging the relative importance of these struggles, to avoid hindsight. J.H. Plumb has written of the conviction of the elder Pitt, and of 'the hard-headed practical men who supported him', 'that France was the greatest danger England had to face, and the only rival worth considering in the race for overseas trade . . . ' Pitt was right; and ironically it was the '45 that helped put him in a position to implement his beliefs in the form of government policy.

The French, too, came to realise the importance of the war, and of taking the war to the enemy. The French invasion fleet of early 1744, carrying the troops of Marshal de Saxe, had, though it was dispersed by a 'Protestant wind', represented a serious threat. William Ferguson comments:

'So far, there was little fantasy in the project ... Whether or not the Stewarts were restored, French purposes would have been served by the probability of an ensuing financial crisis in London, especially if this deprived Britain's subsidised allies of money.'

The French government believed in hereditary, indefeasible kingship. They perhaps never seriously contemplated attempting a Stewart restoration for that reason alone, but often their own compelling self-interest reinforced that argument. This was the case in 1744, and remained the case during much of the '45. As Frank McLynn has reminded us, the Duc de Richelieu had a force at Boulogne at the end of December 1745. It may have been there a month too late, and aimed wrongly at England not Scotland when it was there, but the British government at the time did not have the luxury of relishing these miscalculations at leisure.

McLynn further argues that Charles Edward knew that, following the débâcle of 1744, he had to launch a rising in Britain before the French, 'the key to Jacobite success or failure', would be prepared to move. My personal opinion coincides with McLynn's that the '45 was far from being the work of a 'rash adventurer' or Polish blockhead; though on this large question I am reluctant to be dogmatic.

McLynn also points to the problem of divided counsels in France:

' "France" or "the French", denoting a monolithic organisation of decision-making simply did not exist during the Jacobite rising. This fact alone makes it impossible to speak of French "treachery", "duplicity" or "insincerity" ...'

And he sums up the question of French involvement, or relative lack thereof, as follows:

'Had Richelieu landed on the south coast of England in time to co-ordinate with Charles Edward Stuart, the second front thus established would, beyond reasonable doubt, have very swiftly settled the dynastic struggle in favour of the Stuarts. The history of France and the '45 is the story of a great opportunity thrown away by French indecisiveness.'

This goes rather beyond my theme of the causes of the '45, and brings in rather too many military imponderables, for me willingly to suspend all reasonable doubt. But McLynn is surely right to stress the importance of France for the '45. To us, the rule of French assistance may appear to have been jam tomorrow and jam yesterday but never jam today. It didn't look like that at the time.

What of potential Jacobite support in Britain for the '45? Here the Stewarts may have been guilty of wishful thinking, the almost inevitable result of the unreal atmosphere in which these exiles had waited and hoped for so long. In some parts of England and Wales, and of Lowland Scotland, the Stewarts still had their admirers among the landed classes, the men of property who, in terms of the established ideology of the time, were alone fit to rule. And this admiration was not the mere sentimental attachment that many later had to the Stewarts after their cause was finally lost and abandoned. But I judge these admirers to have been too few to pose by themselves any real threat to George II. And the penalties of unsuccessful rebellion made their caution in the event readily comprehensible. Such Jacobites were not cowards; and yet they were capable of writing to James Edward:

> 'The sentiments and inclinations of Sir Watkin (William
> Wynn), Lord Barrymore, and their friends, are known to all,
> they intend they should and even use means to manifest
> them; but they, with great reason, make a vast distinction
> between the owning of their principles, and being engaged in
> any direct or indirect correspondence with Your Majesty and
> the French Court, with an actual design of overturning the
> present government . . . a correspondence of the nature I
> have mentioned, is an overt act of treason according to the
> present laws, the least suspicion of which would bring certain
> ruin upon them . . .'

To have placed reliance upon such honourable but scant and cautious support, and without calculating the possibilities of support from south of the Channel, and from north of the Scottish Highland line, would indeed have been the action of a rash adventurer. I am sure the decision to raise the rebellion was posited on the larger calculations.

People of property may have considered that they alone constituted the 'political nation'. We are entitled nevertheless to consider the evidence for the political opinions of the population of this island as a whole. Leaving aside the Highlands for separate consideration, it can be said that the post-1714 government of Britain does not seem to have been universally popular. Douglas Hay characterises eighteenth-century England as 'a society with a bloody penal code, an astute ruling class who manipulated it to their advantage, and a people schooled in the lessons of Justice, Terror and Mercy.' But no people in history so far has been schooled with total success, and the lesson that at least some eighteenth-century people learned was that of resentment. Their 'betters' feared them accordingly:

> 'The lowest class of the English are very brutish and
> barbarous, much of the nature of their bull-dogs . . .'

But no government in history so far − or in British history at any rate − has been universally popular, and effective expression of resentment and of extra-parliamentary opposition was, and remains, a major problem. Rightly, recent historians have become more interested in the evidence for the opinions of ordinary eighteenth-century people. They have responded, without always realising that they are doing so, to a plea made by Sir Lewis

Namier in 1928 for more research on 'the biography of ordinary men.' But sadly, such evidence remains especially resistant to agreed interpretation. There is a current feeling that disenchantment with Hanoverian rule was at least potentially translatable into positive support for the Stewarts. Maybe so, but I beg to remain sceptical. I would not wish to deny that, as Nicholas Rogers argues, plebeian Jacobitism could constitute a familiar idiom of defiance. But one cannot prove what one cannot first measure. And here Eveline Cruickshanks says what needs to be said:

> '...English response to the rebellion has hardly been touched upon. Obviously, the amount of sympathy there was in England cannot be known, how can one quantify views which cannot be expressed?'

She observes also (and I quote without comment) that 'recent work purporting to show that Jacobites in London consisted mainly of Irish Roman Catholics would seem to illustrate rather the usual behaviour of Irishmen in public houses.'

MacLynn's 1985 survey of *The Jacobites* is similarly guarded, similarly alive to the complexities of the evidence in the following passage:

> 'The occupational groups that appeared so significantly in Charles Edward's army – artisans, shopkeepers, farmers, and labourers – were being rapidly weaned away from Jacobitism to the new creed of Methodism; John Wesley, the sect's founder, was rapidly (*sic*) opposed to the Jacobites. The non-clan regiments ... contained a strong component of weavers, shoemakers and drapers, exactly the same kind of skilled men who by the 1760s were following the banner of "Wilkes and Liberty". The irony here is that the anti-Scottish and anti-Catholic sentiments of the Wilkesites were sometimes cited as evidence that the English mob could never have held Jacobite sympathies. The truth is rather that in an era of aristocratic politics the urban masses would follow whichever deviant political dispensation seemed to pose most of a challenge to their "betters". '

In attempting, then, to conclude this part of my argument, I take my stand on the commendably bold assertion by Roy Porter:

> 'Yet the political fabric – much abused, pulled, torn, tattered, and patched – was never ripped up. If the socio-political nation really had been verging on anarchy or revolution, the Jacobite rebellions of 1715 and 1745, or the Gordon Riots, would have sparked explosion. But crypto-Jacobite sympathies – though widespread – did not lead to people taking up arms in England ...'

Porter proceeds to a sophisticated and convincing explanation of why this was so. Bruce Lenman travels much the same road by means of a brief and back-handed encomium on Sir Robert Walpole and his legacy. Neither Jacobites nor Protestant nonconformist groups, Lenman suggests:

> 'could seriously shake a system which both appealed to the baser instincts of the political classes, and displayed a remarkable sense of its own limitations. In politicians who have reached the heights of power cynicism usually goes hand in hand with a burgeoning conceit which can easily lead on to megalomania and hubris. Not so in Walpole. He was cynical, corrupt, and vain, but he remained, at the apogee of his vanity, realistic about what was possible and what was desirable.'

> 'God bless the King, I mean the Faith's Defender;
> God bless – no harm in blessing – the Pretender;
> But who Pretender is, or who is King,
> God bless us all – that's quite another thing.'

Thus John Byrom (1692-1763) and perhaps better known for 'Christians, awake! Salute the happy morn.' When I turn, as I do now, to the Highland clans, or to some of them, I am again turning to 'quite another thing'. To me this is the most fascinating part of the exercise. This is not because I prefer the local to the international, or Scotland to other places. Rather, it is because, in order to test out the connection usually made between some clans and Jacobite sympathies, we have to examine the innards of a society of great antiquity that has since been transformed beyond comfortable recall. This examination has never been carried out with complete success, and possibly never will be, no doubt because it is simply too difficult. Neither do I claim that I will succeed here, nor that my linguisitic and other qualifications will remotely bear comparison with some of those who have tried and failed. I had better now simply promise not to name those enquirers to whom I would claim to be superior, and then get on with it.

The following passages from R.W. Munro's *Highland clans and tartans* (1977) seem to me to provide a sound basis for a systematic discussion of clanship, such as he himself then expertly supplies, and which for reasons of space cannot be supplied here. The rugged terrain of Highland Scotland:

> 'encouraged the growth of a tribal system, where great families came to be established under their own patriarchal authority. This was part of 'the ancient Gaelic polity' (in the historian Macaulay's phrase) which Celtic immigrants brought with them from Ireland, and most of what we know of its early character is derived or deduced from Irish literary sources.
>
> The Gaelic word *clann* means children, and the central idea of clanship is kinship. A clan is a family and theoretically at least the chief is father of it. Such a community structure was not peculiar to the Highlands and Islands, or even to

Scotland, but in some form it survived there longer as a basis of society than in other places . . . '

R.W. Munro shows also that many chiefs in fact as opposed to theory have shared a Scottish, rather than exactly a common, ancestry with many of their people; other chiefs, of Norman antecedents, probably at the start had a blood-tie with few or none of their people. And he discusses the gradual interpenetration of the kin-based and the feudal social orders within Scotland as a whole. Such a scholarly treatment as his serves to illustrate why there can be no final consensus on this topic, amounting as it does to little less than the social history of an entire people.

The more extreme scholarly opinions tend not to exist, but to be phantoms suggested by the truncated summary of one scholar's opinions by another. The society I am describing might be expected to be more than a little resistant to change. But I am not aware that anyone has ever seriously suggested that it was, over the period from Cù Chulainn to Charles Edward Stewart, literally static or unchangeable. Yet the careful Frank McLynn asserts that:

> 'It is often said that the clan system had two fatal defects. Like the ancient Greek city-states the clans found it impossible to cooperate for any length of time, and moreover they represented a closed society impervious to change.'

His attack on the first defect 'often said' to have existed is devastating. As he shows, the saying isn't true, and isn't relevant anyway. 'The impossible' is an absolute category, just as 'never' is on a different plane of meaning from 'for rather a long time'. His attack on the second defect 'often said' to have existed is interesting but less conclusive. He argues that the saying isn't true. But, unless he's prepared to settle for 'relatively closed' and 'relatively impervious', he ought to have added that it isn't said either. I should emphasise that I write as Dr McLynn's fellow-labourer, subject to the same sins against semantics, and not as the lord of the vineyard!

Of course this disagreement, no doubt more apparent than real, is about the precise dating, and the exact speed, of change within a *relatively* slowly changing society. McLynn names Donald Cameron of Lochiel as a good example of those clan leaders who 'were able to develop their interests as minor capitalists', and he is absolutely right.

I am prepared to describe some aspects of Highland society as 'relatively closed' and 'relatively impervious to change'. I fear that this defence by means of repeating an adverb may not render me safe from attack by Dr McLynn, or by Bruce Lenman. Lochiel in Lenman's account reminds me of Andrew Carnegie, 'a hard man who ran his little territorial empire with an iron fist . . . Social discipline he maintained ruthlessly. Men were hung for thieving . . . ' We are warned not to see the 'Gentle Lochiel' as a 'simple, just patriarch'. But the Jacob of *Genesis* was one of the early patriarchs, and look what he got up to. Lenman asserts that 'even the vaunted solidarity of Clan

Cameron concealed inner tensions and submerged groups'. *A groyser kunst*! must be the reply of anyone who has studied the Jewish patriarchs through the works of Joseph Heller and Leo Rosten.

Lest it be thought that I am less than serious here, I should say that Lenman's revisionism, as deployed now in two major works, seems to me to be serious and scholarly enough itself to be worthy of a robust challenge, if a challenge is in order at all. He points to 'the assumption that there was a peculiar relationship between the Highlands and the Jacobite cause' and a following 'conclusion that this relationship must have been rooted in the distinctive culture of the Gaelic-speaking Highlands . . .' Before questioning the assumption and conclusion, he then names the two works that have given 'depth and great intellectual distinction' to this viewpoint, namely Audrey Cunningham's *The Loyal Clans* (1932) and George Pratt Insh's *The Scottish Jacobite Movement; a Study in Economic and Social Forces* (1952). Next, Lenman properly observes that 'of course, (Cunningham's) argument was much more complex than this' and 'a summary (of Insh) is bound to be distorting', while yet giving as scrupulous a summary of both works as anyone could wish. The question is whether, in his following pages, he effectively refutes the arguments of these works. The problem is whether, given that clans were not simple mechanisms of uniform size, and given that ideologies are less quantifiable still, such ideas as the following can be described as essentially 'true' or 'false', as opposed to 'helpful' or 'unhelpful'. My preference among the four is for 'helpful'. What follows is Lenman's final summary of Insh:

> 'To him therefore the Jacobite rebellions were almost a
> cosmic drama in which an ancient civilization, with many
> spiritual virtues, hurled itself unsuccessfully against the
> inexorable advance of the hard-faced politicians, businessmen
> and merchants who within the framework of the Hanoverian
> state were building the foundations of an industrial Britain.'

I must regretfully omit any discussion of Lenman on Insh's view of North-East Scotland (i.e., in this context, primarily the shires of Aberdeen and Banff). Lenman has some very pertinent things to say here, notably on Episcopalianism; but the issue turns more on the North-East's rôle in the '15 rebellion than in the '45. When Lenman turns to the Highlands, he rather naughtily professes to be looking in vain for 'an elemental clash between Gael and Anglo-Saxon.' These two terms may originate in linguistics, but we know now that linguistic geography is too cluttered and fragmented a field for elemental clashes to occur therein. 'Gael' and 'Anglo-Saxon' therefore carry us back behind Cunningham and Insh to the nineteenth century, when linguistics and race theories were too close together for comfort. There are thus extra and sinister undertones to the words, which I am sure the author did not intend.

To be fair, the ensuing discussion is methodical, restrained and full; it traverses much the same ground as R.W. Munro's discussion cited above;

and it does nothing to minimise the complexities of clanship. Rather, I would contend, even Lenman's scrupulous approach does not enable him to build all the complexities into his model. He suggests that in most clans the kinship element 'was at its most genuine and effective in relations between the paramount chief and the tacksmen . . .' Surely these were the people who counted, as formers of opinion.

When Lenman discusses the penetration of the feudal social order into the Highlands, he bravely essays a generalisation:

> '. . . by 1700 it is clear that most effective clan units were formed of a combination of feudal and ancient Celtic elements, and of these two the feudal element was the more important.'

I disagree with this relative order of importance. More significantly, I don't see how the matter can be as clear to either of us as Lenman suggests. I wonder if the strength of his conviction comes from the fact that Highland history sometimes gets read backwards? Thus Frank McLynn considers the results of the '45 and proposes, (to be fair, in order to question,) the notion that:

> 'The dissolution of the clan system as a result of both the purging of its human element in the pogroms of 1746-47, and the legal attacks on it in the form of the abolition of wardholding and hereditary jurisdictions and the interdiction on the wearing of the plaid, all seem part of the ineluctable process whereby Scotland was integrated into a mercantile-capitalist society . . .'

Abolish the feudal tenures. See the clan system dissolve. So the clans must have been basically feudal all the time. Q.E.D.. I disagree with this too, and I see the dissolution of the clan system as no less agonising for being much longer in working itself through, working from socio-economic causes and not from short-term political and legal causes. Again, this topic merits its own discussion on another day.

Lenman contrasts two great regalities, that controlled by the Duke of Argyll – more kin-based in its operation – and that controlled by the Duke of Atholl – more feudal, or even princely. The point is well taken. But if the Campbells were a clan, and they were the greatest of clans, it is hard to make Archibald, Duke of Argyll in 1745, into any kind of 'Gael'.

> 'I should perhaps be cautious about classifying someone who went to school in England (Eton) and to university in Scotland and the Netherlands (Glasgow and Utrecht). But I think I would call him a Londoner, who knew his way around Lowland Scotland, but apparently never visited Inverary between the 'Fifteen rebellion and his accession to the dukedom in 1743. He was making the wilderness bloom on Hounslow Heath long before it was clear he would ever have the chance to 'improve' his ancestral home.'

It is true that he understood the workings of his own clan very well, but this shows *his* ability to adapt, not that of Clan Campbell.

The Campbells were notable, but far from alone, in being a clan not remotely interested in flirting with Jacobitism. And if the Campbells were for Hanover, *ipso facto* some of their neighbours would be for the Stewarts. This might be held to remove the need for Audrey Cunningham's theory about a patriarchal ideology that linked Stewart kings and Jacobite chiefs. Not necessarily so, since the house of Argyll by its success over the centuries had often made Stewart kings and rival chiefs alike rather frightened.

Lenman sees Highland society as 'potentially fluid' and 'unlikely to have a history of stability', with the dynamic in the early modern period 'provided by the expansion of three great imperialist clans' (Campbells, Gordons, and Mackenzies). I would be foolish to quarrel with this. What Lenman, in my view, underplays is the extent to which the early modern Highlands were destabilised, were made more warlike, by deliberate crown policy. Charles Edward Stewart's ancestor James IV forfeited the Lord of the Isles in 1493 without being able to replace the Lordship's authority by his own. Jenny Wormald says that James IV, 'who spoke Gaelic himself, never showed the utter contempt for Gaelic society and Gaelic culture that was so marked an attitude of James VI.' But the house of Argyll also understood Gaelic society and Gaelic culture, and were better placed to fill the vacuum left in 1493 than was the monarch. James IV, like Prince Charles Edward, believed in a policy of calculated risks, but the best calculations 'gang aft a-gley'.

Highland society had changed in the centuries before the '45, but Lowland society had changed faster. One can list Jacobite clan chiefs who were nascent capitalists, just as one can list Labour Party supporters who are full-blown capitalists. The exceptions test the rule, but I have yet to be persuaded that they overthrow it. Highland society stood out, by 1745, as the main British area of potential support for the Stewarts. In the end, I believe that McLynn is reasserting what is basically the correct position when he writes that the 'Forty-Five:

> '. . . in Scotland produced a genuine civil war, almost along the lines of the North/South divide in the American Civil War basically between those who had done well out of post-1688 mercantile and financial capitalism and those who had not.'

Not all the clans were Jacobite, nor did all those who came out for the Stewarts come out with unmixed feelings. A sense of obligation, and other more covert pressures, certainly played their part.

Highland Catholics tended to be Jacobites, but they were thin on the ground. Highland and North-Eastern Episcopalians, indeed Episcopalians in general, tended to be Jacobites or crypto-Jacobites, and Bruce Lenman has shown their significance. William Ferguson calculates that the '45 'was supported mainly by Episcopalians and Roman Catholics in the proportions of 70 per cent to 30 respectively.'

Speaking Gaelic would hardly of itself make anyone a Jacobite. But the Lowland hostility to the Gaelic language might. And Gaelic enshrines some of the finest utterances of Jacobite defiance to the southern enemy. There is no sentimentality, and no defeatism, in most of what John Lorne Campbell assembled in his *Highland Songs of the Forty-Five*. Alasdair Mac Mhaighstir Alasdair, the MacDonald who has been credited by a Campbell with writing 'the most passionately patriotic Gaelic poetry ever written', admitted to no doubt, at least in his poetry, that there should be *another* rising to avenge Culloden and its aftermath. All that such a Highlander asked of Charles Edward was that the expedition should be adequately prepared, and be soon. (The translations are those by John Lorne Campbell):

> Coma mur an tig thu idir,
> Mur an tig thus nis a chlisgeadh;
> Ar call 's ar sgainnir nach fidir?
>   Thoir a nis, a nis an ionnsaigh.

> We care not if thou comest never
> Unless thou comest at this moment,
> Heedst not our loss nor our dispersion?
>   Make *now* the invasion.

> Diùbhlaidh sinn air cuilean Dheòrsa
> Na rinneadh oirnne de dhòibheairt,
> Ma dh'fhòghnas claiginn a stròiceadh,
>   'S an cuid tòn a sgiùrsadh.

> We'll revenge on George's puppy
> All the mischief he has done us,
> If to split their skulls asunder
>   And scourging backs suffices.

There is room for debate on the exact nature of Highland society in the eighteenth century. This might dispose us to forgive London government at the time its ignorance on the subject; what is more culpable is its lack of any desire to find out. Rosalind Mitchison tells the story of this government ineptitude which, if it did not actually provoke the '45, failed both to prevent it and to contain it once it had broken out. It is, as she says, a 'lamentable story'.

Let me raise, without being able to resolve, one final question, the question whether the '45 was a manifestation of Scottish nationalism. In one sense it probably was. When McLynn speaks of a Scottish civil war in 1745, he adds that, 'in political terms, this manifested itself in respective support for and opposition to the Act of Union of 1707.' but as Eveline Cruickshanks observes:

> 'In his declaration, Charles Edward had promised to dissolve the Union, but he had no desire to be King of Scotland only, nor could he have been for how could an independent

Scotland have been defended from King George and his
allies?'

When the Jacobites decided to retreat from Derby, military considerations may well have been uppermost in their minds. Eveline Cruickshanks,
who describes herself as 'part English, part Scottish, and part French', thinks
not. It is perhaps the Scottish part of her that leads her to place the blame on
the Scots:

> 'The real reason for their decision to retreat, however, was a
> narrow kind of Scottish nationalism. All along they had
> complained that Charles Edward was "occupied with
> England" to the exclusion of Scotland the land of his
> ancestors, and some of them even told him 'they had taken
> arms and risked their fortunes and their hopes, merely to seat
> him on the throne of Scotland; but that they wished to have
> nothing to do with England.'

None of us can write about the '45 in a completely dispassionate spirit.
It may be that, then and now, if the Stewarts had not existed the Scots would
have had to invent them. Scotland as such did not fight for Prince Charles
Edward Stewart. And maybe Scotland was right – that is altogether too large
a question for this essay. Alasdair Mac Mhaighstir Alasdair, at any rate,
found a way to fuse together his vision of the Stewarts, of Gaeldom, and of
an ideal Scotland:

> Nach nàr dhuit féin mar thachair dhuit
>   O Albainn bhochd tha truagh,
> Gann làn an dùirn de Ghàidhealaibh
>   Fhàgail ri h-uchd buailt'?
> Nach sumain thu do chruadal mór,
>   Shliochd Scòta sin nan lann?
> Us diùbhlamaid air muinntir Dheòrs'
>   Fuil phrionnsail mhór nan Clann.
>
> O Scotland! art thou not ashamed
>   At the poor part thou'st played,
> Leaving a handful of the Gaels
>   To face the foeman's blade?
> Come, summon up your mighty strength,
>   O warlike Scotia's sons,
> Let us revenge on George's folk
>   The royal blood of the clans.

Art is necessary: sometimes it provides the synthesis that life cannot.

Dr William Ferguson has kindly read and commented on this essay. All responsibility for the errors and infelicities in it is mine.

SELECT BIBLIOGRAPHY

John Lorne Campbell, *Gaelic in Scottish Education and Life* (new: edn: 1950).

John Lorne Campbell (ed:), *Highland Songs of the Forty-Five* (1984).

Eveline Cruickshanks (ed:), *Ideology and Conspiracy: Aspects of Jacobitism*, 1689–1759 (1982).

Eveline Cruickshanks, *Political Untouchables: the Tories and the '45* (1979).

H.T. Dickinson, *Liberty and Property: Political Ideology in Eighteenth-Century Britain* (1977).

Victor E. Durkacz, *The Decline of the Celtic Languages* (1983).

William Ferguson, *Scotland: 1689 to the Present* (1968).

Margaret Fosster, *The Rash Adventurer* (1973).

Bruce Lenman, *The Jacobite Clans of the Great Glen, 1650–1784* (1984).

Bruce Lenman, *The Jacobite Risings in Britain 1689–1746* (1980)

Frank McLynn, *France and the Jacobite Rising of 1745* (1981).

Frank McLynn, *The Jacobites* (1985).

Rosalind Mitchison, 'The Government and the Highlands, 1707–1745', in N.T. Phillipson and Rosalind Mitchison (eds:), *Scotland in the Age of Improvement* (1970).

R.W. Munro, *Highland Clans and Tartans* (1977).

Alexander Murdoch, *The People Above: Politics and Administration in Mid-Eighteenth Century Scotland* (1980).

W.A. Speck, *The Butchers: The Duke of Cumberland and the Suppression of the Forty-Five* (1981).

Katherine Tomasson and Francis Buist, *Battles of the '45* (1967).

Jenny Wormald, *Court, Kirk, and Community: Scotland 1470–1625* (1981).

2

THE TITULAR CHARLES III
AND THE STEWART CROWN
OF SCOTLAND
by
Hugh Douglas-Hamilton

Lord Hugh Douglas-Hamilton, was born in 1946. He has
travelled very extensively in Europe and the U.S.A., where he
studied at the University of South Carolina. After learning to
fly, he worked for the Outward Bound Trust both in Wales and
in Scotland, and later worked with the Royal Scottish Society
for Prevention of Cruelty to Children. Joining the Scottish
National Party in 1973, he was subsequently included on their
candidates' register. As curator of his family's collection of
paintings and state papers at Lennoxlove, East Lothian, he
assembled the present library and the Hamilton and Douglas
Clan Museum there. He became associated with the Gaeltacht
Island of Tory, taking part in sponsoring and organising the
first international exhibition of the native school of artists from
the island.

He is a member of the Society of Authors. He has a son
Brendan, and a daughter Kitty, and lives on a farm in East
Lothian.

IT IS AN IRONY that some men and women, in spite of merit
and courage, become agents of destruction to their fellows and even to whole
ways of life. A measure of such fate fell to the lot of Prince Charles Edward
Stewart, warrior, exile, and man of myth. He was born on the 20th December

1720, at the Palazzo Muti in Rome. His father was James Francis Edward Stewart, declared by his followers to be James VIII of Scotland and III of England and Ireland, sometimes called the Chevalier of St. George and known to his enemies as 'The Pretender'. Charles's mother, before she became a Queen, was Princess Mary Clementina of Poland and was the grand-daughter of King John Sobieski, who had thrown back from the gates of Vienna the mighty armies of the Turkish Empire, extinguishing their hopes of a Europe under Islam.

This first-born child was baptised Charles Edward Louis John Sylvester Maria Casimir. Among his titles were those of Duke of Rothesay and Prince of Wales.

The family into which he was born, while on the whole one of un-doubted genius, has sometimes been judged as remarkably unsuccessful. It has been said that Scotland would have been fine if it had not been for the Stewarts, but they were as much part of her reality as the Cheviot Hills or the Rock of Dumbarton. Personally unhappy and even unstable as many of them were, they showed a remarkable capacity as a dynasty for outlasting unpopularity and, latterly, surviving their own doctrines concerning their divine right to rule.

The monarchy of the Scots is by far older than the name of Stewart (altered to Stuart during the French residency of Mary, Queen of Scots and France, the letter 'w' not existing in the language of the latter country.) Fergus, King of the Scots of Antrim and Argyll, was the first to rule over a then small kingdom in the West of Scotland. He is said to have died in 501 A.D. and brought with him from Ireland to his new colony the name Scot, once synonymous with Irishman, and in his person the beginnings of our Ulster founded Royal Family of today, who owe their crown to his blood.

About 350 years later, Fergus's descendant, King Kenneth MacAlpin, united the nation of Dalriada in Argyll with that of the Picts of Caledonia into one kingdom, known as Alba, the Gaelic name for Scotland. She is the oldest nation in these islands. However, it was not until much later that Strathclyde, Lothian, and part of the present Cumbria and Northumbria were added to the Gaelic north. This meant that Scotland was largely Celtic, with a considerable share of the Welsh speaking variety. Later descendants of Fergus, particularly David I, called 'The Saint', invited in folk of other backgrounds, among them Flemings and also some Normans. These welcome immigrants were of much value to their new country, which they often defended against their kinsmen of England.

The Wars of Independence, at the turn of the 13th and 14th centuries, virtually bankrupted Scotland. These were the result of the land greed of the ageing paranoiac Edward I of England, who had already slaughtered the Welsh Royal Family and swallowed into his own territory their principality. At the same time the struggle provided Scotland with her strongest leader, the hero King Robert I, the founder of the Bruce dynasty and ancester of the Stewarts. Out of this time also grew an enduring faith in the Nation.

The Stewarts were also descended from the Great Steward of the Realm, one of David I's immigrants, whose line was joined with Robert's by marriage to his daughter Marjorie. After a slow start they proved an often brilliant, though sometimes quixotic Royal Family. For five hundred years they held on to power, though not always to their lives; for another hundred they fought for their claim to the crown with the sword and the pen until their line died out in the nineteenth century. In their time Scotland, a small and largely desert land on the periphery of the civilised world, again and again made her mark on international culture in letters, art and military prowess. The desires of the English to take ownership of the country were contemptuously extinguished by all the Stewart monarchs except Anne, the last *de facto* ruler of that family.

Many of the dynasty died violently and not all were conspicuously brave, but on the whole they commanded great popularity and frequently gave their subjects much to talk about. Most of them can hardly have been secure or happy, but they could never be called brutal as a family. Their small fortresses and palaces were intensely gorgeous and their nobles, who were often little more than tribal chiefs, were second to none in pride.

Until the Stewarts became kings of Britain perhaps the greatest quality that the Scottish Crown allowed, a thing comparatively uncomprehended south of the Border, was accountability. Towards the conclusion of Robert I's struggle with England, when Scottish independence had become assured, the nation's parliament wrote a petition to the Pope for recognition. This memorable letter of 1320, known as the Declaration of Arbroath, contains, among other points concerning the nation's freedom, one remarkable and crucial statement. It runs thus:

> 'Yet if he (the King) should give up what he has begun, and agree to make us or our Kingdom subject to the King of England or the English, we should exert ourselves at once to drive him out as our enemy and a subverter of his own rights and ours, and make some other man who was well able to defend us our king ...'

In the ensuing years this could be read to imply, among other things, that the subversion of the rights of the subject by any king provided constitutional grounds for his deposition and that no monarch could simply take the crown for granted.

In the case of James III, his disregard for the law, his over-sumptuous designs for his own self-aggrandisement and his unwanted plan for the invasion of England can be seen as stepping stones to the rebellion in which he was murdered. Nevertheless his reign provides a classic example of how a Scottish monarch might be checked by his subjects. James had surrounded himself with a coterie of favourites drawn from his personal servants. They included, among others, his tailor, his musician, his architect, and his swordsman. He has been suspected of having amorous relations with these men. He certainly made them rich and indeed created one of them an Earl. From this clique the old nobility, accustomed to counsel the King, were largely excluded. In 1482 James set out with his army to meet an English attack. With him went his soldier nobles, but he also took his favourites. Far from invading England his army penetrated only as far as Lauder, on the periphery of the Scottish side of the Border country. There his generals of the old school seized and hanged all the favourites that were to hand. They then marched the army back to Edinburgh with the King captive. What was perhaps most remarkable was that thereafter James was still allowed to keep his crown, which is a different thing altogether to being allowed to do as he liked in the manner of an autocrat.

Of thirteen Stewart Kings, six died in blood, so it was natural that the Head of State should become a good ear. Liable to the possibility of replacement by deposition or assassination as he was, we find a Head of State such as James V to have been far more accessible to, and interested in, ordinary people than can have been his English counterpart Henry VIII. Perhaps in this attitude can be seen something of the Highland notion that a Chief is but *princeps inter pares*, which is to say, the first among equals, obliged to take the hand of the least of his clan (or literally 'children'.) As Chief of Chiefs, the King was not without those who considered themselves his equals except in the right to wear the crown. During the Jacobite campaign of 1745, the fact that his Generals and chief officers expected Prince Charles Edward to be accountable to them can be seen as an ardent example of the Scottish attitude that a ruler should be seen in the context of his council.

Deviation from this principle of accountability served the Stewarts ill after their accession to the English throne. In this time they scarcely left their larger English kingdom for Scotland, except to attack or recruit from their subjects. This produced a strange confusion. Scottish intervention decided the course of the English Civil War for that land's parliament; yet, when Charles I's life was threatened, there was a second Scottish intervention, backed by her parliament and on a considerable scale, for the purpose of rescuing him. It was as though the nation was saying 'We are loyal to the King, but not necessarily to his every action.'

This loyalty, which continued despite the Royal absence and the oppression which took place in the King's name in the Covenanting period after the Restoration of 1660, reached its apotheosis in the Jacobite campaign of Killiecrankie, while the Scots Convention was once again deliberating changing its King.

Charles Edward was brought up with a Protestant tutor at his father's insistence. Although this caused a major rift between his parents, it was assumed that he would remain a faithful Roman Catholic. It was not until four years after his cause was smashed at Culloden that he became a convert to the Church of England, removing an incubus in the eyes of most of his countrymen, too late to have any effect except on his own habit, thereafter, of carrying the English Prayer Book while out walking Sundays, although there was no Church of that denomination for him to attend. From the age of thirteen when he served as a General of artillery at the Siege of Gaeta in the Kingdom of Naples, the Prince was noted for his courage rather than his piety. During this successful action on the part of the Spanish against the Austrians, he was described as showing 'not the least surprise at the Enemies, even when the Balls were hissing about his ears.'

By the time he reached manhood Charles was accomplished at field sports and the martial arts. He was also a golfer and a competent cellist. In later life he possessed a microscope. He was a tall young man, slender, fair haired with a high-browed oval face. Historians differ as to the colour of his eyes which are large and alert in his early portraits.

In 1744 he left his father at the Palazzo Muti on a secret journey for France by land and sea, his boat outsailing a British ship in hot pursuit. France and Britain were locked in the War of the Austrian Succession, and an army of seven thousand French under the command of Marshal Saxe set out for England with the Prince aboard, only to be driven to confusion and wreck by a great storm during embarkation. Charles returned to port and impatiently cooled his heels in expectation of another prospective invasion. Preoccupied in defeating the British at Fontenoy under Prince William, Duke of Cumberland, who was of an age with Charles, the French showed but a flagging interest in the fortunes of the Stewart Prince. At last privately he equipped two ships and on July 5th 1745, without the knowledge or consent of Louis XV of France, he set out for Scotland. He was disguised as Mr. Douglas, a divinity student.

An action took place off Cornwall with a British man o' war, after which Charles's larger supply ship, the sixty-eight gun frigate Elizabeth, returned, crippled, to France with considerable casualties including her captain. She took back with her seven hundred men and much of the expedition's arms. The Prince, notwithstanding his seasickness, had been eager for his own small vessel, the brig Du Teillay, to engage in the action, but her master prudently held off despite him, and on the 23rd July Charles set foot on the Isle of Eriskay in the Scottish Outer Hebrides.

How the Prince, by force of personal magnetism, gained the support of Lochiel and the MacDonald chieftains, against their better judgement, is well known. From the raising of his standard at Glenfinnan on the 19th August 1745 until the fall of Carlisle at the turning of the year, his forces suffered not a single reverse. He had come with seven friends and hardly any arms. One of his followers, MacDonald of Tirnadris later declared on the scaffold that he would have followed him had he been a Mohammedan. Lord Balmerino, in the same plight, spoke of 'the incomparable sweetness of his nature, his affability, his compassion, his justice, his temperance, his patience, and his courage.' Certainly the young man of twenty-four showed powers of leadership and inspiration throughout the campaign, marching in Highland dress on foot with his men, who are recorded as having had considerable difficulty in keeping pace with him.

At Corrieyarrack the Highlanders won a totally bloodless victory, taking up a strong position in the Pass there. On this occasion General Sir John Cope's advancing army beat a retreat before there could be an action, eventually taking ship for the Lowlands.

Edinburgh was captured by Lochiel without bloodshed, and, marching from the capital, the Prince surprised and routed Cope's army at Prestonpans in seven minutes at dawn on September 19th. The Highland charge led by Lord George Murray and Charles himself, involving as it did such terrible weapons as scythes and the Lochaber axe, cast the Hanoverians into such a miasma of terror as was only to be dispelled by the atrocities at Culloden and the ensuing genocide in the glens, on the public gallows and in the prison hulk ships to which the Jacobite prisoners were at last consigned to languish or die of malnutrition and disease, long after the cause was finally lost.

The campaign of '45 to '46 is now legend as well as history. The stories, songs and verse it inspired in Gaelic, Scots and English, bear witness to the Messianic nature of the Prince's appeal. Scotland, aching for the mystique and dignity of her monarchy, had bled copiously over its cause on both sides since the days of Montrose. No King had stood on Scottish soil since Charles II had invaded England with Scottish arms in 1651. Before he succeeded in 1685, James VII, it is true, had, as Duke of York, served as Viceroy of the Scots. For the ensuing sixty years the Scottish people, with all their sense of a kindred Kingship, had not witnessed a single member of their Royal Family on their soil. Indeed it was more than seven and a half decades later that George IV was to become the first Prince of the blood to follow his great uncle Cumberland to the Northern nation at a time when Jacobitism had become transmitted from a lost cause to high fashion. Thus to those who adhered to the government the Prince with his Highlanders must have appeared as another Attila the Hun, while to his followers it was as a Second Coming. Royal neglect of the land and people which had given Britain her Kings in the first place, from the Union of 1603 on, had drained the cultural, traditional and political life of the nation. At her heart was a vacuum. On his advent into this leaderless human wilderness, Charles must have represented to many Scots far more than a mere paragon of kingly virtues and leadership.

The Derby Campaign, which began six weeks after the victory at Prestonpans, showed Charles in a different light altogether from the apparently gifted amateur who had stated his wish to match the Hanoverian reward on his own head of £30,000 with a corresponding one of £30 for the person of George II, and who had sportingly forbidden any public rejoicing for the defeat of his father's subjects in Cope's army. The incursion into England had more of the nature of a skilled professional raid than anything else. The operation amounted to a guerrilla strike, numerically estimated as being of between four and five thousand men commanded by such hill-fighters as Murray and Lochiel, tactically able, but strategically canny and determined enough to force Charles to turn back when they considered the odds too high. The whole campaign resembles far more an extended 14th or 15th century Border foray reaching far into enemy territory, than an invasion on a national scale of the kind that ended at Flodden and Preston. It was the sort of exercise at which Scottish arms had always excelled and, within its limitations, was as successful as almost all her greater campaigns were diastrous. The entire operation took only six weeks. There had been no Jacobite reverse and, in terms of the warfare of the past, it was a supremely executed military achievement. Tragically to the Prince it represented disaster. Staking, as he did, all on reaching and holding his father's throne in London, the failure was to him perhaps more abject than if the campaign had never taken place at all. Even his subsequent overwhelming victory at Falkirk on the 17th January can have little assuaged the disappointment. Psychologically the rising lost its edge at Derby at the zenith of its achievement. Charles's instinct for a 'win or lose it all' bid for a *coup d'état* in London might just have paid off. The road from Derby led inevitably, by however many tactical successes on the part of Lord George Murray, to the perennial cataclysm destined at the end for the few pitted against the many.

Culloden was the first Jacobite defeat in the field as well as the last battle on Scottish soil. Both the hopeless conduct of that action and the Prince's complete belief in the ensuing defeat precluded the probable regrouping of his forces and made the act of conquest total. It is said that more Scots were by then in arms against Charles than for him. Cumberland's victory represented the ascendant of the new economy and civilisation over the oldest ruling order in Europe, the Gaelic kinship. To his dying day the Prince never came to terms with the results of that manifestation of 18th century civilisation, associated as it was with genocidal brutality. In his old age the mere recollection was enough to make him collapse in paroxysms on the floor.

Much has been said about the decay of Charles's character and his 'ingratitude' to those who had suffered for him. Had he been struck down like the groom at his side at Culloden, or had the *Heureux* been blown out of the water by British men o' war after her rescue of him from Loch nan Uamh in Moidart, there would be no moral qualities but the good remembered of him. His heroism and spirit of comradeship while a fugitive on the run are not only legend, but also historically attested. There is no weight to criticisms that can be convincingly made of his conduct and person apart from those of the usual military and technical variety. At this time there is no reason to doubt his honesty, courage, generosity, and virginity. Balmerino's speech on the scaffold (see above) could have been his epitaph. After all, his ancestor, Henry, Lord Darnley, King Consort to Mary, Queen of Scots, has gone down in history as weak, villainous, diseased and murderous, and he did not live to be as old as was Charles at the time of '45.

Why then has the memory of such an attractive, charismatic and effective strike commander and Regent of Scots as Charles been overlaid with a dreary catalogue concerning his moral degeneration? Among the personal faults recorded of the Prince in later life are word breaking, sexual looseness, woman beating, filial ingratitude, and apostasy. In his relations with Lord George Murray, his brother, his father, his faithful servants and adherents, and indeed with the entire French nation, he was to become obsessionally embittered to the point of paranoia. He was never to see his father again for the remaining twenty years of the old King's life. The long unnecessary years of hiding under aliasses and his surrounding of his mistress's and subsequently his wife's sleeping arrangements by barricades with bells attached, amounted to delusions of persecution. The reduction of such a fearless and generous nature must seem mysterious.

The late 18th century had perhaps some parallels with our own recent past. In both ages permissive licence became accepted as normal. Both saw increased social freedoms linked with great public cruelty. Ours has witnessed the advance of women's liberation and sexual toleration as it has the killing of the unborn and the phosphorous bombing of civilians. Charles, a contemporary of Voltaire, Rousseau, and Hume, in the age of enlightenment, had to rest in the knowledge that, among others, the officers he had left to defend Carlisle on his retreat from England had been disembowelled before their own eyes while yet living, by the forces of the Crown for which he had been making his bid and for their support of his ambition. His time witnessed the liberating sentiments of the American Declaration of Independence. Had he lived a year longer he would have known of the most brutal excesses of the French Revolution.

Perhaps the truth is that permissiveness can be very cruel, and that toleration so often in practice leads to insensitivity.

The 18th century was an age of vastly excessive drinking. Six small bottles of port at night were considered a manly consumption. The Prince is said to have developed a taste for brandy, while on the run, and is reckoned to have been fattened by it at that time. In his melancholy condition after his return to France, particularly after that country and Britain had made peace at Aix-La-Chapelle in 1748, culminating in his arrest and deportation on the orders of Louis XV, made his predilection for liquor likely to become an addiction. And it did.

The diametric character change seen in his behaviour needs little further explanation than that of alcholic disease. Initially self-inflicted, as such illnesses often are, this had become a condition of malady as beyond his control as if he had suffered from rheumatoid arthritis. The 18th century, for all its enlightenment and licence, was not an understanding age in such matters, and the man, who might today be considered to be in the throes of a form of insanity, was judged in terms of defects of behaviour. Charles Edward should not be so assessed any more than a man's account of himself should be accepted on what he has accused himself of while in a delirium. We know what he was capable of when young and fit. For most of the rest of his life he must have been in a state of sickness to a greater or lesser extent, which totally destroyed his chances of a secondary military career or other employment.

It is something of a relief to learn that for quite protracted periods he was able to at least to moderate if not altogether to stop his drinking. He did so for a year after his marriage to Princess Louise of Stolberg in 1772. The marriage of the teenage bride to the fifty-two year old Prince was a disaster, Louise eventually deserting him for the dramatist Count Vittorio Alfieri in 1780, by which time Charles had again become the long term victim of what

Cardinal York referred to as 'the nasty bottle'. Perhaps because of his alcoholism, perhaps because he had been a member of the Church of England, the Pope never recognised him as King Charles III, and this was an added disappointment. In 1784, Charlotte, his daughter by his ex-mistress Clementina Walkinshaw, came to live with him and look after him. For the remaining four years of his life he drank less and recovered some of his past dignity.

He died at the age of sixty-seven, at the Palazzo Muti, in the arms of Charlotte. The Cardinal Duke of York, administered the last rites of the Roman Catholic Church to his brother and succeeded him as Henry IX.

By Charlotte, who was loved by a French Archbishop, Charles had three grandchildren. His great grandson, Charles Edward, Count Rohenstart, lived into Queen Victoria's reign and died in Scotland. There is reason to suppose that Charles died unaware of the existence of these descendants of his line.

The issues for which Charles Edward had fought so valiantly were resolved long before the end of the 18th century. The manner of his life and the character of the man may seem overlaid, or indeed buried by the great body of historical events since those times. But sometimes a light flashes across the years and, by the remembrances of two or three lifetimes' experience, brings the past near to us. Recently I received a letter from the Scottish explorer and author, the Rt. Hon. John Buchan, 2nd Lord Tweedsmuir, B.E., who was born in 1911. In it he recalled that during the first World War, when he must have been three or four years old, his home was visited by a quaintly dressed, aged gentleman, a great-uncle or some other close relation of his father. This man when young had been nursed by a very old English lady. She had told him how as a child, she had been frightened by the triumphant entrance of Prince Charles's Highlanders at Derby.

BIBLIOGRAPHY

History of the Rebellion of 1745-6 by Robert Chambers, Edinburgh 1840.
Prince Charlie by Compton Mackenzie, London and Edinburgh 1932.
Death of a Legend by Peter de Polnay, London 1952.
Culloden by John Prebble, Harmondsworth, Middlesex 1961.
Battles of the '45 by Katherine Thomasson and Francis Buist, London 1962.
The Prince in the Heather by Eric Linklater, London 1965.
The Edinburgh History of Scotland General Editor, Gordon Donaldson:-
    Vol.4: Scotland 1689 to the Present by William Ferguson, Edinburgh 1968.
Bonnie Prince Charlie by Moray McLaren, Bungay, Suffolk 1972.
Charles Edward Stuart by David Daiches, London 1972.
The Last Stuarts by James Lees-Milne, London 1983.

3

THE '45:
A DISASTROUS MISTAKE
by
The Reverend G. V. R. Grant

G. V. R. Grant (Jim) was educated at Stowe and Oxford, and
has an Honours Degree in Jurisprudence. In 1940 he was
commissioned into the Cameronians and served in the
Waziristan and Burma campaigns. After the war he studied
Divinity at St Andrews, was ordained in 1948 and later inducted
into the Highland charge of Urray and Kilchrist where he was
parish minister for thirty-three years. He served on many
different committees of the General Assembly and was Vice-
Convener of the Church and Nation Committee, after being for
many years convener of its Scottish Interests sub-committee. He
now lives in the Stewarty of Kirkcudbright.

He takes a keen interest in history and politics. He is a
member of the Electoral Reform Society and also of the
Campaign for a Scottish Assembly and looks forward to the time
when there will once more be a Scots Parliament in Edinburgh.

ONE OF THE GREAT PECULIARITIES of Scottish
history is the extremely strange way that the Scots have treated it.
Understanding what really happened hardly ever gets beyond the old
traditional myths that have been trotted out for many years.

Although during the 19th century many original documents were
published by the Bannatyne and other Clubs, Scottish historians preferred to
ignore them and instead turned their attention to English history. There

was, in short, historical loss of nerve that led to Scots losing their sense of the Scottish past. Neither in the secondary schools nor in the four universities was Scottish history given its due place, being practically ignored. On the other hand the history of England was taught extensively, and when British history was taught it turned out to be English history once more. Only at primary school level was Scottish history taught to the children, and then it consisted of the myths and legends. In the past few years however Scottish history has begun to be properly studied, but so far modern research has largely been ignored by the writers of 'popular' histories.

To the casual observer, Scottish history consists of William Wallace, Robert the Bruce (who is never called Robert I, thus implying that he was not a real king), Mary (who is invariably referred to as Mary, Queen of Scots instead of just Queen Mary), and Bonnie Prince Charlie, who is portrayed as though he really were a most admirable character: in the words of the famous song – 'Charlie is my darling, the young Chevalier.'

What a romantic tale has been woven around these characters; and with the exception of Robert I how tragic in the end was their fate! Unfortunately, as a result of this romantic, tragic outlook, over the years the Scottish people have been conditioned to believe that they themselves belong to a tragic, romantic people – a people who, if only things had turned out differently, might have had a much better existence. Alas, all attempts to bring that about were in the end doomed to failure. If their own cherished heroes could not save them in the past, they cannot now be saved from the present or the future. Instead, with girning and grumbling they must grimly thole whatever befalls them, remaining fawningly grateful for the crumbs that fall from the rich table of their neighbour in the south.

So until recently most Scots averted their eyes from the true facts about how the Treaty of Union was brought about. Probably this was because it was such a traumatic event. Far from being 'the voluntary union of two proud peoples' as stated by the Royal Commission on Scottish Affairs 1952-54 (Cmd 9212 para 15) the Treaty was brought about by threat of English invasion and bribery. The might of England forced the Scots Parliament to agree to an imposed incorporating union, although the Scots themselves wished for a federal one – a union moreover which contained no proper safeguards for Scottish interests. In addition it has recently been revealed that the leader of the anti-Union party, the Duke of Hamilton, was secretly working hand in glove with the English government in order to get the Treaty through the Scots Parliament.

The concealment of these facts has in the course of years made the Scots so ambivalent and uncertain about their own abilities and the true wealth of their country, that they acquiesced first of all in the 40 per cent rule in the Referendum of 1979 and then failed to vote in sufficient numbers to overcome that rule and so obtain a modest amount of self-government. Then with hardly a protest they tamely submitted to the repeal of the Scotland Act by the British Parliament, in spite of the facts that the Scots M.Ps. voted against the repeal by 43 votes to 19, and that the Conservative Party had only received the support of 24 per cent of the Scottish electorate. Scotland had done what no other country had ever done. Not only did it give up its independence in 1707, but when a small amount of self-government was offered in 1978 it allowed this to be snatched away by deviousness and misrepresentation. But how could a romantic, tragic nation do anything else, when it had been nurtured on a diet of romantic, tragic history, based largely on myths?

Chief among the myths is the popular account of the '45. A bold, charming, attractive Prince, a direct descendant of the Stewart Kings of Scots, lands in Scotland. Immediately the clans, charmed by his courtesy and pleasant manner, flock to his support at the call of their chiefs. By audacious marches, within one month the Highland Jacobite army enters Edinburgh. Six weeks later, having won the Battle of Prestonpans, they follow their Prince loyally and lovingly as far south as Derby, only 130 miles from London. The Government is in a state of panic. The Hanoverian king, George II, makes plans to flee to Hanover. Nothing stands in the way of the Jacobite army and London except the Brigade of Guards – but then Lord George Murray and some of the other Jacobite leaders refuse point-blank to continue! Ignoring the tears, the pleadings, the implorings and the beggings of their gallant Prince, they insist on turning back. The Crown of England as well as the Crown of Scotland is in his grasp, only to be dashed to the ground for want of a little more courage, a little more boldness, a little more pluck. Back the army marches, to be defeated at Culloden. The clansmen scatter. The Prince flees, but although a price of £30,000 is placed on his head, such is the loyalty of the clansmen that no one can be found to betray him. It is indeed a romantic story: so near to success, yet ending in tragic failure.

The actual truth, however, is somewhat different. The chief character in the traditional romantic account, Charles Edward Stewart, was not really an estimable young man. Although his manners and courtesy were impeccable, he was irresponsible, and completely self-centred and egotistical.

That may seem a harsh judgment, but consider the facts. Towards the end of 1743 serious plans were being made for a French invasion of England to take place in January 1744. The plans were drawn up by the French government, the Jacobite court, and English Tories who were sympathetic to the Jacobite cause. Although the Earl Marischal of Scotland pled for a separate Scottish expedition the French were determined not to dissipate their invasion army, thus illustrating their belief in one of the most basic military principles, namely the concentration of force. Ten thousand men were asembled at Dunkirk, and naval cover was provided by the French fleet based at Brest. The landing was planned to take place at Maldon in Essex, where the Royal Navy did not patrol. Not only was Maldon merely 48 miles from London, but the capital could be reached without having to cross the Thames. However, the English Jacobites began to demand changes in the plans and they also wanted to put back the date of the invasion. The British government learned of the plan, and when the French fleet set sail at the end of February 1744 it was met by the British navy. A violent storm arose which battered the French fleet and caused great damage to the transports waiting at Dunkirk. The effect was that the invasion had to be called off.

Meantime, in the years since 1715 the Union with England was gradually being more and more accepted in Scotland, for by around 1740 the promised economic benefits appeared at long last to be coming. Moreover, as the years went by death began to take its toll of the dedicated Jacobites. The result was that those who remained had become convinced that action was more and more imperative because it would soon be too late. One of the most impatient of the Jacobites, William MacGregor of Balhaldie, tried to bring about a rising in the Highlands in 1743 by greatly exaggerating the strength of the Jacobite movement. The more responsible Scottish Jacobite leaders were appalled at his attempts and sent John Murray of Broughton to Paris in August 1744 to tell the court of St. Germain of their own assessment of a possibility of a rising. The upshot was the Highland Jacobite chiefs promised to raise their clans provided that certain conditions were met. These were that Charles Edward should come in person to Scotland, and should bring with him 10,000 French troops, adequate supplies of arms, and 30,000 French gold pieces. If these conditions were not fulfilled they would be unable to do anything.

Had these conditions been met it is possible that around 10,000 clansmen might have been raised. But when the projected invasion of England was abandoned after the great storm in February 1744, the following year Charles Edward, with the secret connivance of the French government, set out and landed on Eriskay. He brought only seven followers, who were mainly Irish Jacobites, a ship-load of arms and 4,000 French gold coins.

Charles Edward must have been toying with this rash foolhardy adventure for some time, since he had told John Murray of Broughton when they met in France that he would come to Scotland by himself 'though with a single footman' – whereupon Murray had warned him that if he did so he would be lucky to raise 4,000 men from a few clans in the Western Highlands. It is quite obvious that the French regarded the expedition purely as a diversion, designed to tie down British troops which otherwise would be sent to the continent, at the cost of complete ruin to those Scotsmen who took part. Charles Edward himself had nothing to lose, while those who followed him had everything.

When he landed in the Hebrides on 23 July 1745 the local chiefs were horrified and begged him to return to France, while chiefs like MacLeod of Dunvegan and MacDonald of Sleat refused to join him on the grounds that the conditions laid down had not been kept. As a result few recruits came from the Western Isles, the main area of recruitment being Western Inverness-shire, North Argyll, North-east Perthshire, and limited areas in the North-east.

As for the belief that the clans flocked to his standard, the facts are quite otherwise. In 1745 the fighting strength of the clans was roughly 22,000 men, yet only 2,000 joined Charles Edward in the five weeks that followed his landing, and at the Battle of Prestonpans outside Edinburgh his army was still tiny, consisting of not more than 2,500 men. What made the rising possible was the adherence of Cameron of Locheil who brought 700 men – but Locheil came out only after having received explicit promises from Charles Edward that French aid was definitely coming – and even then he insisted that Charles Edward guarantee to reimburse him for the value of his estates should the rising fail.

It seems clear that force or the threat of force was frequently used in order to obtain men for the Jacobite army. To give only two examples: Locheil threatened to hang Allan Cameron of Collart when he tried to withdraw from the rebellion. In the Inverness-shire parish of Alvie, out of 43 who went out only three went willingly, the rest being forced out, sometimes by 'violent methods, such as burning their houses, carrying off their cattle, and breaking their heads'.

Indeed after making allowance for the natural anxiety of those taken prisoner during the rebellion to claim that they had been forced out, the evidence that was obtained by the courts after the rising was over is conclusive that a large proportion were indeed forced out. The normal technique was to threaten local lairds with the herschip (ravaging) of their lands with fire and sword unless a specified number of men was produced. The same method was used for obtaining provisions and the cess (tax).

It is therefore obvious that the rebellion was founded on a lie spoken by Charles Edward: that French aid was coming. It was this lie that brought out Locheil, and it was a lie that was repeated again and again. For example, after Prestonpans Charles Edward wished almost immediately to march on Berwick, but found that that was impossible since it was doubtful whether he could have collected as many as 1,500 men to follow him. When later on he did march into England by way of Carlisle with an army of about 5,000 (half of whom were Highlanders) and 400 cavalry the decision to do so was only agreed after Charles Edward had overcome the great opposition of the majority of his council by insisting again and again that extensive French help was coming and that he had been promised massive support from the English Jacobites. That was another lie. Had the truth been known the tiny Jacobite army would never have invaded England for, according to the war diary kept by David Wemyss, Lord Elcho, '4,500 Scots had never thought of putting a king upon the English throne by themselves'.

Throughout the campaign Charles Edward showed himself selfish and brash. His inability to get on with Lord George Murray, much the most able soldier in the Jacobite army, is a good pointer to his character; he even dismissed Lord George after the fall of Carlisle, but had to reinstate him when the Highland chiefs told him that they would only fight under Murray.

Much has been made of the nobility of Charles Edward's character and how he was willing when a fugitive after Culloden to share the humble lot of those who befriended him. It is not so well known that, when it was necessary to pay the semi-starving 1,500 men who had rallied under Lord

George Murray at Ruthven, the money that Charles Edward sent to be distributed to the men was soon recalled by him for his own use – a clear example
of his selfishness.

The retreat from Derby was not the action of a faint-hearted leadership
refusing to obey their flamboyant fearless leader, but was a wise strategic
decision, since it was clear that no English Jacobite support was forthcoming, other than that of the Manchester regiment. Three armies were
already approaching the Jacobite army. Wade was following in the Prince's
track, and the Duke of Cumberland was west of Lichfield in the Midlands.
Both armies were much larger than Charles Edward's; while in front of him
in London lay the Brigade of Guards. Moreover it is untrue that George II
was getting ready to flee to Hanover, for George understood the strategic
position perfectly well. Charles Edward, in fact, stands convicted by his own
lies and self-centred optimism.

The '45 was therefore a rash, feckless, foolhardy enterprise which only
got as far as it did owing to two fortuitous circumstances – the abolition of
the Scots Privy Council in 1708, and the lack of troops in the country (there
being only about 4,000, most of whom were of very poor quality). This
meant that there was no real government in Scotland able to take decisive
action to crush the rebellion as soon as it had started. The Jacobite army
simply walked from Glenfinnan to Edinburgh without opposition.

The effect of the rebellion upon the Highlands, upon the Episcopal
Church, and upon the general Scottish ethos was catastrophic. Whereas
Charles Edward was for a time turned into a hero by the French and was
made much of by Louis XV, his luckless followers were left to the tender
mercies of butcher Cumberland and others like him.

The atrocities that followed the Battle of Culloden and during the so-
called pacification of the Highlands were all documented by Bishop Forbes
in *The Lyon in Mourning*, and also by others. But, to the shame of Scottish
and English historians, until recently these were glossed over and as far as
possible ignored. However, it must be added to his credit that Lord Mahon,
an English historian, said that the cruelty shown by Cumberland's forces was
'such as never perhaps before or since has disgraced a British army'. The
savagery that took place was due to deliberate policy – Gaelic-speaking
Highlanders, wearing a peculiar form of clothing, were regarded as being
little more than sub-human and were treated more or less like the Slav races
were treated nearly 200 years later during the Second World War by the
German armies acting on Hitler's orders. Lord Chesterfield, the Lord
Lieutenant of Ireland, urged genocide, suggesting that Cumberland
massacre the peasantry, and when General Campbell tried to get meal from
Ireland to feed his semi-starving Government troops, Chesterfield refused to
allow the export of any food, being ready as he said 'to starve the loyal with
the disloyal'. The Duke of Richmond told the Duke of Newcastle in March
1746 that he would much prefer the rebellion to be crushed with heavy
slaughter rather than end in a quiet surrender. On the ground there were

men like Captain John Ferguson of H.M.S. Furnace and Captain Caroline Scott, both favourites of Cumberland, who were without self-control in their actions, ignoring the promises made that the ordinary rebels who surrendered and gave up their arms were to be released with a certificate that they were not to be troubled by the Hanoverian army. Under the rule of the Earl of Albermarle who succeeded Cumberland as commander-in-chief in August 1746 the atrocities continued, and commanders like Major-General Blakeney were perfectly willing to make use of torture during their expeditions through the Highlands.

At the same time there was a great wave of anti-Scottish feeling in England. A pamphlet published at the end of 1746 called *Old England* declared that 'A Scot is a natural hereditary Jacobite, and incurable by acts of lenity, generosity, and friendly dealing', while Albermarle and his successor General Bland displayed blind hostility to the Scottish aristocracy and gentry.

The Highlands, which had gradually been changing during the previous 200 years, now had their society torn apart. A development that was proceeding along natural lines was destroyed without anything worthwhile being put in its place. The former relationship between the chiefs and the clansmen was broken and the chiefs were turned into landlords. Instead of there being ties of interest and kinship the landlord system meant that many of the chiefs soon began to look upon their people merely as tenants, who when the time came could be 'cleared' to make way for sheep − hence the dislike and suspicion of Highland landlords to this day. Had the '45 not taken place the Clearances would never have been carried out with such ruthlessness, and perhaps might never have been carried out at all.

As it was, a bewildered, defeated people in the Highlands, for in the end Hanoverian and Jacobite Clans both suffered, turned to emigration in order to obtain a better life. Emigration increased greatly as a result of the Clearances and the habit grew up of accepting it as being normal. So the population of the Highlands during the nineteenth and twentieth centuries fell, and although here and there during the last 10 or 15 years there have been pockets of increased population, on the whole the haemorrhage of a losing population has not been staunched. The modern Highland problem can therefore have its origins traced back to the '45 and to Charles Edward's insistence upon a rising against all advice from those living in the area. His selfishness had disastrous consequences for Jacobite and Hanoverian clans alike.

A second result of the '45 was the enactment of the Penal Laws directed against the Scottish Episcopal Church. From 1581 the Church of Scotland had been a Presbyterian Church which, during what are called the First and Second Episcopacies (1610-38 and 1661-90), had had bishops grafted on to its Presbyterian system of government and worship. Broadly speaking, the Church included not only those inclined to Presbytery but also those inclined to Episcopacy. This was due to a great sense of the unity of the

Church. Throughout the existence of the Second Episcopacy, for example, there had been very little difference between the Episcopal and the former Presbyterian worship except that the Episcopalians used the Lord's Prayer every Sunday. No surplices were worn, there was no prayer book, extempore prayer was used, communion was infrequent (being dispensed only twice during 28 years in Glasgow Cathedral), and the Church's doctrinal standard was *The Scots Confession* of 1560, drawn up by John Knox. In addition, Church government was by Kirk Sessions, Presbyteries, and Synods, with bishops acting as perpetual Moderators of the Synods.

After the Revolution of 1689 the bishops, who had recently addressed James VII as 'the darling of heaven', and a good number of the ministers who had also sworn oaths of allegiance to James VII, felt that they were bound by them and refused to take fresh oaths of loyalty to William and Mary. William II had been disposed to maintain Episcopacy in Scotland but the failure of the bishops to support him was fatal, and in 1690 he agreed to an Act restoring Presbyterian Church government. In many parts of the country, however, non-juring Episcopal ministers continued in their parishes until they died, for their congregations could see no real difference between the two systems; and when the Presbyterians did gain control of the kirks frequently a large number of folk in the congregations remained loyal to the disestablished Episcopal Church.

The non-juring Episcopal ministers, who kept to the old ways of worship and had Kirk Sessions in their congregations, believed that re-establishment of Episcopacy would be achieved through the restoration of the Stewart monarchy. They were encouraged in this belief because at least until the end of the 1730s James Edward, the Old Pretender, insisted that the right of episcopal appointments belonged to him and this had been accepted by the College of Bishops. They therefore kept alive the Jacobite cause in their congregations while they looked forward to the reign of James VIII.

The members of the Church of Scotland were utterly opposed to the rebellion, and those who took part in it were almost all Episcopalians or Roman Catholics (approximately 70% Episcopalian, 30% Roman Catholic). Although only about 3,500 Episcopalians at the most openly supported the rebellion the great majority of them were Jacobite by inclination. Since this was widely known, Cumberland was determined to destroy Episcopal chapels and meeting-houses wherever he came across them. During his march north from the Tay to the Spey many were burnt, and after Culloden even more were burnt and destroyed. But that was not all. Between 1746 and 1748 the Penal Laws directed against the Episcopal Church were passed by the British Parliament. Among the provisions were these: All clergy of the Episcopal Church had to take the oaths appointed of loyalty to George II by 1 September 1746 and pray in public for the king and royal family; all meeting-houses and chapels where the clergy did not comply were to be closed. Clergy who officiated after this date were liable to 6 months' imprisonment for the first offence and transportation for the second. A meeting-house was defined as a meeting or congregation where five or more persons in addition to the members of the family, if in a house, or five or more persons where no family was residing, had assembled for public worship conducted by an Episcopal clergyman; laity attending such prohibited meetings were liable to a fine of £5 for the first offence and two years' imprisonment for the second offence. Only letters of orders given by a bishop of the Church of England or Ireland would be regarded as being fit for registration after September 1746. Ordinands had to seek ordination in England or Ireland, and those ordained by Scottish bishops were forbidden to officiate anywhere except in their own houses. (The intention of the Penal Laws was to suppress the Scottish Episcopal Church and to grant toleration only to those who derived their orders from English or Irish bishops.)

In time means were found to keep the letter of the law but to overcome its provisions. For example, a house might be built containing several separate rooms with the inside walls not going up to the ceiling. This meant that five people could gather in each room, see and hear the service, yet keep within the law. Nevertheless, by the time George II died in 1760 the Episcopal Church had been reduced to what Sir Walter Scott called 'a mere shadow of a shade', and when the Scottish Episcopal Church, with the help, encouragement, and approval of the General Assembly of the Church of Scotland, succeeded in having the Penal Laws repealed in 1792, it had only four bishops and about 40 clergy.

The qualified chapels (Episcopal Churches where the oath of loyalty had been taken and the Hanoverian royal family prayed for) were staffed mainly by English and Irish clergy who used the Church of England prayer book. After the Penal Laws were repealed the formerly persecuted Scottish Episcopal Church began to draw nearer to the qualified chapels. The effect of this was that gradually the Church turned its back upon its history and traditions as a Scottish Church and instead, during the nineteenth century, became more and more like the Church of England, until today the common expression among ordinary people for the Scottish Episcopal Church is 'the English Church'. So Charles Edward by his reckless impetuosity has a considerable responsibility for the anglicisation of the Episcopal Church. Had there been no '45 and had the non-juring Episcopal clergy accepted the fact that neither James VII nor 'James VIII' would ever be restored, there is every reason to suppose that the Church of Scotland and the Scottish Episcopal Church might have come together, since they both sprang from the Church of the Reformation. The idea of the unity of the Church was still extremely strong, and from Reformation times men and women had been willing to accept things that they disliked rather than leave the national Church. The anglicisation of Scotland would thus have been greatly lessened.

Finally, it seems obvious that Charles Edward's obstinacy, his self-centredness, and his blind egoism which had caused the rebellion and which kept it going to the bitter end on the field of Culloden is in part responsible for the lack of any Scots Parliament to this day!

The atrocities after Culloden, the open violation of the Treaty of Union, and the virulent expressed hatred of things Scottish and of Scots themselves by most English, persuaded many Scots that the Union was there to stay, and that the only thing they could do was to accept it and become as 'English' as possible if they were to get on. Therefore the educated classes tried to ape English ways and began to apologise for Scotticisms in their speech. Lord Cockburn said that the 18th century was the last Scottish century, and during the 19th century distinctive Scottish traditions and outlook began to wither away. To give a few examples: the word England was used in Scotland (as it still is in England) to mean Great Britain. No protest was made when the brother of George IV ascended to the British throne as William IV, although it was perfectly clear as shown by the Act of Abjuration of 1712 that it was intended to number the sovereigns afresh as rulers of Great Britain.

However, many protests were made at the accession of Edward VII and the statue to him in the forecourt of the Palace of Holyroodhouse merely calls him 'Edward, King of Great Britain'. More protests were made about Edward VIII and Elizabeth II including one by the then Conservative Secretary of State for Scotland for the Cabinet records for 1953, when released under the 30 years rule, revealed that 'during the Cabinet discussions of the Coronation oath, the Secretary of State for Scotland, Mr James Stuart, made a vigorous bid to have the Queen styled simply Queen Elizabeth, on the grounds that she was not Elizabeth II of Scotland' (*The Times*, 3 January 1984). To their shame, neither *The Scotsman* nor *The Glasgow Herald* saw fit to mention Mr Stuart's bid.

The Lyon Court accepted the English quarterings on their tabards when fresh ones were sent from London during the 1830s. The Reform Act of 1832 meant that Scots M.Ps. did not have to be Scotsmen and soon many of those representing Scottish constituencies were English who knew little or nothing about Scotland.

At the same time there grew up, as a counter-weight to all this, what has been called 'Balmoralism'. This consisted of a sentimental sickly attitude towards Scotland, illustrated by the many 19th century Jacobite songs that dripped with synthetic, cloying loyalty to the King over the water. Even Queen Victoria claimed to be a Jacobite! Few Scottish historians bothered themselves about Scottish history, but were prepared to perpetuate the myths; and what history books were written often finished with the collapse of the '45 – possibly because this saved the authors from having to detail the atrocities that took place afterwards.

Moreover, it was easy to claim that after 1746 the history of Scotland was contained within the history of Great Britain, since Scotland had no separate existence. Thus Scotland sank into North Britain. While various attempts have been made to reverse this process, sometimes with a certain amount of success, at the present time the future looks bleak. Ever-increasing centralisation has played havoc with the Scottish economy. Nearly all decisions nowadays are taken furth of Scotland, with the result that except when there is a tremendous effort, generally speaking the decisions work towards

Scotland's detriment. From having one-fifth of the population of England in 1707, Scotland now has only around one-eleventh.

Many Highlanders after the '45 were encouraged to join the army during the Seven Years War (1756-63) because, as explained by General Wolfe, if they were killed, it would only be the death of some potential rebels; and since then Scotland has played more than its fair share in the wars of the British Empire. For example, during the First World War 20 per cent of those killed were Scots although the population was about 10 per cent of that of England. Field Marshal Montgomery told an audience of St Andrews University students towards the end of 1945 that while he always tried to avoid casualties, when it came to 'a real killing match' he invariably chose the Scots divisions. He meant this as a compliment to the fighting qualities of the Scottish soldier . . . but yet . . . was that all?

What has all this to do with Charles Edward? How can he be held partly responsible for Scotland's lack of a Parliament to this day? The answer is this. Those nations who were ruled by another and who have gained either complete independence or autonomy in internal affairs during the last hundred years, did so because their people knew their history, were proud of it and were determined to pass it on to their children. Hungary, Czechoslovakia, Poland, and the Republic of Ireland gained their independence. Corsica received some self-government from France; the Basque region of Spain and Catalonia received some from Spain; Sicily, Alto-Adige (south Tyrol to the Germans) received some from Italy; while in 1946 the Faroe Isles received some from Denmark. (It is interesting to compare what happened here with Scotland's experience. The Danish government held a referendum on home rule. There was a low poll, 66.4 per cent of the electorate, with a majority in favour of home rule of 161 out of a total vote of 11,640 : 5900 for and 5739 against. Denmark accepted the result, and now the islanders are full of self-confidence and have been able to do many things for themselves that previously had been left undone.)

But in Scotland the myths of the '45 among others dogged the teaching of Scottish history. As was stated at the beginning of this essay, for years it was not taught in the universities and in schools, except in the romantic, tragic manner at primary school level. Scotland's history was a story of failure, and therefore people lost confidence in their country.

Only when the '45, and other so-called romantic episodes of Scottish history are taught properly, and Charles Edward's character revealed for what it was, will it be possible to get away from the unhealthy, sentimental, and romantic image of Scotland. Only then will the Scots nation begin to feel pride in their country and expect to be responsible through a Scots Parliament for their own affairs.

BIBLIOGRAPHY

In writing this essay, I make no claims to original research, but have made use of the following books:

ASH, M., *The Strange Death of Scottish History*. Ramsay Head 1980.

BARRON, E.M., *The Scottish War of Independence, 2nd Edition*. Carruthers 1934.

DONALDSON, G., *Scotland: Church & Nation through Sixteen Centuries*. S.C.M. 1960.

DRUMMOND, A.L., & BULLOCH, J., *The Scottish Church 1688 - 1843*. St Andrew Press 1973.

FERGUSON, W., *Scotland: 1689 to the Present*. Mercat Press 1968.

GOLDIE, F., *A Short History of the Episcopal Church in Scotland*. SPCK 1951.

LENMAN, B., *The Jacobite Risings in Britain 1689 - 1746*. Eyre Methuen 1980.

PREBBLE, J., *Culloden*. Penguin 1967.

SCOTT, P.H., *1707: The Union of Scotland and England*. Chambers 1979.

STEPHEN, W., *History of the Scottish Church Vol II*. Douglas 1896.

TAYLOR, I.C., *Culloden*. National Trust for Scotland 1972.

4

SOME HIGHLAND CAUSES
OF THE '45
by
Donald C. Fraser

Donald Cameron Fraser was born in 1944 of good Highland stock. He belongs to Glen Urquhart on his father's side with Grant, MacCallum, Cumming, MacGregor, and MacDonald of Glengarry blood, and on his mother's side has roots in Lochaber and the Black Isle in Ross-shire, with Cameron and MacKenzie blood. An ancestress on that side of the family, a Naomi Munro whose people had a small farm at Loch Gorm in Inverness (where the railway station now stands) remembered the Redcoats after Culloden coming into the house and taking the meal from the girnel.

Donald Fraser was educated in Plockton Senior Secondary School under the headmastership of Sorley MacLean to whom and to his own mother he is indebted for the maturing of an interest in history. He attended Edinburgh University, and afterwards taught English at Lochaber; for the past five years he has been itinerant teacher of Gaelic in the regions of Ardnamurchan, Sunart, Morven, Ardgour, and Moidart.

THERE IS PROBABLY no episode in the long and varied history of Scotland which is as universally known as that brief blaze of glory in which all hopes of a Stewart restoration were finally consumed.

The very mention of Scotland to the foreigner who has but scanty knowledge of our history brings to his mind immediately a vision of tartan, bagpipes, and Bonnie Prince Charlie. Those who prey on the tourist present an image of Scotland in terms of tartan novelties; yet only slightly more than two hundred years ago the sight of tartan and the sound of bagpipes brought alarm to a large proportion of Scots. It is only now, when the great Highland warpipe has been domesticated in the British Army and the race who wore the kilt has been absorbed by the majority, that the rest of Britain can look benignly on these erstwhile symbols of the Gael. What has brought this change of attitude?

In a very real sense it would be true to say that Culloden was the watershed for it was there that the military power of the Scottish Highland clans was proved once and for all not to be invincible. After Culloden it was no longer necessary for the London or Edinburgh establishment to cast nervous glances northwards whenever the political climate became un-settled. The policy of deracination which had begun before ever the Stewarts ascended the throne of Scotland, has continued with increasing acceleration, especially from the time of Culloden, until today the Gael of Scotland nowhere can rely on an inviolable heartland where a viable ethnic com-munity can be maintained.

This is the legacy of the '45. No-one acquainted with 20th century 'Gaeldom' will question that; yet it is only right to ask whether the fate of the Gael would have been any different had the Stewarts been victorious and returned to London as monarchs, constitutional or otherwise. The history of Stewart interaction with the Gael of Scotland or Ireland does not incline one to believe that a Stewart King, Scottish by descent but English by upbring-ing and education, would have had any more love for his Highland subjects and their 'barbarous tongue' than had the wee German lairdie and his English descendants. One English Jacobite cynically remarked of the political reality that it did not much matter whether it were George or James the King was called – things would be much the same for the ordinary man. Nevertheless, the history of Jacobitism is so intricately bound up with the history of the Gael during this period that we must ask ourselves what caused the Highlanders to be so well-disposed to the exiled dynasty.

Much ink has been spilled by writers of history and fiction, of all shades of bias and of varied professional calibre and standing, whose researches have shed a flood of light on the fateful events which took place between August 1745 when Charles Edward Stewart, animated by high hopes, landed in Moidart and September 1746 when the Prince, a hunted fugitive, was picked up by the French ship *Le Prince de Conti* in Loch nan Uamh. That year was filled with the very stuff of romance, and no-one who studies this period can fail to admire the undoubted courage of the principal actors and the unshak-able loyalty of many ordinary men and women. But it is that very glamour that has clouded the real issues. In truth the Jacobite movement in all its tortuous politics and socio-political interactions can be likened to nothing better than the intricate twists and knots of Celtic Art. The simple explanations so often given to explain the origins of the '45 in the Highlands are just too simple. It has been concluded that the rising was the last stand of a dying civilization – the pastoral belt versus the industrialized materialistic Anglo-Saxon. Others have seen it as the final efforts of the spirit of the Counter-Reformation to achieve its ends by political and military means. Still others have seen it in terms of a large-scale opportunity for plunder and looting, and the clans who rose as a motley crew of brigands. The idea that a loyal Catholic people rose to throw off the shackles of Presbyterian tyranny has long been in circulation, while the anti-Campbell bias of many neighbouring clans has seemed to provide yet another basis for the rising. The causes of the '45 spread like some vast cobweb across the continent of Europe from Sweden to the Mediterranean and from Ireland to Russia. Jacobitism was no parochial matter but part and parcel of the international scene involving all the great names of contemporary Europe and an integral part of that long struggle between France and England which was yet to have so powerful an influence on the course of world history and be played out in all five continents of the globe. It is in its wider background that we must place the '45 in order to understand its failure apparently within an ace of success, and it is in this context that we can appreciate the magnitude of the issues that turned on this hinge of fate.

Donald MacLean in *The Literature of the Scottish Highlands* says:

> 'The debacle at Culloden, which terminated the wasteful devotion of a splendid fidelity, was more inglorious and less beneficial to the victors than to the vanquished. The genius of the people that had hitherto expressed itself in wars and conquests, in feats of valour ... now found room for expansion in other spheres. The feuds and conflicts, the jealousies of ruling chieftains and the restlessness incidental to all these, were not fitted to foster an interest in literature and art. With the collapse of the Stewart cause, the Highlanders ... awoke to a true appreciation of their new opportunities, the wider outlook afforded by these and the possibilities for asserting their power in other domains of life than those in which it had already excelled. The power of the chieftain was broken, the clan system was largely abolished and with it slowly disappeared the pupilage which was its peculiar feature. Improved means of communication brought the north more in touch with the commerical centres of the south, the standard of living was raised, cattle gave way to sheep, tillage was improved and argiculture showed signs of prosperity.'

John Lorne Campbell in the preface to *Highland Songs of the Forty-Five* says:

> '... I now consider that the rising of 1745 was the natural reaction of the Jacobite clans and their sympathizers in the Highlands against what had been since the coming of William of Orange in 1690 a calculated official genocidal campaign against the religion of many and the language of all

Highlanders, and that however inopportune the choice of the
moment of the rising may seem to have been, it must have
appeared to many men and women as the best possible chance
to throw off the Whig yoke. The relative relaxation of this
political persecution that came with the accession of George III
in 1760 could not have been foreseen fifteen years earlier. The
subsequent history of the Highlands, with the Clearances still a
vivid memory, has not been so happy that anyone can say that
the men who rose with Prince Charles in 1745 did not have a
cause that was worth fighting for.'[2]

The contrast in these two views, expressed by eminent Gaelic scholars,
doubtless reflects their own religious background but at the same time high-
lights the ambivalent attitude of many Gaels to the events of these fateful
days. What was the attitude of the contemporary Gael in Scotland to the
rising of 1745? Indeed what was the attitude of the Gael to the House of
Stewart?

We know the attitudes of the chiefs and tacksmen from contemporary
records and autobiographical material. We can find out the attitude of the
clergy – Presbyterian, Episcopalian, and Roman Catholic – from church
records, but who speaks with the authentic voice of the common people? Is
it the bards? The only contemporary Gaelic comment extant apart from the
songs of the bards is the history of the MacVurichs, which is more baldly
factual than expressive of the actual feelings and reasoning which lie behind
the actual events. There are two main sources of Gaelic political thought
available to us, viz. the songs of Ian Lom of Lochaber and the political songs
contained in the Fernaig MS. The standpoint is strongly Roman Catholic in
the former, and just as strongly Protestant in the latter. Between them they
may give us an entrée into the contemporary Gaelic mind: if we bear in mind
that neither Ian Lom nor Duncan Macrae of Inverinate, compiler of the
Fernaig M.S., were of the common people. They were representative of the
cultured class, the native aristocracy, albeit not wielding executive power.

Ian Lom was a member of the chiefly family of the MacDonells of
Keppoch, and as such could trace his descent through Alisdair Carrach first
chief of Keppoch (and incidentally a prominent figure in the battle of Harlaw
1411 when he supported the claims of his brother, Donald, Lord of the Isles, to
the Earldom of Ross, and again at the battle of Inverlochy 1431 where he supported Domhnull Ballach of Islay against the Royalist forces under the Ear of
Mar) to the Clan Donald kings of the Isles. It may be worth noting also that
Alisdair Carrach's mother was Lady Margaret Stewart, daughter of the High
Steward of Scotland who later became King Robert II and founder of the
Stewart dynasty. The immediate family of Ian Lom descended from a branch
which had been deposed from the chiefship and no doubt in economic standing the bard was as poor as any other tenant-at-will in the Keppoch lands, but
poverty or riches would have meant little in establishing the status of a man of
his descent and a bard to boot with a most powerful command of invective.

It has rashly been assumed by certain writers (even scholars) that the Highlanders had no understanding of politics. This assumption is not borne out by the facts. How could a race whose Protestant sons were to be found in the armies of Gustavus Adolphus during the great religious wars in Europe and whose Roman Catholic sons were to be found in the armies of France and Spain be ignorant of the wider European political and religious scene? We will see that cultured men such as Ian Lom and Duncan Macrae took a keen and intelligent interest in the political scene as it had reference to Great Britain as a whole. We would do well to bear in mind that the chiefs and tacksmen of even the remotest and most patriotically Gaelic clans were well able by the 18th century to speak English and well able to accommodate themselves to the customs of the southern parts of the realm.[4] It is interesting to note that Mackinnon of Strath, the only one of the three Skye chiefs who went out in the '45, was a son-in-law of Archibishop Sharpe of St Andrews, while Sir Ewen Cameron of Lochiel married as his third wife Jean, daughter of the Quaker, Col. David Barclay of Urie. The town of Inverness was a centre of English before the advent of Cromwell, as is witnessed by the fact that Robert Bruce, minister of St Giles, Edinburgh during his exile there in the days of James VI preached in that language regularly and with profound effect. The towns of Inverary and Campbeltown had English speakers as the result of the pro-Covenanter policies of the Argyll family. An interesting indication of literacy in English is provided by the quaint orthography adopted in his manuscript by James MacGregor, Dean of Lismore[5], (died 1551) a native of Glen Lyon in Perthshire. A similar orthography was adopted by Duncan Macrae of Inverinate in Western Ross for the manuscript he began to compile in 1688 – the Fernaig M.S. In both cases the standard Gaelic orthography was set aside in favour of a phonetic spelling based on Lowland Scots.

A most potent instrument of Anglicisation was the policy adopted by the Crown and Estates of Scotland towards the Highlands during the 16th and 17th centuries – a policy expressed in the Statutes of Icolmkil (Iona) 1609 where we find in the 6th Statute:

> 'The quhilk day, it being understand that the ignorance and
> incivilitie of the saidis Iles hes daylie incressit be the
> negligence of guid educatioun and instructioun of the youth in
> the knowledge of God and good letters for remeid quhair of it
> is inactit that every gentilman or yeamen within the saidis
> Ilandis, or any of thame, haveing childerine maill or famell,
> and being in goodis worth thriescore ky, sall put at the leist
> their eldest sone, or haveing no children maill thair eldest
> dochter, to the scuillis in the Lowland and interteny and bring
> thame up thair quhill that may be found able sufficientlie to
> speik reid and wryte Inglische[7] (Register of Privy Council
> 1609, IX 28-29).'

The bulk of the Highland people were completely untouched by this enactment and even its effect upon the chiefs may not have been so great; but it is a clear indication of the attitude of the Scots establishment towards Gaelic (and so towards the racial integrity of the Gaels). This hostile attitude was fully concurred in by James VI, indeed he was a prime instigator of it. Charles I in a letter to his bishops (1626) referred to the establishing of schools 'for the better civilising and removing of the Irish language and barbaritie out of the heigh landes'. James VII was no more friendly to the Gael, as is evinced by a study of his vice-regal period in Scotland as Duke of York. To quote Bruce Lenman:

> '. . .it would be quite wrong to conclude . . . that James was a particular friend of the Gael, a king who turned his back on the traditional hostility of his house to Celtic civilization . . . His religious views apart, that monarch's prejudices were in virtually every respect those of a typical patriotic and insular Anglo-Saxon Briton, with all the dislike and distrust of the Gael which that implies'[8]

The Instructions which he drew up in exile for his son bear out well the truth of the above opinion.[9]

Commerce again was a means of drawing the upper échelons of Highland society into social intercourse with their Lowland peers. The Highlands held a rich store of timber both in the native pine of the Caledonian Forest and the huge oak woods of Lochaber and parts of north Argyll. There were also mineral deposits which were worked by outside companies such as the Leadmining Company of Sir Alex Murray of Stanhope which worked the lead deposits of Strontian in the early part of the 18th century, whose workforce became the butt of some scurrilous verse by Alasdair MacMhaighstir Alasdair. Charcoal burning took place in suitable deciduous woods – Strontian is one place where the remains of the charcoal ovens can still be seen. Charcoal and lead were of course in great demand for military purposes. There was considerable local trade with the garrison of Inverlochy (later to become Fort William). It stands to reason that meat, milk, and such commodities would have to be found locally to feed the garrison although oatmeal was brought in by sea. In spite of the famous skirmish at Achdalieu where Ewen Cameron of Lochiel only saved his life by biting out the throat of his assailant, that famous Jacobite did very well out of the fort during the Cromwellian ascendancy.[10] That is not to say that he was unpatriotic or even that his loyalty to the Jacobite cause was hypocritical – he was just a good pragmatist.

His grandson, Donald, the 'Gentle Lochiel' of the '45, was a sophisticated landowner who managed his estates with sound business acumen, having at the same time business interests in North America and the West Indies. Sir Ewen had bought an estate in Jamaica and this was run by Ewen, brother of the Gentle Lochiel, who is described in contemporary records as planter.[11] We must remember too that many of the West Highland aristocracy, particularly those of Clan Donald, were 'guests of His Majesty' in Edinburgh for various lengths of time as actual prisoners or as hostages for the good conduct of their clans. Those clans who were more predisposed to the establishment line had law agents residing in the capital, e.g. the Campbells and the MacKenzies. From all this we can see how there was a continuous contact between Highland chiefs and Lowland nobles and so can assume with certainty that the Highland chiefs and their immediate circles were as politically aware and just as sophisticated as their Lowland peers.

What was it that brought about that remarkable change among clans which had been in a state of endemic rebellion against the Crown? Loyalty to the Stewart kings was not the normal attitude of those clans subsequently to become the very core of the Jacobite cause as the records of the Scottish Privy Council make abundantly clear. To quote George Pratt Insch: 'Why was it that the Stuarts, flouted in the days of their prosperity, were cherished by the Highlanders in the days of adversity?' This is indeed a riddle wrapped up in an enigma which we from our totally alien 20th century standpoint will never be able to solve with complete satisfaction. The world of the 18th century Gael had features which would have been familiar to Homer or Cuchulainn, social mores which the Middles Ages had failed to have any impact upon, yet we are not dealing with an Iron Age Celtic tribal society. We are not even dealing with a homogeneous society. The clan was not the patriachal society so often protrayed, nor on the other hand was it the feudal society sometimes postulated. There was an unstable and volatile mixture of these systems. When we consider the origins of the clans we begin to have some insight into their complicated nature. The archtypal Highland clan is probably in popular opinion the great Clan Donald whose head was regularly referred to as Rex Insularum or Righ nan Eilean (King of the Isles) by the Irish annalists. Yet their founder, Somerled, was of mixed Norse and Gaelic ancestry as his name, Somhairle mac Gille Brighde, indicates. The much maligned Campbells, in spite of their own fiction of Norman ancestry, were Gaelic as their alternative name O Duibhne clearly proves. The Camerons – who more renowned than they? – were not even a clan but a confederation of small tribes, perhaps not even racially akin, brought together under the authority of the family now known as Lochiel.[13]

The mixed racial origin of the Scottish Highlanders could not fail to have modified the Celtic tribalism of the original Gaels. The tensions between the partiarchal/tribal and the feudal, based as they were on mutually exclusive ideology, could only lead to friction. This was exacerbated when the chief was not the feudal landlord because legal authority lay with the feudal superior and actual power with the clan chief. The classic example of this was Keppoch where the MacDonells refused to acknowledge the feudal superiority of Mackintosh over their lands which they held by right of ancient settlement and protected by the sword. In other words, they were there first and what business was that of Mackintosh? It is worth noticing in passing that the MacDonells of Keppoch at the time of the revolution in 1689 were in a state of rebellion against both James VII and William of Orange. Lochiel was also in the position of not being the feudal superior of his territories which as it happened were the only lands held by Mackintosh directly from the Crown. Argyll and Huntly were at continual loggerheads over the feudal superiority of Lochaber. Is it a coincidence that it was these very lands of Lochaber which were the focal point of the '45? Audrey Cunningham claims 'The beginnings of Jacobite loyalty were rooted in the discontents of a patriarchal people at the anomalies of a feudal system of government. Highland devotion to the Stewart monarchy was not a novel and romantic sentiment but an inevitable outcome of political growth'[14]

It is more difficult to concur in her claim: 'Experience of royal government which was more merciful than that of the feudal lieutenants and withal more effective since it was more just, confirmed the native belief of the Highlanders that the rightful king was the surest defender of their race and liberties'. The fifty Highland chiefs arrested and imprisoned by James I at Inverness in 1428 (particularly Matheson of Lochalsh and those who were executed with him) might beg to differ. Gregory holds that the education of the sons of the rebellious chiefs in the Lowlands as required by the Statutes of Icolmkil brought about the great change:

> 'It is a fact which may appear startling to many, but is not the less evident on that account, that the first traces of that overflowing loyalty to the house of Stewart for which the Highlanders have been so highly lauded, are to be found in that generation of their chiefs whose education was conducted on the high church and state principles of the British Solomon. There is no room to doubt that the chiefs who followed Montrose in the great civil war were actuated by a very different spirit from their fathers, and it is well worthy of notice that this difference was produced in the course of a single generation, by the operation of measures which first began to take effect after the year 1609.'

The anti-Campbell feeling which clearly and justifiably existed among the clans of the West Highlands contributed no small vigour to the enthusiasm with which the Lochaber clans espoused the Jacobite cause. Yet let us never forget that the Campbells continued to have social intercourse with the most perfervid Jacobites, e.g. Sir Ewen Cameron's mother was a daughter of Robert Campbell of Glenorchy, Alasdair Og of Glencoe was married to Sarah Campbell, daughter of Lochnell. The romantic writers have conveniently forgotten that the Mackenzies of Seaforth and the Gordons were just as aggressive, devious, and shabby in their own spheres of empire building as was ever the house of Argyll. Yet the Campbells managed to pick up the best prizes by making the most astute use of prevailing circumstances. This brings us back to the feudal v. tribal conflict and the weakness of central government. Had the King of Scots been strong, law and order could have been maintained by him without being beholden to his feudal magnates. As it was, the general policy was to play one magnate off against another or to use a strong noble to subdue his unruly neighbour. It was this policy that led to the fall of the Clan Donald (not without their having brought it upon their own heads) and the rise of the house of Argyll. James VI was the first king of Scots to be independent of his powerful feudal vassals, and that simply because he had the might and money of England behind him. From this time on the king distanced himself from the feudal lieutenants and was seen as separate and perhaps the royal prerogative could now be seen as a refuge for those oppressed by the clique of nobles who happened to be in power at the moment.

Was the '45 the last fling of the Counter-Reformation, as some have claimed from the Protestant side, or was it a last despairing effort of loyal Roman Catholics to break the iron bands of Presbyterian tyranny, as has been claimed by some with Roman Catholic inclinations? A survey of the religious state of the Highlands in the years leading up to 1745 will hardly support the idea that religion was the most powerful motive impelling the clans to rise. It was chiefly among the MacDonald clans in Moidart, Morar, Glengarry, and Lochaber that the Roman Catholic Highlanders actually rose for the prince. Clanranald himself (persuaded by his cautious brother Boisdale) did not rise, and the men of South Uist and Barra were not in arms in the '45. It is significant that these islands so staunchly Roman Catholic today did not feel any overwhelming urge to rise. The mainland Roman Catholic clans of Keppoch and Glengarry being close to the garrison at Inverlochy (Fort William) felt more strongly.

Just as harassment had only strengthened the resolve of the Covenanters, so harassment of the Keppoch folk only strengthened their religious resolve. Sites of open-air and clandestine masses are still pointed out today in Glen Roy. But the majority of these Highlanders who took up arms in the '45 were Protestant – mainly Episcopalian although some were Presbyterian. Two ministers, Thomas Man of Dunkeld and John Grant of Glen Urquhart, were accused of active sympathy for the prince. In general however, the Presbyterian ministers were strongly against the Stewarts, and as the established clergy of the Church of Scotland since the Revolution Settlement they no doubt exercised a restraining influence over flocks whose sympathies tended towards the Prince. Rob Donn of the Mackay country – that staunchly Protestant area of Gaeldom – composed a song of welcome to Prince Charles Edward which would suggest Jacobite sympathies among the ordinary people in a most unlikely area. When it came to rising, however, much latent sympathy remained just latent.

The imputation of base motives to those Highland clans who did rise was part and parcel of the propaganda of the Whigs. It is true that certain clans had a propensity for plundering and reiving – the MacDonells of Keppoch and the MacDonalds of Glencoe were notorious, and the Camerons and MacDonalds of Glengarry were not far behind – and that certain individuals like Coll McDonald of Barisdale were little better than brigands, but in general loot and plunder was not the reason for even the Lochaber clans rising. In connection with this we may note the economic situation. The chiefs were burdened with a complicated system of debt as were the tacksmen and also many of the Lowland Scottish and English nobility. The standard of agriculture was poor, affording bare subsistence at the best and the dark prospect of famine was only too common an occurrence. Summer grazing was plentiful in the Lochaber glens, but winter keep was something of the future. It is little wonder that the cattle stocks were replenished from more favoured areas by the time honoured method of the 'creach'. The ordinary people who worked the land probably were more concerned with making a living under adverse circumstances than with politics. The ground was poor and the climate does not appear to have been any better than it is now so that subsistence agriculture was a hard and wearisome grind.

I am inclined to agree with Stevenson when he finds the origin of Highland Jacobitism in the 1640's during the struggle between king and covenanter:

> 'The anti-Campbell clans had come, in resisting that clan and the policies of the Covenanters' régime, to claim to be fighting for causes wider than that of the individual clan. Catholicism provided one such wider cause but it was not shared by all the clans involved; of much greater importance in getting the clans concerned to work together was their fighting in the name of the king. This royalism might on occasion have been almost entirely nominal, a useful expedient rather than a genuine belief, but it was none the less significant. Fighting in a loose negative alliance with the Stewart cause, an alliance based on hatred of common enemies, the clans were imperceptively to develop sentiments of positive loyalty to the monarchy. If Highland Jacobitism was to be born in the 1680s it had been conceived in the 1640's.'

It should be borne in mind that in this period the Episcopal Church of Scotland entertained and promulgated high monarchist doctrine, and that the execution of Charles I sent shock waves throughout Scotland – episcopal or covenanting. That and the Cromwellian invasions led to a nascent feeling of nationalism among the clans which found its outworking in loyalty to the old Scottish monarchy represented by the House of Stewart. How great the change of attitude was can be seen by comparing the early history of the Jacobite clans in respect of the central government and the sentiments expressed by Dr. Archibald Cameron before his execution in 1753:

> 'I thank kind Providence I had the happiness to be early educated in the principles of Christian loyalty, which as I grew in years inspired me with an utter abhorrence of rebellion and usurpation, although ever so successful; and when I arrived at man's estate I had the joint testimony of religion and reason to confirm me in the truth of my first principles.'

The idea of the '45 as being a rising of the Highlanders to preserve the ancient Gaelic culture of the Highlands is worth investigating. That there was a real sense of a Gaelic identity is quite clear from the bards and that this identity included the Gael of Ireland is also clear. How much, however, this was a literary identity and how much the ordinary Gaelic speaker in Scotland felt his kinship to the Irish Gael is a difficult question. It is a matter greatly to be regretted that the Reformation inhibited the commerce of language and persons betwen the two countries and placed a wedge between Gael and Gael that was driven home with such good effect by British politics, from Elizabeth Tudor's time on, that Scot and Irishman became virtual strangers and so Gaelic linguistic strength was greatly weakened and the Gaelic cultural integrity was breached, leading in the long run to the parlous state of Gaelic today.

The political power had long resided with the so-called Anglo-Saxon hegemony, more accurately Anglo-Norman, whose cultural heirs still hold political sway from Westminster. Before the Union of the Crowns, English – whether in its southern form or its northern variation Scots – had been the language of the courts of Scotland and England, the language of education and of commerce. In the 18th century as surely as in the 20th century English was the key to advancement, politically and materially. The Lowland Scots looked askance upon their 'barbarous neighbours' with their foreign language and strange culture. Not unnaturally they regarded the Gaelic language as the *radix malorum*, the great root of evil, which must be dug up and destroyed if the Highlanders were to become civilised. Once the language is gone the culture will follow and the Gael will be assimilated to his southern neighbours. History has proved how clear-sighted this view was. No doubt some who held this view sincerely believed that what they intended was for the real benefit of the Highlanders in the same way as the Victorians equated civilisation with the adoption of the English language and European culture. Others certainly were motivated by political desiderata and anti-Highland feeling, *mi-rùn mór nan Gall.*

In this light we must view the work of the various types of school set up. To my mind one of the most damaging influences upon the Gaelic language has been education. This is not the place to discuss a matter which really belongs to the post-Culloden era; it will suffice to say that the psychological attitude that Gaelic is a backward-looking language and a drawback to progress was so well established that it still exists among Gaelic-speaking parents to a quite remarkable degree. The main culprit for this was the Scottish Society for the Propagation of Christian Knowledge, whose policy towards Gaelic was to 'extirpate the Irish language'.

Shades of the Statutes of Icolmkil! The minutes of the Society show quite clearly that Gaelic was only to be used in case of dire necessity and even then only as a means towards the acquistion of English. The teaching of reading in Gaelic was forbidden. It is known that some S.P.C.K. teachers interpreted their remit in a very flexible way, e.g. Alexander MacDonald (Alasdair Mac Mhaighster Alasdair, the great bard) in Ardnamurchan, James

Murray in Struan in Atholl, William Mackay in Durness in Sutherland. But this was frowned upon by their employers.

Just how much the ordinary people realised the nature of this policy is impossible to say. They were innocent of English and illiterate in their own language. The chiefs and tacksmen who were in a position to understand the policy of the S.P.C.K. had mostly come to terms with anglicisation before this to an extent that left such shrewd observers as the Clàrsair Dall uneasy. We find that after 1660 most leading chiefs paid at least one visit to the court in London. The anglicisation of the chiefs, as Stevenson so rightly points out, meant the subverting from the top of the ideals of the old warrior society. The chiefs then could hardly be the leaders of a Gaelic backlash.

The tacksmen were in the best position to understand what was happening. Many of them were well educated, yet their economic status provided less temptation to become anglicised. Placed as they were socially between the chiefs and the common people they tended to have a stronger interest in the literature of their own race, and were the great patrons of the bards. If any Highlanders were aware of the dangers from the schools it must have been the tacksmen, yet we have no evidence of a deep resentment of the schools on any scale that would have provided an impetus to the rising of 1745. In this connection let us remember that Latin was not yet obsolete as the language of education, and thus the idea of another language as the vehicle for education would not seem so strange as it does to us in the twentieth century.

The Highlands, as far as the common people were concerned, presents the picture of a monoglot mass of Gaelic speakers of monolithic proportions, to whom the idea of English supplanting Gaelic, if ever entertained at all, must have been preposterous.

The siting and density of the S.P.C.K. schools in proportion to the mass of population does not suggest that in the heartland of Jacobitism (as reflected by actual willingness to rise) the resentment caused would have been very intense: e.g. Mull, Morvern, Ardnamurchan, and Laggan had each one school, and the fact that there were three each in the parishes of Kilmallie and Kilmonivaig is largely negated by the vast extent of these two parishes. What the distribution of S.P.C.K. schools does reveal is a persistent gathering along the borders of the Highlands and a very scanty coverage of the remoter parishes even of the mainland.

We must beware of reading back into the 18th century the modern phenomenon of politico-linguistic awareness which really began in the following century. The man who perceives that his langauge is teetering on the edge of extinction has a very different perspective from his ancestors to whom their language was as much part and parcel of everyday life as the hills and lochs and even the very air they breathed. In saying this it may be conceded that minor irritants could have coalesced into that feeling of unease among the Highlanders which helped to predispose many to take up arms in 1745; a feeling of unease which militant Presbyterianism, military roads, and strategic forts had already aroused.

In conclusion we shall let contemporary views be expressed by two acute political observers already referred to:

Iain Lom

In his *Lament for the Marquis of Huntly* Iain Lom addresses Charles II:

> 'Gur mor an trian sluaigh dhuit
> A bhith an uachdar na corach
> Gu t'athair a dhioghailt
> Air na h-eucoraich dheòmhnaidh, 587-590

(It is worth as much as the third of an army to you that your cause is just, to avenge your father on the devilish unjust).

> S mor an sgeul san Roinn Eòrpa
> Gur h-i chòir tha ga sracadh
> Fhir a cheannaich o thùs sinn
> Cuir ar cùis an treun taice
> Air na Banndairibh brèige
> Chuir an eucoir an cleachdadh.   613-619

(It is the talk of Europe that justice is being torn apart. Thou who redeemed us from the beginning lay our cause firmly and boldly on the shoulders of the lying Covenanters whose practice is injustice).'

In his lament for Montrose we find the following sentiments

> Tha Sasannaich gar faireigneadh
> Gar creach gar murt s gar marbhadh
> Gun ghabh ar n-Athair fearg ruinn
> Gur dearmad dhuinn s gur bochd.

> Mar bha Cloinn Israeil
> Fo bhruid aig Righ na h-Eiphit
> Tha sinn air a chor cheudna
> Chan eigh iad ruinn ach Seoc.

> Ar righ an deis a chrunadh
> Mur gann a leum e ùr-fhas
> Na thaisdealach bochd rùisgte
> Gun ghèard gun chùirt gun choisd.

> Ga fhar-fhuadach as àite
> Gun duine leis de chàirdean
> Mar luing air uachdar sàile
> Gun stiuir gun ramh gun phort.   663-678

(The English are oppressing us heavily, pillaging, murdering, and slaying us. Our Father has become angry with us, we are forgotten and in evil case.

Just as the Children of Israel were in bondage to the king of Egypt so is our condition; the only name they have for us is 'Jock'.

Our king after being crowned and before he had barely reached maturity is a poor exposed wanderer without guard or court of parliament.

He is banished from his rightful place and none of his friends is with him, like a ship on the sea without rudder or oar or harbour to make for).'

In a long and bitter poem to King William and Queen Mary, Iain Lom pours out his soul in scathing indignation. The poem is too long to quote in its entirety (cf. Orain Iain Luim pp 202 - 213) but in it he castigates the royal couple as unfilial and unnatural – a sentiment found elsewhere in the political poetry of this period – and compares what they have done with Absalom's unnatural rebellion against his father David, hoping that the same fate will befall them as befell Absalom in the just ordering of God. We have already seen in some of the quotes given how the sense of justice had been outraged by the revolt against Charles I and then against James VII. The idea of taking arms against the king is treated in terms of a high doctrine of the Divine Right of Kings – God must be angry with the nation when the king has been murdered or driven into exile and it will be a mark of His Divine favour when the king is restored to his rightful place. No doubt the fact that the 'usurpers' were the English Protestant extremists and the Presbyterian interest in Scotland exacerbated the situation to a loyal Roman Catholic such as Iain Lom. We can also see a note of anti-English feeling beginning to emerge which the Cromwellian pacification of the Highlands had brought into prominence. It was the English who had murdered the rightful king and by so doing had alienated many even of the Covenanting party who were their natural allies. From this anti-English feeling it is but a short step to Scottish patriotism which was fanned into flames by the Act of Union 1707. Many Scots of quite other sentiments than Iain Lom regarded the Union of Parliaments as a betrayal of Scotland (a sentiment which with the benefit of 280 years of hindsight it seems very hard to argue convincingly against). The 'Song against the Union' echoes the sentiments of contemporary Scotland in its insinuation that the Scottish Estates were betrayed for English gold.

A deep hatred of the Campbells, which is only to be expected in a MacDonald bard, runs through Ian Lom's poetry. The astute way in which the House of Argyll had manipulated the law and the weakness of central government to its own advantage, at the expense of its neighbour clans in Argyll especially the MacDonalds, MacGregors, and MacLeans is well known and needs not to be entered upon here but it gives point to the gibe:

'The sgriob ghiar nam peann gearra
Cumail dion air Mac Cailein
Se cho braithrach ri parraid na chòmhradh.
(Oran do Mhac Gille-Eathain Dhubhaird)

(The sharp stroke of the short pens protects Argyll. He who is
as eloquent as a parrot in conversation.' (*Song to MacLean of
Duart*) lines 1764 - 66).

The fact of the matter is more complicated. Had the MacDonalds and
MacLeans not engaged in a bitter feud over Islay, and had the MacDonalds
themselves not been so suicidally divided, the Campbells would not have had
the opportunity of fishing in drumlie waters. Nevertheless, anti-Campbell
feeling and an understandable feeling of nervousness among the neighbouring clans as they watched with dismay the seemingly insatiable territorial
aspirations of Mac Cailein Mor were undoubted encouragements to take the
opposite side.

Turning now to the Fernaig M.S. we move to Ross-shire to the more
settled territory of the Mackenzies, unthreatened by territorial ambitions of
great magnates – the Mackenzies themselves in a less obtrusive way and on
a lesser scale had carved out for themselves an empire in the same kind of way
as the Campbells. The religion of the majority here was Protestant ever since
the Reformation, but not the Church of Scotland in her Presbyterian garb.
The people of Ross-shire at this time were strongly Episcopalian and
remained so long after the Fernaig M.S. had been written and Duncan
himself was gathered to his fathers. As late as 1726 Aeneas Sage, newly
inducted Presbyterian minister of the parish of Locharron, received a warm
welcome from his flock when an attempt was made to burn over his head the
house in which he was sleeping. Indeed wherever the writ of Seaforth ran
there was strong opposition to any settlement of Presbyterian clergy
attempted after the Revolution Settlement.

As in the songs of Iain Lom the political songs in the Fernaig M.S.
exhibit a deep loathing of the *unnatural* conduct of both William and Mary:

'Mac a pheathar – fath an euchd –
Comh-cheangailt ris air dha ghleus;
A chliamhain, fheoil agus fhuil;
Dh' imich da dheoin gu dhi-chrunadh dhuinn.

(The son of his sister – unworthy the deed, doubly bound to
him, his son-in-law, his flesh and blood, moved willingly to
uncrown him for us).   XLIX.4

A king must have more than might to be a rightful ruler. He
must have right on his side and do justly. With the true king
enjoying his divine right the kingdom will prosper. With a
usurper everything will go to the dogs.

Gur fad on là chualas
Gum b'fhuarail a' chleamhnas
Na dhearbh iad san uair-sa
Le fuath mhor is gamhlas
Mac a pheathar da fhuadach
Se fuaighte ris seabhrach
Measg Thurcachaibh truaillidh
Cha d'fhuaradh namh shamhladh.

Ged tha'n creideamh mar sgàil aca
Is tur dh'àicheadh iad Bìobull
Fhuair Achitophel àite
Ann am Màiri cheart rireadh
Dar a threigeadh leò càirdeas
Agus Caritas dìreach
S a bhrist iad gu gràineil
Air an àithn a thug Crìosd daibh.

An Dia chòirich bàidh dhuinn
Umhladh gràdh agus firinn
Ni'm bheil e mar chàs air
A chàraid -sa philltinn;
Ach reir s mar thachair a Dhaibhidh
S a mhac àlainn d' a shior-ruith
Thig Righ Seumas gu àite
Dh' aindeoin cràbhadh
Phresbitri.   LII, 19-21

Ach s mor m'imnidh 's mo smuaintinn
Thaobh gach cuis a ta 'g eirigh
Gum bi Breatunn deth ciùrrte
S fuil bhrùit ann an Eire
Gum bi bristneadh a chnaimh
Eadar Mairi is Seumas
S gum bi 'n smior aig an Fhrangach
Mun cheannsaich sibh a cheile.

Dhè dh'òrduich na rìghrean
Chumail sìth ris gach duine
Bho is tusan is brioghmhoir
Na gach ti dhiubh siud uile
Caisg fein le do mhìorailt
An t-srìth-sa gu h-uile:
Ceartaich robairean Sheumais;
Bath reubaltan Uilleim.   LII, 23-24

(It is long since we heard that his relationship was cold [ie. as son-in-law to James]. They proved this to us at the time with strong hatred and malice – the son of his sister truly connected to him driving him into exile. The like was never found even among the base Turks. Though they have religion as a stalking-horse they have utterly denied the Bible. Achitophel has found his place in Mary well and truly when they abandoned filial duty and love and broke abominably the command Christ gave to us. It is no difficulty to the God who claims of us kindness, obedience love and truth to turn back this pair. But even as it fell to David hard pressed by his handsome son, King James will return to his rightful place in spite of Presbyterian hypocrisy . . .

But my anxiety is great and my concern because of all the circumstances arising that Britain will be damaged by it and blood spilt in Ireland, that the bone will be broken between Mary and James and the Frenchmen will get the marrow before you subdue each other. O God who ordained Kings to keep each man in peace, since Thou art more glorious than each and all of them still thyself by thy miraculous power this whole strife, bring to justice those who have robbed king James and drowned William's rebels.)'

Once again we have the strong belief that rebellion against the king is rebellion against the King of Kings and cannot go unpunished by Divine justice. There is also a very shrewd political insight as to the harm this civil war is doing Britain and no one stands to gain but the French. Duncan Macrae as a staunch Protestant would not view French Catholic supremacy with equanimity. This anti-French and even anti-Catholic feeling was certainly a factor in forming the attitudes of the Protestant Highlanders towards the Jacobite risings which took place later on. The fact that so many of them on weighing up this strong feeling as against their duty to rise for the Stewart kings chose to rise is an indication of the powerful pull that loyalty to the old line exercised upon the Highlanders.

By the time of the '45 it had become obvious to men of political sagacity that a Jacobite rising could not count upon the support of the majority of Highlanders, let alone Scots, and must rely upon foreign military support to have any chance of success. The nation had become used to the *status quo*, yet the adherence of Lochiel and Lord George Murray – to quote two men who joined against their own better judgement – to a cause which seemed foredoomed and eventually involved themselves and their followers in hardship and loss is an eloquent testimony to the hold that loyalty to the one they regarded as the rightful king had taken upon the Highland clans. The subsequent history of Prince Charles as a hunted fugitive also bears testimony to that same loyalty as expressed in the actions of those who, while officially on the other side, made no attempt to betray the son of their king and in many cases actively assisted his escape.

BIBLIOGRAPHY

1. *The Literature of the Scottish Gael:* Donald MacLean (Edinburgh) 1912

2 *Highland Songs of the Forty-five :* John L Campbell 2nd ed. 1984

3 *Orain Iain Luim, Songs of John MacDonald,* bard of Keppoch Edited by Annie M Mackenzie. Scottish Gaelic Texts 1964

4 *Argyll in the Forty-five :* J Ferguson 1951

5 *The Book of the Dean of Lismore* ed. W J Watson. Scottish Gaelic Texts 1937

6 *Lamh-sgriobhainn Mhic Rath :*Dorlach Laoidhean do sgriobhadh le Donnchadh Macrath 1688 ed. Malcolm MacFarlane. The Fernaig M.S. Dundee 1923

7 *Gaelic in Scotland* 1698-1981. C.W.J.Withers (John Donald) 1983

8 *The Jacobite Risings in Britain* 1689-1746 Bruce Lenman (Methuen:London) 1980

9 *The Jacobite Movement :* Sir Charles Petrie 3rd Edit. (London) 1959

10 *Alasdair MacColla and the Highland Problem in the 17th Century :* David Stevenson (John Donald Edinburgh) 1980

11 *The Camerons, a history of Clan Cameron :* J Stewart of Ardvorlich 1974

12 *The Scottish Jacobite Movement :* Geo. Pratt Insch

13 *Bygone Lochaber :* Somerled MacMillan

14 *The Loyal Clans :* Audrey Cunningham

15 *The History of the Western Highlands :* Donald Gregory 1881

16 *The Blind Harper* (An Clarsair Doll) The Songs of Roderick Morison and his music, ed. Wm Matheson Scottish Gaelic Texts 1970.

5

THE PRINCE AND THE GAELS
by
William Gillies

William Gillies was born in Stirling in 1942. He grew up on a farm in Argyll and now lives in Edinburgh. He is married to the poetess Valerie Gillies. They have three children. He was educated at Oban High School and studied in Edinburgh, Oxford, and Dublin before joining the Celtic Department at Edinburgh University in 1970. He succeeded Professor Kenneth Jackson in the Chair of Celtic in 1979.

His scholarly interests are varied and his publications range from the Middle Ages to the contemporary Gaelic scene. He recently edited the criticism and prose writings of Sorley MacLean and is currently working on the Red and Black Books of Clanranald. His curiosity about the Gaelic sources for Highland history was first stimulated in early boyhood by being told a traditional account of the Appin murder while standing on the spot where the Red Fox met his death. His particular interest in Highland attitudes towards *Bliadhna Thearlach* (Prince Charlie's Year) has been fostered by discussion of the Gaelic texts with his University classes over a number of years.

I HOPE TO provide, in what follows, a re-appraisal of a sometimes neglected source of information about the '45: contemporary Gaelic song and poetry. Like any other historical source it can be mishandled if one neglects to learn its particular codes. But there is nothing mysterious about the codes themselves, once one takes account of them; and the exercise is worthwhile in terms of the end-product, which is a coherent and credible set of views, from an important perspective, on the Prince and his adventure.

The songs themselves were mostly composed for oral circulation, and some of those cited below have been sung continuously down to the present day. In such cases, however, the fullest texts we have are usually in sources written down much nearer the time of composition.

The most prolific composer of all the Jacobite poets, Alexander MacDonald (Alasdair mac Mhaighstir Alasdair), saw his works printed as early as 1751; and although the earliest published anthologies of Gaelic verse (Ranald MacDonald's Collection and the Gillies Collection, published in 1776 and 1786 respectively) tend to be reticent as regards the songs of the 'Forty-five', later anthologies, from Turner's Collection (1813) to John MacKenzie's *Beauties of Gaelic Poetry* (1841), were less inhibited; and some of the manuscript collections made from the later 18th century onward supply further items as well as independent versions of songs appearing in printed collections. A substantial selection of these texts is available with English translation in John Lorne Campbell's excellent *Highland Songs of the Forty-Five.*

Despite very few exceptions the political orientation of these songs is overwhelmingly Jacobite. There is a good reason for this. By our period there had evolved a polarisation between two sorts of clan – one group royalist, Catholic (or at least non-Presbyterian), and culturally traditionalist, and the other parliamentarian, Presbyterian, and culturally progressive. The former axis, which included *par excellence* the Clan Donald and its satellites, was the one which provided the more favourable circumstances for the composition of Gaelic poetry in the mid – 18th century and for its trans-mission subsequently. Of course, there were chiefs and leaders within that axis who had accumulated good reasons for toeing the Government line by the time of the '45; but the old attitude died hard amongst their followers. Indeed it is noteworthy that even in areas where the leaders were staunchly Hanoverian, such as Argyll and the Reay country, poets like Duncan Bàn Macintyre or Rob Donn Mackay follow an ambivalent or even a Jacobite line.

Our poets range from educated gentlemen and officers with access to the military thinking of the Jacobite leaders, through traditional Gaelic bards accompanying their chiefs on the expedition, to womenfolk waiting at home for news or lamenting the deaths of their loved ones in battle. While some of the Gaelic songs are 'Jacobite songs' in the same sense as their Scots counter-parts, complete with toasts and exhortations to the converted and loyal messages 'over the water', others, especially the anonymous women's songs, provide us with something very different, much nearer to the ideal *vox populi.*

A fair amount has been written about the motives of the Highlanders who came out in support of the Prince. Were they impractical idealists, or caterans on a glorified cattle-raid, or men driven to desperate action by cultural and religious persecution? Dr. Campbell, who favours the last alternative, has justly complained that too many historians have attempted to answer this question without reference to the testimony of Gaelic sources. Although they require to be handled carefully, the Gaelic songs of the time can tell us a good deal about the psychology and motivation of Highland Jacobitism.

The ultimate reason for taking action is consistently presented as a moral imperative – *còir* 'right, what one should do', *ceart* 'what is right, just' and *dlighe* 'what is due (to and from one)' being the operative terms. The action prescribed is to drive out the usurping ruler and to restore the rightful one. Some powerful old concepts underpin this prescription. First, the older Gaelic bardic poetry had always laid great emphasis on the existence of a compact between rulers and poets, in which the latter were supposed to set the seal of acceptability on a king's rule by giving it their praise, or conversely to withhold that praise if the king's justice faltered – the point being that in mediaeval times the poets' censure was held to be a blemish on a king, and (in theory at least) a blemished king could not rule. This belief in the possibility of a people's rejecting a monstrous ruler, together with the conviction that it fell to the poets to expose his shame, lies somewhere behind the readiness of the Gaelic Jacobite poets to resort to personal satires against members of the House of Hanover.

In the second place, Gaelic political mythology clung to the ancient notion that the just king's reign was accompanied by plenitude and fine weather, while storms and poverty were signs of something rotten in the State. To the Gaelic poets the rule of the House of Hanover constituted such a state of outrage. The various ills and grievances which Highlanders laboured under as a result of present or past Government policies, including the Union, became tokens of the rule of an unjust king and were used to establish King George's ripeness for deposition. Thus, when the poets rehearsed their 'case for the prosecution' by declaring the blemishes of the royal house, they often made use of the conceit that Nature reflects the quality and justice of the present King's rule. Alexander MacDonald, for instance, begins one of his poems:

> 'Every day is cold and raining, every night cold and stormy. Miserable and grim is every day, oppressive and heavy with mist. But waken up, people, and banish your dejection. Cast away your sorrow: Aeolus and Neptune are about to make a pact covering sea and sky, and every sort of ease will attend it.
> Fair weather will come with the [rightful] King ...'

In order to find out what the House of Hanover had actually done wrong one has to wade through the mass of conventional abuse – the animal similes, the physical and mental debilities, the accusations of criminal behaviour and unnatural vices, and other tokens of misrule, which are primarily the currency of satire. It boils down, quite simply, to a question of genealogy: as Alexander MacDonald puts it later on in the poem already quoted, George's *còir* to the throne was based not on heredity, since there were 'fifty better qualified' than he to succeed, but upon a mere Act of Parliament (i.e. the 1714 Act of Settlement). It is open to us, of course, to regard this complaint also as a mere label, a cipher for something deeper and inarticulate, rather in the way that we have to look beyond 19th century satires addressed to sheep or shepherds to find the real causes of the Highland Clearances.

Nevertheless, I believe that the poets' repeated references to *fuil* ('blood') should be understood as a serious and self-sufficient concern. For we are dealing here with the tail-end of an intensely conservative aristocratic tradition in which birth counted for everything, and some clans traced their descent back to the Kings of Scots, or even claimed kinship with the Stewart kings. Moreover, this sense of having a stake in the continuance of the Stewart line became a particularly attractive aspect of the past in the eyes of more conservative Gaels (including, *par excellence,* the poets and shennachies) at a time when the traditional bases of Gaelic society were rapidly crumbling away. Alexander MacDonald could have been touching a deeply responsive chord when he referred to the Gaels as *àlach gun mhàthair* ('a motherless brood') in the absence of a Stewart ruler, or when he addressed the Old Pretender as 'our earthly father under the heavenly Father', whose coming would put an end to present tribulations.

In contrast to the terms of dispraise which Gaelic poetry mostly employs when dealing with the House of Hanover, Charles and James, being 'rightful rulers', fall to receive the standard accolades of Gaelic panegyric. This involves a value-system whose virtues include not only qualities which one can strive to embody (such as justice) but also some which conventional ethical systems would regard as morally neutral, and which are more the product of nature than of nurture – e.g. physical strength, comeliness of appearance, and nobility of birth. Rob Donn nicely articulates this in his song to Prince Charles :

> '[The Stewart prince] is a haven in time of distress, our stout rock to steer by, supremely endowed with virtues, and the people have taken him to their hearts.
> When one considers his heredity the depth and completeness of his culture come as no surprise: (he is) like Solomon, just in dispensation; like Samson he is strong of arm; like Absolom he is fair of face; he is a shield and bulwark to his friends.'

The Stewart king over the water is not infrequently presented in an almost messianic light. He is 'the one we desire', the 'awaited' or 'longed-for' one. Thus in one of Alasdair mac Mhaighstir Alasdair's best-known songs:

> 'O hì ri rì, he is coming,
> O hì ri rì, the king we desire,
> Let us take our weapons and battle-dress
> and the tartan kilt plaided up.

I rejoice, he is coming, the son of the rightful king we desire, a great kingly frame well-suited to weaponry, the broadsword and patterned targe.

He is coming over the sea, the tall man most handsome in appearance, the high-spirited rider of the chargers, who would go lightly in the pursuit.'

The next verse is a fine example of MacDonald's capacity to get carried away by his own words, raising the poetic stakes dramatically. The following translation does no justice at all to its rhythm or density or to the menacing onomatopoeia of the last line (in Gaelic *sgoltadh chorp mar choirc' air cluain*):

'His appearance is like the stormy close of Winter, the chill breeze before a squall, a glimpse of a storm-riven rainbow; a slender blade in his hand to make carnage, scything through bodies like oats in a field.'

On a few occasions the awaited leader becomes 'the Promised One', 'the Prophesied One'. In the aftermath of Culloden John Roy Stewart is able to anticipate better days:

'If . . . the French prevail in Flanders I have confidence in the old prophecy that an army to sustain us will come over the seas.'

However, this theme is not so developed in surviving Jacobite poetry in Scotland as it is in Ireland. More common are Old Testament parallels between the Gaels and the Children of Israel: the Gaels, like Israel borne down by the oppression of Pharaoh in Egypt, await the appearance of their Moses; or again Charles may be seen as playing David to King George's Saul.

The idea that 'God is on our side' in fact occurs in various guises, and should be taken seriously in view of its importance in 'royalist' thinking in general. Not every poet goes so far as Alexander MacDonald, who actually claims Jacobitism as a *soisgeul* ('gospel') and even after Culloden claimed that the inheritance of the Gaels was 'to be loyal — yes, that is our creed'. But the sense that the coming war is a Crusade is strong in a number of the poets. Thus Aonghas Mac Alasdair (MacDonald) addresses the Jacobite clans:

'Clans of the Gael, who have traditionally been 'loyal', give service now to Charles as his loyal followers. Attend him, every one of you, without dragging of heels; do not dwell upon the danger to you but put your trust in Christ.'

Mac Mhaighstir Alasdair himself addresses the Almighty with the following prayer:

'O God of all, do not let might overpower right . . . Remove from us the Pig and his oppression . . . and clean out

Whitehall completely on behalf of that Royal Family whose
ancestors resided there.'

Not only is God on the Jacobite side, but there are signs that the present
time is propitious. Where Rob Donn talks about the way weather and crops
bear testimony to the rightfulness of the Pretender's claim, Mac Mhaighstir
Alasdair regards 1745 as the moment when history is about to be made:

> 'Historians of the Clans, arise and write effective history;
> historians of the present time, seize pen and paper: this is the
> special year . . .'

Even more pointed are references to a Jacobite belief that a new star
appeared for the first time when Prince Charles was born:

> 'The star of his birth already provides knowledge and true
> presage that the one who has now arrived is a "son of
> fortune" whom the Father of Grace has sent to protect us.'

In the poem already cited by Rob Donn the demonstration that Charles
is the 'rightful ruler' includes the following testimony which makes explicit
the Christian parallel and also implies the Messianic message:

> 'Don't you see for yourselves the care which the Heavens
> took to make obeisance to him, when the shining star stood
> out in the line by which people were setting their course –
> the (very) sign which was associated with our Saviour, before
> Charles's coming to this country, when those wise men went
> to Jerusalem to seek Him.'

Finally, we meet a confident insistence that support for the Jacobite
cause will be overwhelming when the Prince comes. In his 'Song of the
Highland Clans' Mac Mhaighstir Alasdair proceeds to a roll-call of the clans
he expects will rise. It includes not only those most obviously likely to
support the Jacobite cause, but also some more surprising names (e.g. the
Campbells); and it furthermore includes reference to participation by
'British' – that is, presumably, Lowland Scots plus English – 'and Irish
Jacobites'.

It should be clear from the foregoing paragraphs that Gaelic Jacobite
poetry of the sort quoted is far from being a neutral commodity.

Alasdair mac Mhaighstir Alasdair, besides being the leading visionary
and intellectual amongst the Jacobite poets, was also a tireless propagandist
for his ideals, using poetry and song in the same way that a political
evangelist in a modern, literary society would use hustings and media, debat-
ing chambers, journals, pamphlets and books. Moreover, as he says himself,
and as not a little of his poetry shows, he was literally 'high' with enthusiasm
for Prince Charlie:

> 'Suppose you were cheerily marching at the head of the
> battalion I would not disturb a single dew-drop as I followed

close behind you, floating on air with high spirits, with
intoxication of battle and of happiness . . .
   . . . your gracious presence that would banish every
deficiency: why, you would turn the pewter of our flesh to steel
whenever we looked greedily into your face.'

But if such verse appears sometimes to lose touch with reality we must
remind ourselves of its functionality within the honour-based, aristocratic
society of the Highlands, and be prepared to tune in to its own wave-lengths.
Thus Mac Mhaighstir Alasdair's already-mentioned roll-call of clans who
would rise is to be seen not as misjudgment, over-optimism, or wishful
thinking, but as invoking the classic bardic carrot and stick of fame and
shame, to say to the Highland gentry, 'Here are the deserved accolades your
fathers have won; this is your opportunity to join their Hall of Fame.' This
was a worthwhile and practical contribution to the Jacobite cause, given that
many of the Highland nobility of the time were not yet wholly purged of a
Gaelic consciousness, and that most Highland families contained some
Jacobite sympathizers, including those houses whose chiefs took the Government line. Even in the case of the Campbells, the precedent of 1715 revealed
some who had defied their clan's 'official' line, and it could be hoped that the
same thing might happen again; while the tone of some of Duncan Bàn
Macintyre's comments suggests that in territory which was nominally under
Hanoverian direction there could be different sympathies amongst the non-
Campbell tenantry and peasantry. And at a quite different level of
explanation one should not forget the tradition that 'The Song of the
Highland Clans' was one of a set carried to Paris by Jacobite relatives of
MacDonald's and used to help persuade the Prince that the time was ripe for
him to come to Scotland!

The question remains, of course, how widely such Jacobite pieces were
disseminated, understood and acted on. The proceedings of the trial of Lord
Lovat contain evidence for the doings of the defendant together with one of
our poets, John Roy Stewart, whose escape from Inverness gaol he had
recently engineered. A prosecution witness alleged that they spent their time
'in composing burlesque verses, that, when young Charlie came over, there
would be blood and blows'. Does that relatively enclosed ambience of
Jacobite gentlemen and agents account for all, or at least much, of the Gaelic
poetry we have been considering? Clearly it played a part; but although our
knowledge of the actual circumstances of dissemination of individual songs
is usually inferential and fragmentary, I believe there are some grounds for
supposing that most of ours were composed (or at least destined) to be heard
by a wider audience than the narrow circle of the wholly converted. In other
words, one may imagine their being sung in inns, at fairs, in *céilidh* houses,
and 'below stairs' in big houses − i.e. not just in the dining halls and drawing
rooms.

The reasons for this supposition are both general and particular. In the
first place it should be remembered that, if we except Mac Mhaighstir

Alasdair's works, the vast majority of the poems under consideration have
been preserved at some stage by oral transmission; and even in MacDonald's
case oral versions of a good number of his poems exist, beside those whose
survival depends entirely on the poet's own scribal and publishing activities.
Secondly, consideration of the metrical-musical form of the poems shows
that in some cases our poets employed 'higher' and 'lower' styles on different
occasions to cover the same subject-matter – which might suggest a
conscious attempt to strike a more communal note in the 'lower' case. Thus,
for example, of John Roy Stewart's three songs on Culloden, one is in the
more 'literary' *amhran* form with its long four-stress lines, while the other
two are in more thoroughly popular metres. And while some of Mac
Mhaighstir Alasdair's poems have more complicated structures corresponding to more elevated language and more recondite allusion, others are
couched in simple song-metres or even adopt the irreducibly popular form of
the women's waulking-song tradition.

Thirdly, while it has correctly been noted by scholars that the anonymous oral-popular song-tradition (as opposed to the productions of the
named poets in the post-bardic tradition) does not offer much evidence for
contemporary composition relating to the '45, the conclusion sometimes
drawn, that the episode meant little to 'ordinary Gaels', would seem to be
less certain. For one thing, it could well be that the principal genres
commonly assumed under the rubric 'oral-popular song-poetry' had ceased
to be regularly productive by that time; for another, the time-lapse between
the mid-18th century and the time when collectors began to take an interest
in such poetry was much longer, and the possibility of non-survival corres-
pondingly greater; and finally, there are a few exceptions, and they do appear
to show the sort of attitudes we should be led to postulate on the basis of the
picture provided by the more 'literary' tradition. The best known such
example is the waulking song beginning *Có a sheinneadh an fhideag airgid?*
'Who would sound the silver whistle?' One of the Barra versions runs as
follows:

> 'Who would sound the silver whistle?
> The son of my king coming to Scotland,
> on a great ship over the sea,
> on the ship of the mariner he has set sail,
> on the ship of the handsome mariner.
> She had a golden helm and two silver masts
> and a well of wine down in her hold,
> shrouds of the French silk,
> with golden pulleys at each end of them.
> Whoever would deny it, he would sound it . . .
> who would sound it but Ewen Cameron?
> Whoever would deny it, he would sound it.
> MacLeod and MacKenzie would sound it.
> When my King comes to his land

> the Prince will be crowned in triumph
> in the White House where the heroes dwell ...'

And another version contains the sequence,

> 'And they would put the foreigners to
>   challenge,
> and they would send King George home,
> away over to Hanover.
> And who will sound the silver whistle?
> Whoever would deny it, I would sound it.
> Who would deny that I myself would sound it?'

Evidence of a different sort is furnished by incidental details in the poems themselves. I have laid stress up till now on their conventional aspects, such as ideological framework, symbolism and rhetoric. But it should be stressed that these are not really part of the message of an individual poem: they function as a sort of *continuo*, rather like the drones of the pipes. Often enough we find realistic and mundane hopes, fears and doubts surfacing in a way which make the poems seem less impersonal and more in touch with a real state of affairs.

For instance, in Mac Mhaighstir Alasdair's '*Oran Nuadh*' ('New Song'), which speaks inspiringly about the new 'gospel' that has reached the Highlands and is galvanizing heroes to action (and so on), we meet with what I presume to be glimpses of reality in such lines as 'Many a man *who is now pretty faint-hearted* will become heroic (when the Prince comes)'; 'You will be comprehensively successful, *if only you show willing*'; however many would drink Jacobite toasts, smash their glasses in the hearth and verbally dispose of King George, 'now the deed is more honourable than any number of (punch-) bowls ...'; and after vaunting the irresistible strength and ferocity of the Highland hosts the poet concludes with a more reflective comment:

> 'It is the small army which has won, often enough, in the
> hard game of battle. Let us march out without being over-
> awed in any way, and let dread not affect us.'

The realities are equally clear from a poem, attributed by one source to John Roy Stewart (though it is anonymous elsewhere), which takes the form of a dialogue between a young girl who is vehement in her support for the Prince, and an interlocutor who counsels a more canny approach, though with a lack of conviction which hints at the poet's own sympathies. It is basically a 'Heart *vs* Head' debate; and the voice of Reason has, as its last word, the following comment to make:

> 'Girl, do not mention Charles, we are little the better off for
> his existing. His enemies are numerous and strong, although
> his friends are not scarce. The 'top drawer' of the nobility are
> denying him (though a certain element amongst them have

treated with him), keeping George around the place despite the desire of the King of France.'

I take it that the two 'voices' in this poem are a device to juxtapose existing views on the political situation in 1745 or 1746, and that, allowing for the discreet loading of the dice on the pro-Jacobite side, they testify to trends of thought then current.

An especially important poem in the present context is Aonghas Mac Alasdair's *Òran Brosnachaidh* ('Song of Incitement'), which gives some palpably practical advice addressed to those who were about to set out to put the Prince on the throne. He begins by advising them to say farewell to their wives, houses and possessions if they have to be away from home, and continues:

> 'Do not let the sound of gun-powder put the slightest anxiety into your bodies, nor blue-black muskets any decline in your hopes; whenever that sound dies away the distress and hurt are at an end, and you will be tackling them at close quarters according to your immemorial practice . . .'

Beyond a doubt these are serious, practical counsels to real fighting men – the advice of a survivor of Killiecrankie and the Rising of 1715. For that reason the poet's enumeration of the objects of the expedition command special attention. Interwoven with the hortatory *cum* panegyric *continuo*, these are as follows. If the Gaels succeed, and 'win a kingdom', their 'fame will spread over the world' and they will enjoy 'the wealth of every land', and not just their own patrimony. The things they will say goodbye to are at least as important as the positive gains depicted:

> '. . . the choicest of land free from import and taxation. You will enjoy ease and comfort, free from hardship and struggle, with goodwill to encourage you and nobody injuring you.'

When Charles attains the throne he will not forget his friends, and the lowly as well as the high-born will benefit from the relief from 'turmoil and harassment'. Church and State will resolve their problems and the various Churches will be respected. Trades will prosper and will always be well-provided for.

Naturally, there is unbounded optimism here, combined with a certain amount of 'pleasure equals absence of pain'. But it would be a poor army that set out without ideals and high hopes; and we know from other sources how confident was the Jacobite assumption that support would be forthcoming from sympathizers throughout the realm as the campaign gathered momentum. I do not believe one can get nearer to the minds of those who followed the Prince than the mix of idealism, calculation, pride and dissatisfaction which emerges from this poem.

The departure of the contingents of fighting men to join the Jacobite army is captured nicely by the traditional accounts of the '45 recorded by Rev. Thomas Sinton in his *Poetry of Badenoch*. According to this source the MacPherson band marched first to the refrain:

> 'We will not return, no, we will not return again,
> Till the King shall be crowned we will not return.'

They then changed to 'the livelier measures of a favourite marching song':

> 'Why should we be miserable?
> Why should we be sad?
> Why should we be miserable?
> We'll all march together!
>
> There's many a wife will lack a son,
> and sister who'll lack a brother,
> and young maid who'll lack her love,
> if we go as we're going.'

Over in Lochaber a MacDonald lady addressed the Jacobite leaders in more formal terms. Prince Charles is 'the Star, the priceless treasure we yearned for' which has now been brought safely to its owners. MacDonald of Keppoch and other leading men are praised and exhorted to heroism, and the MacGregors are urged to throw off the Campbell yoke. On the other hand, Sir Alexander MacDonald of Sleat is roundly criticized for not joining the rising – 'your holding back is becoming tiresome to me'. The general feeling is one of confidence:

> 'The foolish General [i.e. Sir John Cope] was coming to fight against you; it won't be long before he bites the dust, though he advances with head held high. But if he would keep a tryst, as the coward's orders were, there would be many a red-coat without head, without feet, without sight.'

From the point when the Jacobite army left the Highlands we have two viewpoints to take account of: that of the combatants, and that of those who were left behind awaiting news. Because of the ultimate failure of the campaign, the dislocation and confusion which followed it, and the need for all poetic hands to stand to (as it were) to help cope with the trauma of Culloden, surviving participant accounts of the expedition are few. There are, however, several incidental references to Prestonpans in poems addressed to Highland leaders who distinguished themselves there, and similarly with engagements which occurred during the retreat north from Derby. An interesting song from the 'home front' is that ascribed to 'a Stewart lady', *Seo an tìm tha cur as domh* ('This is the time that is doing away with me'). The poetess opens with a complaint of ineffectuality – loss of voice, as she puts it – when what is needed is strong prayer to help 'the rightful king of the Gaels, who will go from us to London shortly'. What I take to be her prayer assumes the form of an invocation of the stout men who will go with Charles, with pride of place given to her kinsman, Colonel John Roy Stewart and to another local hero, Gillies Mac Bean. Mention of them seems to bring a measure of confidence, and she refers proudly to Prestonpans:

> 'In the battle with Cope you won the honour, you were a leader above leaders; why, they all likened you to Claverhouse.
> It is you who would inject disorder into the camp of King George – minus their heads, their legs and their boots!'

A further roll-call of powerful allies comes next. It includes MacDonald of Sleat: was the poetess ignorant of the facts, or powerless to exclude the senior branch from a listing of the branches of Clan Donald, or is this another example of the wish being articulated as a means to bring about the reality? At all events, the list of allies gives way to imprecation against the Redcoats and the Argyll Militia, who, in Thomas Sinton's words, 'were dispersed in parties over various districts in the North, which were favourable to the Jacobite cause, where they rendered themselves very obnoxious':

> 'And if I live five years I will yet see an evil requital exacted from those who are hacking the hides off the cattle, from the people with the red coats and the Militia of Argyll – you will yet see those beasts in an evil way.'

Continuing in invocatory terms but switching back to the Jacobite army, she wishes them the power to ward off lead and powder, and envisages 'English and Campbells' routed 'even if I don't live to see it'. Then, holding the personal note she tells us that she is at present 'in the Braes', away from her relatives, and hearing nothing but the belling of the stag, but will somehow gather her strength and head for home, to the heart of staunch Jacobite territory:

> 'And young Charles Stewart, we shall see a crown on you, and you will yet be scourging the (Hanoverian) brutes.'

The song is noteworthy for its fluctuation between confidence and anxiety, and the whole should be seen as an apprehensive expression of solidarity at a time when hard facts were unobtainable.

When we come to the battle of Falkirk we are more favoured, since we have texts composed by eye-witnesses or participants on both sides. Duncan Bàn Macintyre was with the Argyll Militia on the Government side. He was very probably not yet twenty-one years old, and he was serving as a hired substitute for another man, rather than for reasons of personal conviction. Moreover, the occasion for his song was the loss of his sword – or rather that of his hirer – which he treats in a satirical, mock-heroic way. Nevertheless, in building up a picture of the circumstances of his discomfiture he provides some interesting side-lights on the combatants and action. He shows clearly the confidence of the Government forces:

> 'Going to engage the Prince our side were cheery enough: we thought we would get the better of him and that all we had to do was to seek him out.'

They had not considered the possibility that they might be the ones to be 'driven, like sheep before a dog': after all, they had 'the professionals' on their side – men 'well-armed and trained, devoted to the art of killing'. But then 'panic overtook us in the rout' when the Jacobite army charged downhill and 'Prince Charles and his Frenchmen' were breathing down their necks:

> 'We did not receive a word of command instructing us to smite our enemies – simply liberty to scatter throughout the world; and some of us are still missing.'

The poet then brings the subject round to the sword, its loss, and the repercussions when he returned home without it.

A poem in celebration of the battle was addressed by one Alexander Cameron to his chief, Lochiel, and contains the following verse – the same action as seen from the Jacobite side:

> 'On the day of Falkirk, Hawley's day, you (Camerons) outreached his company when the (Hanoverian) enemy turned in six ranks on the hillside. Stress of battle did not put you (Lochiel) off your stride; you opted for the course of action which was fitting – the hereditary one. When your clan drew together the (Hanoverian) beasts took to flight.'

Aonghas Òg, second son of Iain of Glengarry, was also present on the Jacobite side, at the head of his father's clansmen, but was killed accidentally shortly after the battle. The elegy for him by Aonghas mac Ailein adds some further circumstantial details regarding the battle. After opening with some elegiac verses he continues:

> 'On Falkirk Moor, great was your courage at that time: although the cavalry came up with us they didn't upset you; although they were horrendous to behold with grey blades unsheathed, your word (of command) was efficacious with a view to destroying them all at once.'

In other words, Aonghas was able to hold his men's fire in the face of the cavalry charge until it could have a devastating effect – a reversal of the usual roles in Highland-Lowland confrontations, and one that called for authority, judgement, and nerve.

Aonghas Òg's death was a severe blow to the morale of the Highland army, and especially to Glengarry's men:

'The best news that King George had, since the day you first
joined the fray with him, was your being lost to your fellows.
They have melted away like mist from you since the day they
buried you; no two men of them have remained in rank –
alas that you were not alive until today.

Duke William would not be so oppressive to us, nor
could he be, since you were the one who could withstand
every peril and strike the blows; if the gun had been stayed
and not hit you from the window, sure, Charles would have
been in London before now.'

In this context it should be remembered that, in the pattern of 'limited
warfare' practised by the Gaels of old, loss of the leader entailed an end of
fighting; that this traditional concept was especially relevant in the case of
the Glengarry MacDonalds is suggested by the consistent use of the old term
ceathairn 'band of fighting men' to describe them in the elegies for Aonghas
Òg. In fact the position was more critical than that, since Aonghas's elder
brother Alasdair, the heir, was at the time interned in London. Aonghas mac
Ailein, the bard 'on the spot', puts it thus, speaking first to Aonghas Òg:

'Your band of retainers were tearful, especially since the heir
is not here to take your place; what has happened would have
been no cause for complaint if they had you (Alasdair)
yourself on the spot. What has deepened my grief is that they
have you in captivity in London: woe betide Clan Donald if
King George gets the upper hand.'

He turns now, rhetorically at least, to Prince Charles, and articulates
plainly the conflict of loyalties which the situation imposed on his clansmen:

'But young Charles Stewart, a very great loss has overtaken
you – fine warriors who would not renege on you in the
Cause; the heir of Knoydart and Glengarry imprisoned by the
foreigners – that was the wound; and if harm befalls them
while fighting for your sake it is dearly that we have
purchased your acquaintance.'

In conclusion, however, the poet softens this revealing admission (for
both conventional and practical reasons), though he does not retract it:

But I *would* seek your acquaintance *if* God would so will it
that victory would attend you on every day of battle; long-
term victory, and swift release for my chief – that's what I
would seek if I had my way, and what would dispel my grief
would be for George to be hunted like a fox.'

In circumstances like these, plain speaking (by bardic standards) is
needed if the poet is to rein in the feelings of his fellow clansmen and offer
them a way forward.

The defeat of the Jacobite army at Culloden has been burned into the collective memory of Gaelic speakers everywhere, irrespective of religion or political persuasion. The Jacobite dead, 'without coffin, without shrouds, without even being buried in holes', put a bitter twist into the fulfilment of Mac Mhaighstir Alasdair's bloodthirsty prediction of Hanoverian defeat:

> 'There will be many engaged in stripping corpses in the battlefield – ravens cawing, fluttering and swaggering about; kites ravening, drinking and eating their fill – how sad and feeble in the early morning will one hear the groaning on the field of slaughter.'

Important as the battle was at the time in terms of human loss, it became even more important as a symbol – the symbol of something like the end of independent Gaelic action. The bubble of confidence, the conviction that the Wheel of Fortune was on the turn at last, was rudely burst. And from our present point of view the defeat had the further effect of putting the poets into the front line: there was abundant need for elegies; and equally, if less obviously, for the resuscitation of numbed psyches of the living, by analysing and rationalising the defeat, and preparing men to come out and fight the next round.

This consciousness of a social responsiblity made for a fair degree of un-animity as to the line poetry should take, and in numerous later compositions one senses that the poetic ranks have closed and an 'official version' is being purveyed. The songs of Mac Mhaighstir Alasdair were influential in this process. However, his was not the only analysis, and other poets' on-the-spot reactions contributed to the view which ultimately prevailed. To the question 'what went wrong?' the answers were various, some being more subtle than others. In the synthesis which follows I have drawn heavily on the poems of Colonel John Roy Stewart, which are particularly instructive in that, whatever he says, we must assume that he was *au fait* with the thinking of the Jacobite leaders and as well placed as anyone to interpret the course of events.

In the first place it was suggested that the contest was an unequal one. John Roy maintained that the Hanoverian forces outnumbered the Jacobites by 'more than three to one'. The disparity was increased by the absence of certain leaders and their men on the day. These included some who had in fact been sent up into Sutherland to seek money and reinforcements; but this line of argument also raised the more delicate matter of deserters, late-comers and other non-combatants. Later poets could ignore such inconvenient details; but to John Roy composing while in hiding during the summer of 1746, they had to be dealt with – albeit in a diplomatic way capable of preserving the possibility of 'shaming' such men into participating in the next round.

It was also common belief that the weather and the terrain had been inimical to the Jacobite army in that the Highland charge had been made over rough, sodden heath and bog into the teeth of driving sleet and hail –

'a third of our misery came out of the skies', as John Roy puts it. This in its turn meant that Cumberland's musketry and artillery could take a deadly toll 'fatally pre-empting the brilliance of sword-play'. But facts like these naturally raised questions about the quality of the Jacobite leadership and the wisdom of their tactical decisions. How had they allowed themselves to be manoeuvred into such a position in the first place, and should they have engaged battle in the circumstances? Considerations such as solidarity, not to mention collective responsibility, placed a certain restraint on what John Roy could commit to the poetic air-waves of Gaelic song; and his surviving songs tell us little of the faction and dissension that preceded the battle, and nothing of his own part in the debates. Thus in one of the three songs he composed on Culloden – the most 'popular' in form – he gives simply a circumstantial-sounding, soldier's-eye account of the preliminaries:

> 'They adopted battle order . . . we invited them to meet us half-way . . . (but) they would not come up to meet us.
>   Our commander then shouted out to us, 'We shall be destroyed by wind and rain, (so) up and at them, my beloved ones, we cannot await them any longer.'

Nevertheless, John Roy elsewhere voices some criticisms (admittedly fairly muted and generalised) of 'the leaders' (*an luchd-orduigh*) and the Jacobite tactics. For the rest he has recourse to an expedient which should be seen in terms of the constraints I have mentioned and the audience his Gaelic songs were intended to reach: he seeks a scapegoat, and finds one in Lord George Murray:

> 'If the stories that circulated are true, that there was an Achan in the camp . . . that man was the great General . . . who corruptly sold honour and right. He 'turned his coat' for the big purse, and that brought destruction on King James's heroes.'

In the last resort, however, the Gaelic poetic commentators found it impossible to accept that the defeat could have been engineered by human agency alone – and certainly not that of the Duke of Cumberland, whose military record was by no means awe-inspiring. Many songs, especially those of the more popular sort, reflect a belief that some form of sorcery or witchcraft must have been involved. The implications of all this were clear: it *was* possible to explain the disaster, and there *could* be another day, when the Highland charge would once again prove irresistible and the Hanoverians would be swept away forever.

While this poetic propaganda machine was getting under way with the objective of containing the trauma of Culloden, the survivors were making their way home and the dead and missing were becoming known. John Roy Stewart inserted a roll of honour into one of his songs about Culloden, in which he paid homage to some of his Badenoch friends. But there are also

personal elegies, of which the magnificent one composed by the wife of
William Chisholm of Strathglass is deservedly famous:

'Och, young Charles Stewart, it is your cause which has
ruined me; you have taken from me all that I had, in conflict
on your behalf. It is not cattle, nor sheep that I am
lamenting, but my spouse, (and so it would be) even though I
were left alone without anything in the world but my shift –
my fair young love.

Who now will raise the sword or fill the throne? That is
hardly on my mind now that my first love is dead. But how
could I find it in my nature to deny what I desire, seeing that
my will is so strong to bring my good King to his proper
place? – my fair young love.

It is I who am torn asunder, and if I say it it is no lie,
my cheerfulness has turned to tears since you cannot be
returned from death. It would not be easy to find a man of
your prudence and understanding – and at Culloden there
stood no-one of your sort who was braver – my fair young
love.

I was convinced for a while that my husband was alive,
and that you would come home blithely and cheerily. But
time has gone past and I see no-one resembling you: till I go
to the grave I will not lose my love for you – my fair young
love.'

As for the Prince himself, he was on the run with a price on his head.
Few knew where he was, even amongst his associates. John Roy, skulking in
one of his hide-outs in Strathspey, expresses his anxiety thus:

'All pleasure has departed me, my cheek is frosted with
sorrow, since at present I hear no glad tidings about my
beloved Prince Charles, rightful heir to the crown, who
knows not which way to turn.'

The times are dangerous: 'every trusty man who gave service to the King
is being pursued in headlong flight throughout the deer-forests.' John Roy
himself is an outlaw (ceatharnach coille, 'wood-kerne') with bloodhounds
(coin luirg) on his trail.

By now Prince Charles was no abstract symbol of Kingship to those who
had campaigned with him, but the more homely 'Tearlach Ruadh' ('Red-
haired Charles') – John Roy's 'bonny Red Charles'. We catch further
glimpses of his wanderings at this time in two women's songs, one of them
echoing the courtly tradition and one in a waulking-song fragment. The first
seeks to express the speaker's affection in conventional love-praise terms but
soon breaks out of that mould:

'Young Charles with the lovely tresses, I gave love to you

which was no 'one year love', love which I would not have
given to a Duke or an Earl – how I wish I had never seen you.

Young Charles, son of King James, I saw a great pursuit
following you: they (were) cheerful, I was tearful, the waters of
my head cascading from my eyes.

They killed my father and my two brothers, they destroyed
my clan and plundered my relatives, they ravaged my
homeland and despoiled my mother – and my grief would be
the less if Charles should succeed.'

The second runs as follows:

'Watchman, what do you see?'
'I see An Ùdairn and Rubha Hùinis,
Caolas Rònaidh with mist obscuring it.'
'Do you see the galley beside the Dùn,
flying the white banner of Charles Stewart?
Mary Mother, may grace be doubled for him,
a price on his head and the enemy hounding him;
may the French host come over to help him!'

Eventually, of course, the woman's prayer was granted in that the Prince
escaped safely back to France. We may leave the last word on his Scottish
adventure to Mac Mhaighstir Alasdair. Although self-consciously literary in
form and propagandist in intention, his dialogue 'The Prince's Departure'
has the Gaels speak words which must surely have been felt by many others
besides the poet himself:

'Our thousand blessings go with you, and may God preserve
you in every place. My earnest, open prayer for you is that
sea and land be equally smooth for you; and although sad
misfortune has parted us, one step short of death, farewell,
son of King James, my heart's desire, and return without
delay.'

The Jacobite parts of the Highlands paid the price for their part in the
insurrection, and the Gaelic poetry of this period tells of reprisals and
executions, estates confiscated and leaders in exile. A fragment of song
ascribed to the wife of Fraser of Guisachan and Culbokie is addressed to her
son Ruairidh, who was newly born when the soldiers came and burned down
her home:

'The year that you were born, Ruairidh, that was when they
despoiled us.
Dejected and sad am I trying to keep a one-week-old (child)
warm.
They burned my barn and my byre and fired my floored
house.'

There were exceptions: Alasdair Mac Mhaighstir Alasdair himself, in his vision-poem 'The Ark', includes a certain Captain Duncan Campbell amongst those Campbells who may be saved from the impending Flood because he had been compassionate to the 'bare and poor of Moidart' and 'would not execute the order which his warrant from the Butcher contained'. But in general the impression given is of suffering and misery – as indeed was intended by the victors.

Amongst the various measures implemented with a view to 'pacifying' the Highlands, the Disarming and Disclothing Acts, and especially the latter, attained prominence and a certain symbolic value in the songs of the time. Disarming was, in the circumstances, to be expected, and attracts relatively less comment; but the imposition of Lowland dress on all Highlanders excited indignation and became the subject of a considerable number of expressions of resentment.

In his 'Proud Plaid' MacDonald, after extolling the virtues of the Highland dress in the way that was to become conventional, and declaring that to proscribe it will merely confirm the Gaels in their resistance, continues:

> 'Unless you tear our hearts out and rip our breasts right open, you will never remove Charlie from us until we are snuffed out.
> He is woven into our souls, firmly waulked and tightly locked; and until yon man is cut away from us no-one can prise him free from us.'

In other songs again the calls for defiance and a new rebellion are open and direct in the years immediately following Culloden. Poetry was one of the fires that kept the pot from going off the boil.

It would not be right to conclude this brief account without mention of the ways in which succeeding decades coped with the phenomenon of the '45, as the men who had fought in it or witnessed it died away, and the mixture of grievances and aspirations which had given rise to it yielded to fresh preoccupations, the age of the Clearances, the Napoleonic wars and religious revival. To generalize, one can document a gradual blurring of the image and a process of re-interpretation which eventually left *Bliadhna Theàrlach* appearing either as the height of heroic endeavour or as a temporary and inexplicable aberration. This left the way open for the romantic view of the 'Forty-five to prevail, which it duly did, reinforced by the official respectability of things tartan, in the 19th century; but that is another story.

I have attempted in the foregoing account to pick out some of the most important and interesting ways in which Gaelic poetry deals with the '45. I hope it will have emerged that the ideas and attitudes of the Gaelic-speaking participants do not need to be guessed at, since they are available in the poetry. From the point of view of British historians of the 18th century the Highland perspective is a decidedly 'alternative' one, but it has coherence.

We are fortunate to have it and it deserves fuller and more serious investigation than it has received to date.

A NOTE ON SOURCES

Aiseiridh na Sean Chánoin Albannaich ['The Resurrection of the old Scottish Tongue'] (Edinburgh, 1751).

The anthologies and editions cited most frequently above are as follows; those marked with an asterisk include English translations.

The Poems of Alexander MacDonald, ed. Rev. A. MacDonald and Rev. A. MacDonald (Inverness, 1924).

The Gaelic Bards from 1715 to 1765, ed. Rev. A. Maclean Sinclair (Charlottetown, 1892).

The Songs of Duncan Bàn Macintyre, ed. A. MacLeod (Edinburgh, 1952).

Hebridean Folksongs, ed. J.L. Campbell and F. Collinson, 3 vols. (Oxford, 1969-81).

Highland Songs of the Forty-Five, ed. J.L. Campbell (2nd ed., Edinburgh, 1984).

The Songs of John MacCodrum, ed. W. Matheson (Edinburgh, 1938).

The MacDonald Collection of Gaelic Poetry, ed. Rev. A. MacDonald and Rev. A. MacDonald (Inverness, 1911).

The Poetry of Badenoch, ed. Rev. T. Sinton (Inverness, 1906).

Comhchruinneacha do dh'Orain taghta Ghaidhealach, le Paruig Mac an Tuairneir [i.e. 'Turner's Collection'] (Edinburgh, 1813).

Songs and Poems in the Gaelic Language by Rob Donn, ed. H. Morrison (Edinburgh, 1899).

Sar-Obair nam Bard Gaelach: or, The Beauties of Gaelic Poetry, ed. J. MacKenzie (Edinburgh, 1841).

Note that all quotations in this essay are freshly translated, for reasons of consistency, though they are of course indebted in varying degrees to existing versions. Occasionally they incorporate emendations to printed texts necessitated by sense or metre.

I am indebted to Mr Neil MacGregor for permission to consult his unpublished M.A. dissertation on the poetry of John Roy Stewart.

(For a fuller treatment of the subject, with references and footnotes, see 'Gaelic Songs of the Forty-five', *Scottish Studies* 30, 1989.)

6

THE LONG SHADOWS
A view of Ireland and the '45
by
Owen Dudley Edwards

Owen Dudley Edwards. Born Dublin 1938. After education,
and university teaching in the U.S.A., lectured in History at the
University of Aberdeen 1966-68, since when he has taught at
the University of Edinburgh where he is now Reader in
Commonwealth and American History. His publications extend
widely, but on Irish links with Scotland he has written *Burke
and Hare*; *The Quest for Sherlock Holmes* (a biographical study of
Arthur Conan Doyle); and contributions to David McRoberts
ed., *Modern Scottish Catholicism*, and David Daiches ed., *A
Companion to Scottish Culture*, as well as broadcasts and
journalism. His essay on Patrick MacGill, the Irish writer on
Scots navvies, is in a recent issue of the *Innes Review*. His
analysis of Aodhagan Ó Rathaille's Jacobite poem '*Mac an
Cheannaidhe*' (not discussed in the present essay) will shortly
appear in an Irish review; it was prompted by research for the
present work. He is married to Bonnie Lee, and they have three
children. He has edited an anthology *Edinburgh* with Graham
Richardson. The translations from Irish poetry are by him.

*In Ireland there was peace. The domination of the colonists was absolute. The
native population was tranquil with the ghastly tranquillity of exhaustion and of
despair. There were indeed outrages, robberies, fire-raisings, assassinations. But
more than a century passed away without one general insurrection. During that
century, two rebellions were raised in Great Britain by the adherents of the House of
Stuart. But neither when the elder Pretender summoned his vassals to attend his*

coronation at Scone, nor when the younger held his court at Holyrood, was the standard of that House set up in Connaught or Munster. In 1745, indeed, when the Highlanders were marching towards London, the Roman Catholics of Ireland were so quiet that the Lord Lieutenant could, without the smallest risk, send several regiments across Saint George's Channel to reinforce the army of the Duke of Cumberland.

Nor was this submission the effect of content, but of mere stupefaction and brokenness of heart. The iron had entered into the soul. The memory of past defeats, the habit of daily enduring insult and oppression, had cowed the spirit of the unhappy nation. There were indeed Irish Roman Catholics of great ability, energy, and ambition; but they were to be found everywhere except in Ireland, at Versailles and at Saint Ildefonso, in the armies of Frederic and in the armies of Maria Theresa. One exile became a Marshal of France. Another became Prime Minister of Spain. If he had staid in his native land, he would have been regarded as an inferior by all the ignorant and worthless squireens who had signed the Declaration against Transubstantiation. In his palace at Madrid he had the pleasure of being assiduously courted by the ambassador of George the Second, and of bidding defiance in high terms to the ambassador of George the Third. Scattered all over Europe were to be found brave Irish generals, dextrous Irish diplomatists, Irish Counts, Irish Barons, Irish Knights of Saint Lewis and of Saint Leopold, of the White Eagle and of the Golden Fleece, who, if they had remained in the house of bondage, could not have been ensigns of marching regiments or freemen of petty corporations. These men, the natural chiefs of their race, having been withdrawn, what remained was utterly helpless and passive.

THOMAS BABINGTON MACAULAY, *History of England*, Chapter 17.

'I LANDED WITH 7 MEN', stated Prince Charles Edward. Our concern here is with four of them, the four who were Irish. This is not to slight the memories of those of Irish birth or descent, such as the gallant and tragic Lally Tollendal, who sought to foment distractions in England while Charles Edward marched South from Scotland, or the Irish troops who distinguished themselves in retrieving so much of the disaster at Culloden. It was an Irishman whose ship landed the Prince: the French-born Antoine Walsh, of Nantes, master privateer and merchant who made his fortune in the odious business of the slave trade. It was an Irishman who finally got the Prince away: the soldier of fortune Richard Augustus Warren. But our four men of Moidart are embodied pieces of Irish history, and between them they help us to see the Irish shadows falling across the '45.

The Irish majority at Moidart may appear strange, but in strict numerical terms it had its justice. The only part of the British Isles in which James III and VIII actually exercised regal authority was Ireland. It was a shadow authority, but it was of vital importance. Throughout his majority he was given the right by successive Popes to nominate the archbishops and bishops of the Roman Catholic Church in Ireland. They were outlaws under the existing anti-Catholic penal legislation of the post-Revolution governments in London and Dublin. They lived and worked under circumstances of privation and fear. They were not Jacobite agents in any political sense, so far as we know: a few such charges were made against them by greedy and spiteful accusers, but these seem to have had no substance. They had the grim task of maintaining discipline, recruiting a suitable priesthood, and repelling superstition in their outlaw church. They served a majority of the Irish population, although one reduced to the lowest caste. Their followers had in most instances refused to subscribe to oaths of allegiance under Parliamentary legislation which, while not disavowing Roman Catholicism explicitly, repudiated allegiance to any present or future Catholic sovereign of Britain or Ireland; and they had by definition rejected the benefits in land and status which could follow acceptance of Protestantism. But in most cases allegiance to James went no farther than the refusal to renounce his claims, his Bishops, and his faith. The Bishops whom James nominated seem to have performed their work conscientiously, and it is because of his judgement and their dedication that the institutional structure was kept alive. Had James not insisted on his right to nominate, Irish Catholics might not have been such obvious security risks despite their actual political quiescence; but without his central authority behind their appointments the bishops chosen by six very different Popes could have proved much more disunited and demoralised. By the time of his death in 1766, when the Papacy declined to recognise the succession of Charles Edward (who flirted with Protestantism between 1746 and 1766), the Roman Catholic hierarchy was once more on a secure foundation.

James III (as I style him here when dealing with persons who so regarded him) naturally chose clerics of whose fidelity to him he had no doubts. Inevitably Irish priests at home or in exile who wanted promotion showed no doubts as to the wisdom of his retaining the powers of nomination. Hence the natural leadership element among the clergy, as well as the Bishops themselves, were his loyal supporters. But neither he nor they seem to have sought a political implication for this; it makes him a very unusual figure among Catholic sovereigns who obtained such powers. The system's habitual cancer was the subordination of spiritual to political needs of the sovereign. James did not have the temptation caused by the possession of political power; but he had that induced by the desire to obtain it. But what we know of his nominees argues for their overwhelming spiritual concern. Even here there were dangers enough. Venal clergy, justly reprimanded, could and sometimes did take a terrible revenge by simply denouncing their superiors to the civil authorities. Gaelic itself − the language spoken by most Catholics, and the only language spoken by many − did not prove a natural assurance of secrecy when the apostate decided to look for blood-money with some judicious informing. Small wonder that the only surviving Gaelic sermons by a Bishop of the time are very dark. James O'Gallagher was Bishop of Raphoe (i.e. county Donegal) from 1725 to 1737, and then on James's insistence against a candidate favoured in Papal circles was translated to Kildare and Leighlin serving until his death in 1751. In the first of these sermons he states that God turned away from the world in disgust and anger after the Crucifixion of his beloved Son, who being indissolubly part of Him partook of the sentiment; and only through the intercession of the Blessed Virgin was He led to think kindly of individual persons. O'Gallagher's conclusions seem the fruit of his personal witness of human suffering. The logic is clear: he could not see the unhappy Catholic poor as the authors of their own misery, much though he excoriated individual sins (and much though the majority of Irish Protestants, when they thought of it at all, said it was the Catholics' own fault that their condition was so wretched). So he concluded that the entire world was under sentence of Divine displeasure, and only the holiest of lives could ensure salvation.

Well might such sentiments flourish: about 300,000 are estimated to have perished of famine and disease in 1740 and 1741, i.e. some 6 per cent of the total Irish population in each year. There was a smallpox epidemic in 1745 itself. The Catholic Bishops and priests well knew how little their flocks could contribute to their support inasmuch as the established Protestant episcopalian Church of Ireland demanded its tithes from all in supreme indifference to the Roman Catholic and Presbyterian convictions of the great majority. O'Gallagher and his colleagues worried about clandestine marriage, faction-fighting, alcohol abuse, wild parties at wakes, and the various other self-destructive ways in which their people sought to drug themselves physically and mentally. As for the law, in its worst anti-Catholic forms it was asleep: but it might at any stage wake, and nothing was more likely to wake it than the danger of Jacobite invasion. A very few priests may have fooled around with a little Jacobite conspiracy, but they were lucky enough to go undetected if in fact they existed. For the rest, the clergy were thankful for being untroubled, and took trouble to remain so. Some fifteen years earlier sheriffs visited houses supposedly tenanted by the proscribed religious orders and reported finding no friars; and friars' account-books which have survived list the expenditure of some of their tiny funds on wine with which to treat the sheriffs during their visitations. It is funny, but the humour could hardly be blacker.

The Irish Catholics were decidedly lucky in the Lord Lieutenant who took office shortly after the landing on Moidart: Philip Dormer Stanhope, fourth earl of Chesterfield, wit, letter-writer, and master of elegance. He noted no sign of disaffection in the Catholics, and pointedly tipped off representative figures that if any surfaced, they would find him implacable. The wretched 'mass-houses' officially permitted to function had been closed during the '15. Chesterfield resisted pressure to close them during the '45 (such as they were: a house in Pill Lane, Dublin, had collapsed on 26 February 1744, killing the celebrant priest and nine of the congregation). He jeered at Protestant alarmists, telling one who burst into his chamber in the morning with the news that the Papists in Connacht were rising, that he was sure (examining his chronometer) they were and he had better be rising himself. The only dangerous Papist in the Kingdom, he remarked to another, was the beauteous Miss Ambrose, to whom he also addressed himself rather more directly. But on the rebellion itself his language to the Duke of Newcastle in private correspondence told how the master caste and race saw challenges to its authority and hegemony. 'I am very sorry to hear that any *loyall Highlanders* are to be arm'd at all', he wrote on 6 December 1745:

The proverb indeed says 'set a thief to catch a thief', but I beg leave to except Scotch thieves... Upon my word, if you give way to Scotch importunitys and jobbs upon this occasion, you will have a rebellion every seven years at least. There must be alertness and vigour in crushing of this, and unrelenting severity in punishing it afterwards.

And on 11 March 1746:

For my part I would put a price upon the heads of 'em, and then they would bring in and destroy one another. And why not? There is already a price upon the Pretender's head, who is the only one among 'em to be pitied or justified. And why not put a price upon the Drummonds, the Gordons, the Glengarrys, and the rest of those rascals? They are not enemies but criminals; we cannot be at war with 'em ... I would ... employ only English and Hessians in subduing the Highlands. I would also forbid provisions of any kinds being sent upon any pretence whatever (unless directly to the Duke's Army) into Scotland, and I would starve the loyal with the disloyal, if the former thought to remain with the latter. ... I have taken effectuall case that the *Loyalest* Highlander shall not have an oatcake from hence.

And the Irish Parliament on 11 April 1746 responded to the crisis by three acts which showed what bolt-holes were felt most necessary to be stopped. There was an act for licensing hawkers and pedlars and encouraging the foundation in Ireland of English Protestant schools, a recognition that nomads were a security risk, especially when seemingly supported by economic occupation, that 'hedge' schoolmasters were another risk, and that the incentive for smuggling children abroad for education must be countered – however impractically. There was an Act disabling Irishmen in the French or Spanish service from holding property, which it was hoped would at least cut down on the lawful occasions for such knight-errants to revisit their native shores. And there was an Act annulling for the future any marriage solemnized by a Roman Catholic priest when either or both of the contracting parties were Protestant – a reminder that fears of the alienation of Irish Protestant property into Irish Catholic hands remained at the heart of the Irish Protestant ascendancy and its rigid caste system.

The Irelands for which the four men of Moidart stood differed in some respects from that of Bishop O'Gallagher as much as from that of Lord Chesterfield. The Bishop and the Viceroy were conditioned by realities, while being the envoys of Courts much misinformed by rumour and chimera, self-serving courtiers and wish-fathered thoughts, greed and privation, love and hate, hope and despair, faith and fear; they were neither of them prepared to sacrifice the welfare of the people they ruled for cheap popularity. The four men of Moidart ruled nobody. They were where they were because of dreams and memories, and their individual policies partook strongly of both. Their identification with the Irelands they served had some self-service in it; but it never involved the obvious self-service that betrayal of Charles Edward would undoubtedly have brought them. The Jacobite movement in Europe among Irish exiles must not be seen as cut off from Ireland. In certain respects James III was better served by information from Ireland than were the Hanoverians and the oligarchy that ruled in their name, witness his insistence on the effectiveness of O'Gallagher in remote Donegal. Smuggling between Ireland and the European mainland supplied invaluable cultural, social, intellectual, religious, educational and economic links. Goods were shipped in and out; bishops, friars, nuns, unregistered priests, recruiting agents, conspirators, spies and other contraband persons were imported to Ireland, potential students, soldiers and ecclesiastics were exported. The smugglers and privateers, and their employers in mercantile business in Europe, were obviously animated chiefly by economic self-interest. Walsh was all for the '45 in Scotland, where it could be trusted to draw off British shipping from the sea-lanes productive of most profit to himself and his associates. Among his colleagues with larger views could be found ideas of isolating Ireland from British rule by establishing a limited Stewart restoration there, with obvious economic advantages to Britain's continental rivals; but to James, Charles, and the Jacobites in Ireland it was restoration to the three Kingdoms of Ireland, England, and Scotland, or nothing. The four men of Moidart all seem to have agreed with their sovereign on that point.

There were Irish Jacobites still surviving among the Irish descendants of pre-Reformation English settlers who had remained true to Catholicism – an ancestor of the vigorously Protestant Violet Martin, the 'Martin Ross' of Somerville and Ross, was said to have tried unsuccessfully to support the Stuart forces in the '45 – but the Moidart four by patrilinear descent at least were of Gaelic origin. Two, however, were of Protestant antecedents. The Protestantizing of Ireland had been almost invariably subordinated to land confiscation, and its maintenance, but certain attempts were made to bring the reformed faith to the Gaelic-speakers by persuasion and instruction. Sir Thomas Sheridan derived from such a case. William Bedell (1571-1642) was made Protestant Bishop of Kilmore and Ardagh by Charles I in 1629: he dropped Ardagh, a good indication in itself as to his unusual non-materialist priorities, and, concentrating on Kilmore, took an interest in a young fellow known as Dennis Sheridan who had been brought up as a Protestant in the household of the Dean of Kilmore. The boy was certainly born Donnchadh Ó Sioradáin of an old Cavan Gaelic sept. He seems to have worked for Bedell in the Bishop's great design of translating the Bible into Irish, and certainly played a critical part in saving the manuscript later. Bedell ordained him priest in the Church of Ireland, and stood godfather to his eldest son.

Kilmore, lying in South-West Ulster, had a Protestant population thinning out from the large masses imported from Lowland Scotland and the Borders when James VI became James I and found that a deep frontier of tough, independent, radical Protestants had suddenly become a liability. The Irish Catholics in Ulster not only saw their masters change but themselves driven off their old land, and in 1641 exploded in a bitter insurrection against Protestants. Sheridan seems to have retained enough Gaelic associations to possess immunity and powers of protection, but Bedell, allowed sanctuary under his roof, died of fever contracted from the number of other Protestant refugees crowded into the same dwelling. Sheridan saw to the funeral, where the Catholic insurgents greatly startled the mourning family by accompanying to his grave the Bishop whom they had driven from his Palace, loudly declaring him to have been 'the best Englishman', and giving him military honours with drum and musket-volley.

Irish historical crises have very long shadows, and none longer than that of 1641, recalled down the centuries as a warning to Protestants of the fate in store should they relax their vigilance against the dispossessed Catholics. Montrose undoubtedly met his doom in part for the hatred extended to him for having brought the dreaded Irish aborigines to Scotland: there was a sense in which he was held guilty of treason to his race. As the immunity of Dennis Sheridan makes clear, the Lowland Scots and the English were not the only ones to see the conflict in proto-racial terms. Cromwell's slaughters in Drogheda and Wexford were explicitly in retaliation for 1641, and one of the greatest counts in the indictment of James VII and II in the minds of Protestants was the fear that he would unleash the Irish Catholics. But Dennis Sheridan's family had a different tradition, one of terms being made across the religious frontier.

Dennis had four sons. William was given his Godfather's See of Kilmore in 1682, refused to take the oaths to William and Mary, was the only Irish Protestant Bishop to be deprived of his See as a Nonjuror, and died after twenty years in poverty and insanity. Patrick was a short-lived Bishop of Cloyne, likewise appointed by Charles II; James, the youngest, also remained in Ireland (his son Thomas was a friend of Swift: *his* son Thomas was actor, elocutionist, and father of the playwright Richard Brinsley Sheridan). Thomas, Dennis's third son, was an intellectual of secular rather than spiritual bent, becoming Fellow of the Royal Society; he frequented Court circles, married a reputed bastard of James Duke of York, and defended himself during the Popish Plot by vigorous asseveration of his Protestantism, but was nevertheless identified with James, who made him Chief Secretary for Ireland when he had succeeded Charles as King.

In Dublin James's boldest Irish proconsul, the Earl of Tyrconnel, wishing to have some thousands of Irish (but non-Gaelic) Catholics incorporated in the English army as a counterweight to hostile Irish Protestants, was opposed by Thomas Sheridan who declared that the O's and Mac's were ten to any one of the rest: Thomas evidently inherited Dennis's confidence in his own people. And he also remained true to Dennis's Protestant tradition by opposing Tyrconnel's dismissal of Protestant army officers solely because they were Protestants, for which, he told James, Tyrconnel hated him.

The Sheridans exemplified the principle of Gaelic Ireland making the best terms it could with a Stuart monarchy, and fell with it. Thomas fled with James, taking his son with him; young Thomas was present when William defeated James at the Boyne in 1690, and then became a page in James's exile Court. Old Thomas disappears. Young Thomas ultimately became a Catholic, was appointed under-Governor to the young Charles and was given an empty baronetcy in 1726. The Prince's Governor, to whom he seems to have preferred Sheridan, was James Murray, the Protestant Earl of Dunbar: he would not be the last Murray whom Charles liked and trusted less than he did his Irish Catholic advisers. Charles wrote his father asking for Sheridan's presence when he made his dash to France in 1744. But however much Sheridan's acceptability was now partly owing to his Catholicism, it is that lost Gaelic Protestant inheritance which makes him so particularly interesting, if ineffective, a figure at Moidart.

The Rev. George Kelly had been a martyr to the Jacobite cause but, by contrast, remained a Protestant to the end. In his case also Gaelic Ireland looms as a shadow in the background, ominous and alien to his fellow-Protestants but not, apparently, to him, and once more with familial reasons for reassurance. He was born in St John's parish, co. Roscommon, just before the Revolution, a short distance westward of Athlone where the Shannon divided hard Gaelic Connacht from the lush, green, Dublin-ruled plains of Leinster. Kelly's father is described on the rolls of Trinity College Dublin as a centurion. A name of Gaelic origin in a Roscommon domicile on the eve of the Revolution invites the suspicion that the centurion supported James at the siege of Athlone and the subsequent disaster at Aughrim; but whether he did or did not, conformed or was killed, George entered Trinity in 1702, obtained an academic post and was ordained Deacon of the Church of Ireland. In 1718 he delivered a sermon expressing sympathy for the exiled Stuarts, at a time of increasing fear of a Jacobite invasion. For this he was expelled. It may have been that his action was based on belief of a Jacobite *coup* of some kind. Jacobite agents were active in Connacht. Disaffected Tories were drifting into Jacobite ranks in Britain. The '15 itself had depended greatly on the anger of dispossessed Protestant episcopalians in Scotland. But in Ireland the Protestant episcopalians, firmly hugging to themselves the seats of socio-political power, had everything to lose from a Stuart restoration. The best guess is that Kelly had drifted into Tory circles in Dublin and London, which with the advent of the Hanoverians were pushed towards Jacobitism for want of prospects elsewhere. James Butler, second Duke of Ormonde, Lord Lieutenant in 1703-05 and again in 1710-11, and then captain-general, was stripped of his office after swearing allegiance to George I, and then went over to the Jacobites. He fled to France and his estates were forfeited in 1715, when he endeavoured to invade England in support of the Rising. His fall would certainly have ended the hopes of many Tory Protestants, and Kelly would have marked in the next years the plums of the Church of Ireland falling to Englishmen. He may already have become an associate of his future patron Francis Atterbury, Bishop of Rochester, deep in Jacobite intrigue from 1717.

It is easy to dismiss Kelly as merely a foolish place-seeker whose isolation in Trinity and removal from his roots led to his ludicrous misreading of the political situation. Yet he cannot have been deaf to the opinions of his colleagues and seniors in the College, and his action required courage and conviction. At worst, he had the nerve of a gambler. His subsequent attempts to recruit his finances through John Law's Mississippi schemes are no simple proof of venality; he had cut himself off from means of subsistence. He migrated to London, where he was put in the Tower as a political prisoner. There he remained for fourteen years, ultimately escaping through the work of a relative, Myles MacDonnell, a Roman Catholic priest. Here is proof of continued if sporadic association with Gaelic kinsfolk, but he subsequently remained true to the Protestant faith as well as the Jacobite cause. He served and survived Atterbury and Ormonde, and seems to have become increasingly a focus of considerable suspicion to his Catholic fellow-Jacobites, including the Irish (and ultimately his cousin MacDonnell). He obtained some personal ascendancy over Charles, and may have had reason to hope for his conversion to Protestantism. And it was probably a further gamble for personal prestige arising from a Stuart restoration aided by conversion which took him to Moidart.

Sir John Macdonald, as he is usually termed, dashes into the story as though anxious to provide Stevenson with a part-model for the Chevalier Burke in *The Master of Ballantrae*. He was noisy, drunken, aggressive, sardonic, intriguing, shrewd, resentful, censorious, and impractical. He was a cavalry leader from the French army in Spain and on the Prince's campaign was assigned a purely titular role as Inspector of Cavalry. His origins and indeed entire career are largely shrouded in obscurity, but one point stands clear. He was from Antrim, and his name was correctly MacDonnell, although with his first language almost certainly Irish its vagaries were probably caused by his thinking of himself as Mac Domhnaill. The last we know of him is that on 26 July 1750, having surrendered after Culloden as a French subject and been exchanged, he sought to secure from James III a vacant See in Ireland for a friend. His lobbying suggests a concern about his place of origin, the still Catholic Glens of Antrim, for the See was Down and Connor. He wanted it to be in what he took to be appropriate hands. He was by now very old, and his motives underneath the alcohol and inferiority complex would seem to have been those of fidelity to his own local origins. Had Charles secured the Kingdom of Scotland, the nearest friendly Irish locality would have been MacDonnell country in Antrim. Charles no doubt had other reasons for enlisting him. The Irish Catholics had by now won a great reputation in the armies of Europe. Most of their prominent figures were careerists, with little hope or even interest in the country of their own or their parents' origin, although those of the rank and file who ultimately reached Scotland suggested a more personal involvement. As recently as the beginning of May 1745 Irish troops had played a great part in winning for the French against the British and Dutch the unexpected victory at Fontenoy. MacDonnell may not have been much of a substitute for their leaders, but his own waning life gave him a desperation absent from wiser heads. When Charles's advisers would decide at Derby against further penetration of an increasingly hostile and sullen South, MacDonnell roared with rage, demanding that all be put at hazard for a dash to London. Despite all common sense, he may well have been right. But from his point of view that was the only solution.

The lack of English support was less an obstacle in his eyes and in those of certain other Irish, not because they were Irish so much as because they were soldiers. The European soldier of his time expected to be resented by civilians through whose homeland he marched and whom he generally regarded as oscillating between a nuisance and a prey. On the other hand in Moidart MacDonnell took the views of the locals very seriously indeed. He evidently thought of the old unity between Gaelic Antrim and Gaelic Western Scotland with a coherence founded on the antiquity of his childhood memories and the traditions embraced in them. What matter that the descendants of Donald had divided across the North Channel several centuries before? Montrose had brought some of them back to Scotland. MacDonnell at first was specifically in favour of returning to France when no local support seemed forthcoming. Then, a little later, as the Prince negotiated with Macdonald of Clanranald, kinship asserted itself when Clanranald hesitated. MacDonnell later wrote in his memoir:

> This indecision lasted nearly an hour during which time he came out of the room several times to come and consult with me as a relation and one whom he could trust. I did all I could to persuade him to do what the Prince wanted, and it was not more difficult than it usually is to persuade people to do that to which they are strongly inclined.

The sardonic Ulster common sense adds credibility to his claim. His Gaelic and that of Clanranald would have been extremely close, much more so than he would have found with that other Irish native Gaelic-speaker at Moidart, John William O'Sullivan of Kerry. Gaelic culture and the claim (rather than the actuality) of kinship would seem to have been the determining factors in any influence he exercised on Clanranald. MacDonnell at this point looks like a man aware of having come home, although to a remote part of home. More than any of the others, even the possibly English-born Sheridan, he stands for an identity of culture and interest to be found in both islands: but it was still a Dál Riada local patriotism. He extended it readily across the Gaelic Highlands, especially for distant cousins:

> Upon the day fixed for the raising of the standard, the two chiefs Lochiel and Capoch [Keppoch] arrived according to promise, at the head of their men. Never have I seen anything so quaintly pleasing as the march of this troop of Highlanders as they descended a steep mountain by a zigzag path.

But if his blood thrilled to such allies, his Antrim heritage also bred in his bone hard suspicions of Scottish Protestants. He would never have had a fully pan-Scots, let alone a pan-British, sense; and his identification with the rest of Ireland, even Gaelic Ireland, would have been markedly limited. The '45 gave him one last chance to fight for the locality he held so dear. And it would have been this which brought him to Moidart.

John William O'Sullivan was also from Gaelic Ireland, but at the polar opposite from MacDonnell. His family was from the island of Dunkerron, in the Kenmare River, and when he was born in 1700 he was at the heartland of the richest Gaelic Jacobite poetry in existence. There flourished and suffered the great Aodhagán Ó Rathaille, passionate patriot, Jeremiah of the old Gaelic noble order and evangel of the exiled Stewart kings. What has come down to us of his work through manuscripts is of extraordinary delicacy of imagination, wealth of symbol, fierceness of anger and almost unbearable sorrow. And its power must have been far greater in its oral expression. In the dark and seemingly hopeless years of its deprivation, Catholic Gaelic Ireland maintained a cultural identity with the dream that somehow it could be restored to its former glory by the return of the exiled Stuarts to the three Kingdoms: Ó Rathaille alluded very clearly to all three. Footballs in European diplomacy, last refuges of English politics, alternative options for threatened Scots lairds and chieftains, the Stewarts remained for the Ireland of Ó Rathaille and his heirs the means of fighting a rearguard literary action for a culture faced with the ultimate certainty of extinction. The Stewarts offered a cause for their present privations, and a heroic justification of their struggle to maintain their identity. The condition of the people induced in itself only a grey despair: the vision of the heroes who would, who must, return gave the poets and their fireside audiences a stature far above the petty misery and pygmy servitude to which their condition condemned them. Their conquerors had made their supposed fidelity to the Jacobites the basis for their reduction to the lowest caste; their poets made that fidelity a means of still reaching to the stars. Ó Rathaille was dead when news came of Charles's return, but Piaras Mac Gearailt sang:

> *Tá lasadh 'san ngréin gach lae go neoin;*
> *Ní taise don rae, ní théigheann fé neoill;*
> *Tá barra na gcraobh ag déanamh sceoil,*
> *Nach fada bheidh Gaedhil i ngéibheann bróin.*

> All day the sun shines noonday tall,
> The moon will never downward fall,
> The tops of trees their stories call
> That Gaels will find their griefs grow small.

To understand John William O'Sullivan it is necessary to think of the ideology and traditions of the Irish poets whose work supplied the cultural heights of his youth. It is only as a latter-day Irish bard that he makes sense. His deep emotional involvement with Charles Edward was personal, but it was bound up with the larger cause of the Stuarts, of Catholicism, and of the old Gaelic order to be restored by their return, on the evidence of James II's Irish Parliament which had called the title of the confiscated lands into question. His love for Charles could not prevent their estrangement when after the '45 the Prince announced his Protestantism. He shared none of the sense of need for diplomatic dealing with the Protestant potential supporters of the Prince which animated Kelly and Sheridan. English was not his native language although his memoirs are written in it: he speaks of fearful English people on the march being reassured by 'Sir Thomas [Sheridan], who spoak their language very well', implying that he was less sure of himself. At moments of emotion his narrative lapses into Gaelic rather than English constructions, as when he describes his farewell to the Prince after their arduous journey from Culloden:

> Sullivan cant containe, he burst out a crying to quit the
> Prince & to see the danger & misery he was exposed to; the
> Prince embrasses him, & holds him in his arms for a quarter
> of an hour, Sullivan talking to him as much as his tears & his
> sobs cou'd permit him, praying him for God sake, if he had
> the misfortune to fall in the enemis hands never to own what
> he was, to go by the name of *Champville* & give himself for a
> Lt in Daufins [the Dauphin's] Regimt of foot. It was a most
> dismal sight to see Sullivan in the Princes arms; the Saillors
> hear Sullivan crying & see the Prince go off, they all cry &
> roar, & looks upon the Prince as lost. The Prince come back
> to them, assures them that there is nothing to fear, that he
> leaves Sullivan with 'em, that they'l hear from him that night
> or next day, that 'we will all joyn again': that does not satisfy
> the men, they double their crys & moans. It wou'd touch a
> heart of flent to see that seperation.

The bard would speak of himself at such a moment in the third person as one observing himself; and he would style himself *An Súilleabhánach* (which he simply anglified as 'Sullivan', without the prefix). It may be that the entire narrative was drafted in Gaelic, and that O'Sullivan could not bring himself to polish so heartbreaking a passage when he had translated it or had it translated. The memoir in general is highly bardic in its endowment of the chieftain with the heroic virtues. These might be expressed in terms of formal admiration, but they could be rendered as comedy such as in O'Sullivan's description of Charles's parole of Captain Swettenham (whose name O'Sullivan recalled in a form more usual in Ireland):

> The Prince gave Captn Switman his liberty upon condition
> he wou'd not serve for a year & a day. This officer behaved
> very gallantly, he frightend the Governors of the Garrisons he
> past by, and even Cope. For he told 'um all, that the Prince
> had six thousand men, & that neither armes or mony was

wanting to 'em; he gave every where the most favourable
acc[oun]t that cou'd be given of the Princes personne &
activety. It is said the Ellector [George II] sent for him when
he arrived at London, & asked him, what kind of a man the
Prince was, he answered that he was as fine a figure, & as
clivor a Prince, as a man cou'd set his eyes on, upon wch
George turned his back, & left him there.

(To gain its full effect, the narrative has to be read with the musical
cadences of a rich Kerry accent.)

The bardic element is also reflected in other aspects of O'Sullivan's
narrative and conduct. The charges of his incompetence are very widespread, and while he makes some case against them, the form in which some
of them are couched and the unfriendly descriptions of his demeanour
around the Prince are consistent with something very unreal about him. It is
as though the return of the Prince in itself is the triumph, however
unsatisfactory its execution. As a military man, O'Sullivan supplies reasons
for the failure of the campaign, and he has the bard's consciousness of his
enemies, notably Lord George Murray, to keep their alleged shortcomings to
the fore in these reasons. But behind his rationalisations is another vision,
which constantly surfaces: the presence of the Prince in his country with his
faithful bard beside him, illustrated by figures who make entrances or exits
and by choruses of soldiers and sailors. Charles's speeches are very Irish
affairs, and Ó Rathaille, for one, would have found it highly appropriate that
he promised deliverance 'from the Slavery' his audience lay 'under'.
O'Sullivan seems to have shocked some of the Scots by his very physical
expression of devotion to the Prince, again a metaphor for the bard's relationship to his chieftain. Ostensibly his memoirs are a report to James III;
actually they are the claim that his hero proved his title as the promised
Redeemer, that the long sought-for Messiah came, that the prophecies have
been fulfilled:

> 'Tis not credible the movement the Prince gave himself, to
> get tember carryed to repair those bridges, as well as to
> reconnoitre the foards, tho' he had people, that he cou'd
> depend upon for those things. As well on this occasion as on
> all others, I cant imagine, how he resisted, in those great
> marches we made. He went alwaise a foot, only when he was
> to come into a Town, & notwithstanding the rigour of the
> season we were in, he never come to his lodgings until he
> saw the guards posted, & the men quarter'd, & to cause no
> jealloussy, marched allternatively at the head of each Regimt;
> every man had acces to him, especially those that had the
> least detail, so that he enter'd into the State of every thing, &
> continued this all the time. He was never heard to say a rash
> word to any man, prais'd most graciously those that served
> well, & treated very mildly those that did not; no Prince can

have a greater tallent to gain the hearts of mankind, nor
keeps his temper better.

Charles is admitted by his bitterest enemies to have shown himself a
noble commander; O'Sullivan declares he showed himself *the* noble
commander. Ó Rathaille had instructed Ireland on the contrast between
George I and James III:

> *D'inniseas di-se, san bhfriotal dob' fhíor uaimse,*
> *Nár chuibhe dhi snaidhmeadh le slibire slím-bhuaidheartha,*
> *Is an duine ba ghile ar shliocht chinidh Scuit trí huaire*
> *Ag feitheamh ar ise bheith aige mar chaoin-nuachar.*

> I told her, and true was my word as any I ever could speak,
> That it shamed her, the bond with that long and most
>   mis'rable streak,
> When of all of the race of the Scots the threefold fairest peak
> Stood waiting to make her his bride of the softest and
>   tenderest cheek.

O'Sullivan transposed the sentiment to their sons, and the poetry to his
prose.

Whether O'Sullivan knew this poem is neither possible nor needful for
us to know: he would certainly have heard others like it. His early years had
been passed with the expectation that he would be a scholar, to which
purpose he was smuggled to Paris for schooling about 1709, and thence went
on to Rome some years later to study for the priesthood. He seems to have
been ordained Deacon – thus resulting in Charles Edward arriving in
Presbyterian Scotland accompanied by Irish Deacons in the Anglican and
Roman Churches. He returned to Ireland when he had come of age, and
found he could only inherit the estates of his father by conforming to the
Church of Ireland. The estates had not been large, but had given some social
consequence: the family would have kept a table, and bespoken the services
of local poets, and the boy as infant or returned heir would have heard song
also in the cabins of the poor. O'Sullivan learned the hard lesson of what the
fall of the Gaelic order meant for him personally: by 1700 only 15 per cent
of Irish land was owned by Catholics and by 1800 that had fallen to 7 per
cent. He went back to Europe as intellectual rather than cleric, becoming a
tutor in the household of the Marshal Maillebois. It was only from here that
he was drawn into military service, under the Marshal, and while he saw
action in Corsica, Italy, and on the Rhine it was not until 1739-40. At some
point after this he became known to the Court of James III at Rome, and
directly attached himself to the Jacobite cause. Apparently he was at one
point a prisoner in England, whether arising from military or espionage
service is unclear. His memoirs simply mention a Captain Talbot as a fellow-
prisoner, noting that 'he was loved and esteemed by enemies as well as
friends': the casual reference conveys that James III, the recipient of the

memoirs, knew all about his imprisonment which suggests a Jacobite implication.

The memoirs are military: if anything, too military. If the author had listened to Irish poets, he almost certainly also had student memories of Caesar's *Commentaries*. Like many intellectuals in government service, he played the soldier. He had the courage and devotion; he also had the impracticality of the listener to prophecy. His bitter conflict with Lord George Murray has all of the recrimination between gownsman and swordsman, but where Kelly was self-evidently that anomaly so hated by Charles's kinsman William III, a cleric in the firing-line, O'Sullivan was careful to represent himself as a soldier. He accordingly acted much with MacDonnell, but he was far more intimate with the Prince than MacDonnell. Both of them had a particular reason for suspicion of Murray, whom they noted as anxious to purge Roman Catholics from the Prince's advisers and officers. 'This was a very nice proposition', recorded O'Sullivan bitterly. They were not simply concerned for their own positions. O'Sullivan probably inspired the Prince's insistence that he could not thus ostracise the 'Duc of Perth', or Sheridan, or the Catholic Highland Chiefs. MacDonnell believed that Murray and his associates wanted to make Charles their prisoner, and knew enough Scottish history to remember the fate of Charles II when a fugitive claimant 'in the same dependence on them'.

Hence behind the bitter feud with Murray lay O'Sullivan's conviction of an implacable conflict between their aims in the '45, and this must colour any view of their mutual hostility. It was a rivalry which seemed to aggrandise itself against the welfare of the Stewart cause; but to O'Sullivan, and almost certainly to Murray, it was essential if that cause was to come to fruition in terms acceptable to them. MacDonnell feared a Stewart restoration tied to a new Protestant ascendancy, and characteristically lumped the strong Protestant Episcopalian presence in Jacobite ranks with Presbyterian sentiment, both taken to be desirous of maintaining the Scottish, English and, it followed logically, Irish, Catholics in subjection. O'Sullivan agreed, but his priorities were much less Scottish. He was not anti-Scots – he was very enthusiastic about the Highlanders, and probably with Kerrymen in mind noted their prowess in the kind of terrain they knew, their fine work if only 'they wou'd but let themselfs be gouverned', and their unfitness for prosecuting sieges. He was grimly aware, again certainly by Irish analogy, of the horror-stories about Highlanders which convulsed the English. But he was implacably opposed to what he saw as Murray's aim of Stewart restoration without Catholic emancipation. He was the Prince's man, but this implied an inextricable commitment of the Prince's return to the restoration of the Gaelic order. Better the Prince should fail than that he should win a victory which betrayed the cause of that order. And if he did fail, his bard stood with him more constantly than ever, through all privations and illness and the discomfort of his corpulent frame. When they were sundered O'Sullivan went berserk over half Europe from Bergen to Versailles in order to rescue his Prince. As for himself, the shadow of a world already doomed, he found his true happiness in shadow, richer to him than any substance:

> I'd never finish if I cou'd recall to yu all the marques of Compassion, generossity, & good neature, that the Prince has given from the moment he landed until he went off, & I set a greater vallu on those marques, than I do on all the proofs, of Vallor, presence & courage of mind that he has given upon all occassions, & that no man can refuse him.

Considered in cold, calm, rational analysis, the '45 was a hopeless failure, Charles was a noble disaster, and the Irish were fighting the wrong war, in the wrong place, in the wrong time. But what has logic to do with the defence of a world which logic has already doomed? It was in the service of the lord of the Munster poets that John William O'Sullivan became the seventh and last man of Moidart.

BIBLIOGRAPHY

The conduct of Irish-European soldiers in the '45 is valuably examined by the late G.A. Hayes-McCoy, leading Irish military historian of his time, in 'Irish Soldiers of the '45', *North Munster Studies* ed. Etienne Rynne (Limerick, 1967). F.J. McLynn, original and incisive, adds 'Ireland and the Jacobite Rising of 1745', *Irish Sword*, XIII. (1977-79), to his very useful other studies of military, diplomatic and ideological questions which likewise are helpful here: *France and the Jacobite Rising of 1745*, *The Jacobite Army in England* and (more ragbag but still seminal) *The Jacobites*. Writings of Richard Hayes on the Irish in 18th century France are crammed with instructive if filiopietistic detail: *Biographical Dictionary of Irishmen in France* is most constructive, and see also his 'Irish Associations with Nantes', *Studies*, XXXVII. (1948), *Irish Swordsmen of France* and *Old Irish Links with France*. John William O'Sullivan's narrative is edited by the siblings Alistair and Henrietta Tayler as *1745 and After* (London, 1938), with annotations quoting appositely and comparatively from Sir John Macdonnell's memoir. My other sources on the '45 are obvious enough: *The Lyon in Mourning*; W.B. Blaikie's edition of the *Itinerary* of Charles; Robert Fitzroy Bell's edition of the *Memorials* of Murray of Broughton; W. Scott, *Waverley*. As the content invites literary perspectives on Prince Charles Edward, I have had particular reason to be grateful for the biographies by Compton Mackenzie, Moray McLaren and David Daiches. The greatest historian of eighteenth-century Ireland was the late Maureen Wall: her *The Penal Laws 1691-1760* may well be unsurpassed as a miniature masterpiece in point of information, analysis, real sense of the country and scholarly authority: all of her other works on the period are vital (and newly discovered MSS by her are shortly to be published), notably her 'Catholic Loyalty to King and Pope in Eighteenth-Century Ireland' (*Proceedings of the Irish Catholic Historical Committee 1960*). Rev. Cathaldus Giblin, O.F.M., 'The Stuart Nomination of Irish Bishops' (*ibid., 1965-67*) makes an essential point. Bishop James O'Gallagher, *Sermons in Irish-Gaelic* is conveniently reprinted in both languages (Dublin, 1877) and is unique as a contemporary work of its kind. Rev. John A. Brady, 'Catholics and Catholicism in the Eighteenth-Century Press', bound with *Archivium Hibernicum* XVI. (1961) is an outstanding presentation of newspaper evidence: other works by Brady and by Rev. Patrick J. Corish, jointly and severally, are admirable. There are many individual editions of Irish-Gaelic poets, but as a start Canon Pádraig Ó Canainn, *Filidheacht na nGaedheal*, a gigantic selection primarily for schools, cannot be bettered; an agreeable bilingual presentation in smaller compass may be found in *An Duanaire* (Seán Ó Tuama and Thomas Kinsella), and Kinsella has included some of the translations in his *The New Oxford Book of Irish Verse*. Oxford's *A New History of Ireland* (still under production) is of vastly varying quality: volumes VIII (chronology) and IX (maps, genealogies, lists), are indispensable, and IV (Eighteenth-century Ireland is (apart from a useful if imperfect bibliography) dispensable. Dublin University graduates are ably charted in G.D. Burtchaell and T.U. Sadleir, eds., *Alumni Dublinensis*, and the *D.N.B.* and Henry Boylan's *Dictionary of Irish Bibliography* have some uses, as have Anne M. Brady and Brian Cleeve, *Bibliographical Dictionary of Irish Writers*, and Robert Hogan ed., *Macmillan Dictionary of Irish Literature*. Edward O'Reilly's semi-mythological *Chronological Account of Irish History* (Dublin, 1820) is actually of chief importance for its calendaring of lost poems. Michael Drake, 'The Irish Demographic Crisis of 1740-41' (*Historical Studies*, VI. (1968)), is of outstanding value as background to Ireland in 1745. The Protestant episcopalian community have received disproportionate if far from comprehensive attention, and the general histories by Froude, Lecky and F.G. James deserve study despite their authors' ignorance of Irish: so do the writings of Constantia Maxwell and R.B. McDowell, with the same *caveat*. Contemporary accounts of Bedell are to be found in *Two Biographies of William Bedell*. Lives of Chesterfield contain some useful quotations, and Sir Richard Lodge's edition of his *Private Correspondence* with the Duke of Newcastle is rich in anti-Scottish venom. The Martins are looked at in Edith Oenone Somerville and Martin Ross, *Irish Memories* and Shevawn Lynam, *Humanity Dick*. The Protestant episcopalian clergy appear in perspective through focus on one of their most attractive members in Sir C.S. King, *A Great Archbishop of Dublin William King*. My approach has been strongly influenced by Thomas Flanagan, *The Year of the French*, with its brilliant foci on so many different Irish vantage-points; 1798 may seem a long way from 1745, but in certain respects it is not so far.

7

LORD ELCHO
AND THE '45
by
Alice Wemyss

Alice Wemyss is a daughter of Admiral of the Fleet Lord Wester
Wemyss, who signed the Armistice in 1918 in company with
Marshall Foch. She was brought up in France and has lived
there most of her life, and so is bilingual.

After the Second World War she went to Germany with the
Red Cross to work for refugees. Later she settled in a village
whose curé had drawn up, on the eve of the Revocation of the
Edict of Nantes, a list of the Huguenot families in his parish.
Having studied their lives she wrote a doctoral disertation, *Les
Protestants de Mas d'Azil, 1680-1830 : Histoire d'une
Résistance,* possibly the first historical disertation on a
community. This was followed by a history of the *Réveil,* the
French-speaking version of the Evangelical Movement.

When her husband died in 1974 she returned to her Scottish
roots and came to live at Wemyss in Fife. At present she is
writing a biography of her kinsman Lord Elcho.

LORD ELCHO, AUTHOR of the well known *Affairs of
Scotland* and a partially published *Journal,* is a controversial figure. Looked
upon as a traitor by latter day Jacobites in whose eyes Bonnie Prince Charlie
is a *chevalier sans peur et sans reproche,* as well as by those of his
contemporaries who had a deep attachment to the crown, he was never seen
as such by his fellow exiles, many of whom had fought with him in the '45.

He has long been a shadowy figure largely through his own fault, for he was extremely reticent about himself. But a close study of the above-mentioned two documents, in the light of other contemporary sources, show that his criticisms of the Young Pretender, which have earned him so much ill will, stem from the very exceptional – not to say unique – position he had within the movement.

He was born in 1723, son of the fifth Earl of Wemyss. His forebears had been zealous Covenanters and the family had supported the Glorious Revolution. But the tactlessness of George I, added to the influence of his young wife, had turned his grand-father into a mild Jacobite. His son – Elcho's father – was a zealot in both religion and politics. He married the daughter of that notorious rake and gambler, Francis Charteris, known to posterity as the Wicked Colonel. But the scurrilous attacks of his enemies were rather motivated by party spirit than by moral indignation, for he was a self proclaimed Whig and an admirer of Robert Walpole. No wonder the wicked Colonel objected to having young Lord Wemyss as a son-in-law! The couple eloped and the marriage, though fruitful, proved unhappy, the bone of contention being Lady Wemyss's refusal to share her husband's convictions.

At the age of five poor little Elcho was wrenched from the nursery and sent to live with an old non-juror clergyman. This was followed by a spell in a Dunfermline school after which he went to Winchester in charge of a zealously Jacobite tutor, whose sole duties consisted in keeping him within the Jacobite fold and preventing him from having any communication with his mother, who had left his father, taking the other children with her. Winchester was then in the grip of party politics, Jacobites and 'Georgites', as he called them, being at each others' throats. But it was to defend the honour of his native land that he learnt how to 'fight with his fists'. The unpopularity of the Scots was to turn him into a Scottish patriot. Yet he never went home for the holidays, these being mostly spent visiting stately homes, as open then to the public as they are today.

His schooling once finished, he started on the traditional "Grand Tour", still in the charge of the same tutor. But in his case it took on a distinctly Jacobite flavour, for before settling in Rheims, where he was to acquire those airs and graces which would fit him for polite society, he was taken on a visit to the garrison towns where he made the acquaintance of Scottish officers in French pay, many of whom were to serve with him in the '45.

Horace Walpole, who was also to stay in Rheims for the same purpose, found the town dull and provincial. Not so Elcho. Delivered at last from those political wrangles he had come to hate, he threw himself into his new life with all the enthusiasm of youth, and became the darling of Rheims society. This was followed by a spell at Angers where he attended an academy – a sort of finishing school for well born young Protestants, who were precluded by their religion from attending the normal priest-run establishments. The curriculum was, however, the same, and geared to forming officers, for all young Frenchmen of noble birth were constrained to military service. He found, to his dismay, that politics were as divisive here as they had been at Winchester, and he preferred the company of the local gentry to that of his fellow countrymen.

He started on the Grand Tour proper by visiting Avignon, then a Jacobite stronghold, where he was welcomed by Lord and Lady Inverness who acted as heads of the colony in the absence of the Duke of Ormonde, then in Madrid where he was seeking support for the cause. His next port of call was Lyon, where he made the acquaintance of a man who was to exert a decisive influence over him.

Sir James Steuart of Goodtrees, Bart, was the son of an eminent Edinburgh lawyer and descendant of an influential Covenanting divine. After finishing his studies at Leyden, he took to roaming the continent. In Avignon he fell in with Ormonde, who was so enchanted with his company – he was extremely witty as well as exceptionally intelligent – that he invited him to come with him to Spain. In Madrid he made the acquaintance of Earl Marischal, who (as a fellow Scot) realised what an acquisition this bright young man would be to the party, all the more in that he belonged to a *milieu* normally hostile to the House of Stewart. A stay in Rome, where the art of winning over promising young men had long been practised, brought the process of conversion to a successful conclusion, and by the time he reached Lyon the cause had no more ardent supporter. Elcho fell immediately under his charm, and what was to prove a lifelong friendship was later consolidated by Sir James's marriage to Elcho's sister, Lady Fanny Wemyss.

After having crossed the Alps and visited Turin, Milan, and Florence, where he made the acquaintance of two prominent young Whigs, Horace Walpole, son of Sir Robert, and Lord Lincoln, heir to the Duke of Newcastle, Elcho received orders from his father to proceed to Rome, possibly at the behest of the Old Pretender who saw in him a suitable companion for his two sons. His reception could not have been more flattering: he was met on his arrival, provided with rooms, called upon by the more prominent members of the household and received in audience by James, with whom he chatted cosily in front of the fire before being presented to the young princes, when he was placed back to back with the elder to see which was the taller.

The winter of 1740-1741 was spent largely in their company, which, however, did not prevent him from exploring the city or frequenting the members of the British colony where he made new friends amongst both Whigs and Jacobites. He felt very grateful to James for having provided him with such a good time, and who he thought might well be a good king if only he were not so devout. He had, however, a low opinion of Charles Edward, and much preferred the Duke of York. One might attribute this to hindsight had not the President des Brosses, who spent that same winter in Rome, expressed similar opinions. The grand tour ended by a stay in Paris, where he made friends with the banker, Aeneas Macdonald one of the 'seven men of Moidart'.

He returned to England after three delightful years on the Continent only to discover that his now bankrupt father had appropriated the very large sum of money he had inherited from his grand-father the Colonel. He was no longer a rich young *milord,* but the penurious heir of a largely discredited Scottish peer. The next three years were spent wandering aimlessly between Wemyss, Edinburgh, London, when he could afford it, and Hornby, a Lancashire place which formed part of the Colonel's large and ill-gotten estate which he had left to Elcho's younger brother Francis, on condition he should adopt the name of Charteris. During this time, Elcho was advised by well-wishers to accept offers by Lord Lincoln, who said he could find him a place at Court, and Horace Walpole who offered him a commission in the army. The most pressing of these well-wishers was Lord Sinclair, who had distinguished himself during the '15 as the Master of Sinclair and who had spent some time in exile. He warned Elcho of how ungrateful the Stewarts were, and he might have carried his point had it not been for Sir James.

In 1743 Elcho returned to Paris as the guest of his brother Francis, who was doing his grand tour in company of the same tutor. He found the Jacobites rent asunder by a quarrel between Earl Marischal and the Jacobite Lord Sempil who, although a Frenchman in all but name, had appointed himself spokesman for the English Jacobites. Elcho, who disliked wrangles, gossip and backbiting, found relief in the company of his cousin and old schoolfellow, Lord Drumlanrig, heir to the Duke of Queensbury, a family much disliked by the Jacobites for the part they had played in the Glorious Revolution.

Their defeat at Dettingen had led the French to plan an invasion of England, as a Stewart on its throne would turn an implacable enemy into a subservient ally. It was to be under the command of no less a personage than the great Maréchal de Saxe. Early in 1744 Charles Edward arrived secretly in Paris bearing his father's commissions for Earl Marischal, who was to lead a smaller expedition to Scotland, and Elcho, who was to raise a cavalry regiment of which he was to be the colonel. Marischal was the first to visit the Prince and was followed, at a fortnight's interval, by Elcho, who was received in a most informal fashion, Charles Edward opening the door himself and brewing a cup of tea for his old companion. Shortly after the two newly commissioned officers were called to Dunkirk, where they found Saxe fuming against the English Jacobites, on whose collaboration the success of the expedition largely depended, and who were proving most unreliable. Marischal soon found grace in his eyes but ran into trouble with the Paris Jacobites, who refused to give him the money he needed to maintain his status as general, and prevented him from receiving the instructions for which he was clamouring. Had it not been for a generous loan from Elcho's brother Francis, he could never have carried out his mission. A couple of gales, during which convoys were sunk and men drowned, provided a pretext for calling off the expedition.

Elcho returned to Scotland against Earl Marischal's advice, who feared he might get arrested. On his arrival he went to see the Lord Chief Justice Clerk, Lord Milton, to whom he was related through his mother. That astute statesman was certainly not hoodwinked by the tale he was told; but he was fond of his foolish young relative and saw to his not being molested. Elcho was now at the very heart of the party, whose leaders could not but be alarmed by what he had to relate about what was happening in Paris. It was therefore decided that Murray of Broughton should go and see how things really stood, and find out what the Prince's plans were for the future. Broughton thought he could combine this with a visit to the Scottish regiments in Flanders, and he invited Elcho to come with him, for he had many friends and relations amongst the officers. The welcome left nothing to be desired; Elcho was made much of and was even allowed to take part in a foray. It was his first experience of war and he thoroughly enjoyed it. It is doubtful, however, that this visit did much to help the cause, for very few officers and not many men were to change sides during the rebellion.

The two now parted, Broughton going to Paris, where he had several secret meetings with the Prince who told him he intended to go to Scotland during the following year, even if it was to be with only one servant, whilst Elcho did a sightseeing trip round Holland. They met up in Rotterdam, where they crammed their secret papers into the barrels of their pistols, intending to shoot them off should they be arrested. Once in Edinburgh Broughton suggested Elcho should found a club, in imitation of London's Cocoa Tree, with a view of preparing for the Prince's arrival. It was called the Buck Club. The membership was soon divided between those who said they would only rise should the Prince arrive at the head of an adequate French force, and those, who were in the minority, who intended to join him under whatever circumstances. A letter was sent to the Prince informing him of the majority's decision, to which Elcho added a personal note pressing the point. But Broughton, whose financial future depended on a successful rising, went on trying to bring members round to his way of thinking. As we all know, the Prince paid no need to Elcho's advice and landed in the Highlands.

On hearing the news, Elcho wrote to Broughton asking him if the Prince had fulfilled the conditions, and received a mendacious reply to the effect that the French were on the point of landing. So he joined the Prince near Edinburgh. Charles Edward must have been immensely relieved, for his following was lacking in lustre, and Elcho was a well known figure in London society. 'We hear of no men of quality or fortune having joined the (Prince) but Lord Elcho . . . and the Duke of Perth, a silly horse-racing boy,' wrote Horace Walpole. During their night-long conversation Elcho offered to lend the fifteen hundred guineas his brother had loaned him for the expedition, whilst the Prince warned his old friend that Lord George Murray was a traitor. Elcho was to become Lord George's most devoted follower, which goes to show what little weight he attached to the Prince's opinions.

During the occupation of Edinburgh he became Charles Edward's constant companion, and people got so used to seeing them together that he was later reported as having been beside the Prince on his drive to Versailles

when he was not even in France at the time! It was a period of intense
activity: he was on the Prince's left hand when they rode to Hollyrood amidst
the cheering crowds; he fought at Prestonpans where he was appointed
colonel of the Body Guard on the field of battle – he was to take part in every
military action with the exception of those in the Highlands, when he was
guarding the Spey – he chaired the committee dealing with the commissariat; he recruited, equipped, and trained the Body Guard – the hours
spent in the riding school at Angers were bearing fruit – and above all he sat
on the Council where he held a unique position, being the only man present
who had a real knowledge of the British Constitution and the workings of
Parliament in which he had taken a keen interest, the other Councillors
being either Irish in French pay, or Highland chieftains who were a law unto
themselves. He soon became alarmed at the Prince's insistence on getting his
own way. Fortunately Goodtrees, who was keeping a low profile, often made
discreet visits to Charles Edward's quarters at Holyrood, thus preventing
serious blunders. Elcho, who was very outspoken, was clearly making a
nuisance of himself, which probably led the Prince to suggest he should go
to Paris as his representative. He was, however, well aware of his
shortcomings and pointed out that his brother-in-law was better fitted for a
diplomatic mission.

At the council-of-war held to decide what the next steps should be,
opinions were equally divided between those, who like the Prince, wished to
march on London, and those who, like Lord George, felt it would be wiser
to retire to the Highlands and await the arrival of the long promised French.
The casting vote lay with Elcho who, surprisingly, opted for the Prince's
choice. He believed himself to be well acquainted with the notoriously
Jacobite Lancashire, with its large Catholic population, and where he must
have drunk many a toast to the 'King over the water' in the company of
inebriate squires; he had even been asked by the town council of Lancaster
to become their M.P. It was an enthusiastic young colonel who rode off at
the head of his smart, well mounted, well groomed and well disciplined
regiment, whose blue uniforms with red facings and gilt buttons formed a
striking contrast to the kilted, bedraggled and often bare-footed Highlanders.

The campaign started with the capture of Carlisle which was followed by
violent dissensions, when an exasperated Lord George wrote to the Prince
that in the future he would fight in the ranks, and that he was leaving Elcho
in charge. Under pressure from the Scots, a reluctant Prince was obliged to
place Lord George at the head of the army with the rank of Lieutenant
General. He chose to command the van and put Elcho at the head of the
advance guard. In this capacity Elcho was to be first to enter the towns, and
being on familiar ground – he had often travelled over this road – he must
have been aware of how hostile the local populations were. Fortunately
Lancashire lay ahead. He took his troop to Hornby, where they were well
received and given a good meal. But the news he gathered must have been
dreadfully disappointing. Far from taking arms for the cause, the Catholics
were being advised by their priests to keep low, even in some cases to desert

their homes, rather than get involved in a movement which might well reawaken the dreaded cry of 'No Popery'. He spent that night in a Lancaster inn conferring with Lord George, and the harsh terms imposed on the town council give some measure of his frustration.

The Scots now felt that the time had come for them to return home. The English Jacobites had not risen, nor had the French landed in the South as the Prince was continually telling them they were about to do. At Manchester Elcho gave a great banquet in honour of St. Andrew's Day when the subject must have come under discussion. It was decided to go to Derby but no further. The council held there proved stormy, and Elcho told the Prince to his face that if he went to London he would be in Newgate within a fortnight.

The march down had been far more disciplined than anyone had expected. But it was a bunch of marauders who wended their way north amidst a hostile population. At Carlisle Elcho was one of those who was opposed to leaving the town in the hands of the Manchester regiment, which did not wish to go to Scotland. It should have been sent home. As it was it had to pay the grim penalties attached to rebellion.

Scotland proved as hostile as England, and Elcho's first task once over the Border was to impose heavy fines on Dumfries for having pillaged the army's baggage before its departure for England. The next halt was Drumlanrig, home of his old schoolmate and friend, which was systematically ransacked. The Rebel army ended up in Glasgow 'the prettiest and most whiggish town in Scotland' which was also to pay a heavy penalty for its attachment to the crown.

In the meantime Lord John Drummond had landed in Scotland at the head of a sizeable French force. He had unfurled the French standard and had proclaimed that the King of France intended to pursue his war against the Elector of Hanover on Scottish soil; and that all those who did not obey the Regent, i.e. the Prince, would be treated as enemies. Elcho must have joined in the general rejoicings, all the more that Lord John was an old friend of whom he had seen a great deal in Paris. But the influx of officers, who were all Irishmen in the French service, tended to increase the tension already existing between the Irish and the Scots, for the former had nothing to lose and all to gain by way of promotion whilst the Scots were sacrificing their all to the cause; the Irish were to win over the Prince completely by means of flattery.

The army, whose numbers had been doubled, put the enemy to flight at Falkirk; but the Prince did not follow up this victory by re-occupying Edinburgh, as he wanted to be present at the capture of Stirling Castle. But the Castle did not fall, and the lifting of its siege coincided with the arrival of Cumberland. But when the Prince went about preparing for another battle, he discovered to his horror that he was now outnumbered, as to some extent the Highlanders had returned home. All he could do was to retire to the Highlands and await the arrival of more French reinforcements. What Lord George had planned to be an orderly retreat degenerated into a headlong flight, through the Prince having omitted to publish the proper orders. Elcho, who had been told to guard a bridge, was forgotten and only just escaped capture. He was very angry indeed, and did not conceal it at the council which met at Crieff on the following day. It was decided that the army should be divided, one part marching through the Highlands with the Prince at its head, hopefully making recruits on the way, whilst Lord George would take the other by the East coast so as to secure the ports for the safe arrival of the French. Elcho was to occupy Montrose which, however, he was soon obliged to leave on the appearance of a naval squadron: he was in no position to repel a large boarding party. The arrival of Cumberland at Aberdeen forced the Rebels to retire behind the river Spey, Elcho being quartered at Forres.

During the ensuing lull he spent a great deal of his time at Inverness, no doubt attracted by the presence of some charming Jacobite ladies, and the balls the Prince was giving in their honour; he dearly loved a party. He became seriously alarmed by a deterioration in the situation, largely caused by lack of funds. The men, who were now paid in meal, were becoming mutinous. More serious was the unashamed preference the Prince was show-ing to the Irish and the way he was treating the Scots as mere mercenaries. By now Elcho had lost all hope of an ultimate victory; but as even the suggestion of a negotiation was regarded as treachery there was nothing to be done. As he wrote: 'le vin est tiré, il faudroit le boire'.

Jacobite intelligence must have been singularly poor, for Elcho and his men were alone on the Spey when Cumberland crossed that fordable river. All they could do was to fire their pistols and gallop away as fast as they could to give warning. The Jacobites now started on an orderly retreat which took them to Culloden where they were joined by the Prince at the head of whatever men he could muster. They were without food, for no bread had been baked at Inverness. Elcho supped with the Prince at Culloden House, where he had once stayed as a guest, Forbes of Culloden having been a friend of his grandfather. He was shocked by Charles Edward's behaviour: 'his boastfulness that night was unworthy of a Prince'. He spent the following morning in sight of the enemy camp where he could see no movement, as the men were busy celebrating the Duke's birthday. That night there took place the notorious march to Nairn when Lord George, feeling it was too late to attack the camp, turned back in direct opposition to the Prince's reiterated orders. Charles Edward felt he had been betrayed and did not hesitate in saying so. The Rebels were exhausted and the 'principal officers' sought what rest they could at Culloden House, 'some on beds, others on chairs, tables etc, and on the floor, for the fatigue and the hunger had been felt as much by the officers as the men.' Two hours later the enemy came in sight and they all took up their allotted places, Elcho's being at the rear of the right flank, his mission being to prevent it from being outflanked by the dragoons, which would have put the Prince at risk. It was the one wholly successful action of the day.

He rode off Culloden battlefield in the wake of the Prince and in company of Lord Balmerino, to whom he was related and who was one of his father's best friends. Balmerino told him that should there be no rally he would give himself up. Elcho expostulated with him, saying that it would lead him straight to the block – but in vain. Life would have no more meaning for the gallant old man. Having ridden five miles into relative safety, the Prince halted and began directing his followers to Ruthven in Badenoch where, he said, they would receive further orders. (These were to scatter and do the best they could for themselves). This must have raised Elcho's hopes. He had been told by Lord George that the Highlands could be held with eight thousand men which would oblige the Government to come to terms, as they would need their regiments in Flanders. He now rode up to the Prince to ask for his orders, and was struck by the fear he was in of the Scots. What then was his dismay to hear himself being told to do as he pleased, for the Prince was returning to France. It was the death knell for Balmerino and many other brave men who had sacrificed their all for the cause. He pleaded for them: the Prince had been alone when he landed; he was now at the head of some eight thousand men and he had always proclaimed his intention of remaining in Scotland as long as he had a single man at his back. Charles Edward was somewhat mollified; not so his Irish *entourage* who hated the Highlands where they had been badly received, and who had no faith in guerilla warfare. So Sir Thomas Sheridan chipped in making Elcho responsible for the defeat by allowing Cumberland to cross the Spey. It was a ridiculous accusation, for what could a troop of horsemen, however gallant, do in the face of a whole army? Elcho was so furious that he would have laid hands on his detractor had not the Prince intervened. So he turned on his heel and took his departure saying 'There goes a damned Italian coward'.* He was never to see the Prince again.

He escaped to the continent, where he lived the life of an unhappy exile, always hoping against hope for the pardon which was never to come. It has been said that Cumberland bore him a grudge for having prevented his dragoons from capturing his Stewart cousin. Elcho never forgave the Prince, and was to spend large sums endeavouring to get him to repay the loan. It was not so much for the money, which he would have probably returned to his brother, but as a way of proving to himself and to the world that old Sinclair had been right in accusing the Stewarts of ingratitude.

* Shocked Jacobite historians have put in doubt the accuracy of these words. But Sir Walter Scott had them from Elcho's nephew, son of Sir James Steuart. Young Steuart was the only member of the younger generation with whom Elcho was familiar, he having grown up in exile. Elcho was, moreover, very fond of him and saw a great deal of him in his later years. What is more, these words fit in with his character. Not only was he outspoken, but he did not hold the Stewarts in awe, having no time for the 'divine right of kings' on which their aura was based, and he had an uncontrollable temper.

8

DUNDEE AND THE '45
by
Annette Smith

In 1970 Annette M. Smith returned from domesticity to academic life and lectured in Scottish history in the University of Dundee until 1988. During these years she worked for various associations forwarding the interests of Scottish history, at one point being Honorary Secretary of the Scottish History Society. Her first major research project was a study of the 1745 Forfeited Estates papers. The results of this were several articles, a doctorate and a book *Jacobite Estates of the Forty-Five*. She then turned, spasmodically, to the 1715 Forfeited Estate Papers, but she has recently been more preoccupied with the history of Dundee. She wrote *The Three United Trades of Dundee: Masons, Wrights and Slaters* for the Abertay Historical Society and, in cooperation with a colleague, is currently engaged in work for a general history of the town. The present article marries the local and national lines of research.

DUNDEE WAS FIRST recognised as a burgh in royal charters of the late twelfth century. During the following eight hundred years, the town has had continuous contacts, both personal and public, with Europe north and south, with the New World across the Atlantic, and more recently in historic terms, with the Far East and India. No research on the town and its inhabitants can be considered complete which does not take cognisance of this vital part of its history. Unfortunately, the combination of the publisher's timetable and the writer's previous commitments have precluded consultation of any archive furth of Scotland, and additional sources might well have led to different conclusions. Nevertheless, it is hoped that some addition can be made to Dundee history and to understanding reactions to the '45.

The response evoked by the several Jacobite attempts to replace the Stewarts on the thrones of England and Scotland in 1689, 1715 and 1745 were very similar in Dundee to those most common over the rest of the Lowlands, but for particular reasons. The events of 1708 and 1719 impinged on so small an area of Scotland that we may legitimately ignore these dates for the purposes of this paper. In 1689, Claverhouse and his Highlanders were viewed with 'stony hostility' from behind the town's walls. Whatever loyalty may have been felt towards James VII at his accession, he alienated the burgesses totally, when he insisted on having James Graham of Claverhouse, hereditary Constable of Dundee, installed as Provost. For a long time, the town had fought the claims of previous holders of this office, the Scrymgeours and then the Maitlands, that they could exercise authority within its boundaries. However efficiently and fairly Claverhouse carried out his duties on the Town Council, he would be seen primarily as the successor of those who encroached on rights and privileges considered properly the town's by those who lived in it. They obtained these legally only in 1747 when the heritable jurisdictions were abolished.

In 1715 a different picture emerges. Over the years, the Town Council had become predominantly sympathetic to the deposed dynasty, possibly for reasons similar to those over Scotland as a whole – poor economic conditions and dissatisfaction with the 1707 union. Episcopalianism was also given more than tolerance, the congregation having been allowed in 1713 to worship in one of the town's churches, the Cross church. Schoolmasters too were appointed with similar proclivities. Partrick Lyon, the burgh master, had 'gone against the Confession of Faith' and was dismissed in 1716. Even so, like the majority of Jacobites, overcome by the suddenness of events in 1714, the Council ostensibly accepted the Hanoverians, unanimously welcoming George I and agreeing to celebrate his accession. A year later, when given a choice, most of the council showed that their loyalties lay with the Stewarts. In July, 1715, the Convention of Royal Burghs had expelled the Dundee delegates, one of whom was being charged with the crime of 'cursing His Majesty' and the other for calling the members perjured rogues. Though the Council agreed to organise a town guard on the prompting of Bailie John Robertson, who reported information – not strictly correct – of 'a sudden invasion by the Pretender with a forraigne force from parts beyond the sea', not all appointed to lead this agreed to act. They excused themselves on the grounds that their business 'took them out of town'. When the Old Pretender did appear early in 1716 with a retinue of 300, he was proclaimed at the Cross, with general approval and the enthusiastic support of Alexander Wedderburn, the Town Clerk, whose family had a long history of unquestioning Stewart loyalty. Wedderburn had to resign after the failure of the Rising, but he refused to hand over the town's documents until he was faced with Court of Session action.

In 1745, there was a change again. The Councillors, the heirs of the pro-

Hanoverian sympathisers elected since 1716, shut their collective eyes and
hoped the Jacobites would go away. They admitted as much in their
apologetic address to the king in 1746. 'We did not give credit to the first
accounts brought us of the beginning of the rebellion, but continued unprovided for resistance, till of a sudden we were overcome by a superior force'.
They did not specify that one of the 'accounts' they must have received came
from Lord Tweeddale, the minister responsible for Scotland, who had
written to the provosts of Glasgow, Edinburgh, Aberdeen and Dundee on 13
August, 1745, warning them of the arrival or intended arrival of Charles
Edward, and asking them to take such precautions as they judged necessary
'to preserve the public peace within the bounds of your Jurisdiction'. (It is
ironic that the only answer recorded is that of the Edinburgh provost, who
was charged with neglect of duty in 1747.) Nor did the Council point out that
they maintained this apparent incredulity, at least for the sake of the records,
when the Jacobite army was at Perth, only 25 miles away, and even when a
small detachment of that army had entered Dundee.

In fact, it is difficult to see what else they could have done. The town was
totally defenceless, with neither military forces in its precincts nor arms
which the burgesses might have used. Rather late in the day, in April 1746
300 stands of arms were provided and promptly laid up the following month,
by which time government forces had arrived. Not only had the town no
means of warding off rebels, it was surrounded by landed gentry of Jacobite
sympathies, many of whom had town houses or commerical interests in the
burgh. In the immediate hinterland were Hunter of Grange at Monifieth in
the east, the Fotheringhams of Powrie on the north-east and north, Sir John
Wedderburn of Blackness to the north and west. They were backed by a
further layer of families who had shown their Stewart sympathies in 1715 –
Thriepland of Fingask, Carnegie of Balnamoon, the Earl of Airlie are only
a few. Estates in Angus had been forfeited after the earlier rebellion, though
some had been regained by the families – by one means or another; the York
Buildings Company was still in possession of the Earl of Southesk's lands.
But there was no saying how these cats would jump thirty years later. In fact,
seven sons of the eighteen children of Thomas Fotheringham and Ann
Ogilvy were active in 1745-6, David the fifth child serving as Jacobite
governor of Dundee; Sir David Thriepland lost a son fighting for the
Pretender, and, while he himself stayed at home, he provided grain for the
rebel army. Sir John Wedderburn of Blackness was executed on Kennington
Common. The Earl of Airlie also remained at home while his son, Lord
David Ogilvie, raised a regiment, the Forfarshire, in which most
Dundonians who joined the Jacobite army are to be found. As late as March,
1746, the earl was still trying to drum up men for his son, despite the
presence of Hanoverian forces in the county. It must be remembered too
that, though Dundee can never be thought of as other than a Lowland town
sharing in the ethos of Lowland Scotland, the Highlands and Highlanders
were near. Glen Esk, which was especially considered a hive of Jacobites,
Glen Clova, Glen Prosen and Glen Shee are none of them so remote that they

did not need to be taken into account, while the north-east Lowland plain from Arbroath north was hardly an area of sure Hanoverian support. In the circumstances, the Council's discretion is excusable, if extreme. On the other hand, despite the presence of the small force of Highlanders from 8 September, and the installation of David Fotheringham as governor with Sir Alexander Watson as his deputy, the Council proceeded with its annual election at the end of the month and swore allegiance to George II on 26 September. The Common Good was rouped as usual on 14 October and proposals were made for the celebration of George II's birthday on 30 October, 'with all demonstrations of joy', the lighting of bonfires and the drinking of the Royal Health at the Cross. As the populace responded to this by chasing the Jacobite governor out of town on that date, the gap in the Council minutes from 11 November until 8 February 1746 is hardly to be wondered at, nor the statement in the 1746 address that many had to flee for safety. The town mob in Perth had also shown signs of popular preference for George II; Laurence Oliphant of Gask, Jacobite treasurer and deputy governor of the town, had had to seek refuge in the council house. Both governors were able to return, of course, in the absence of government troops.

Of course, town mobs are notorious for their volatility, and it is not ever easy to ascertain ordinary citizens' feelings, but this incident does seem to indicate some degree of unity between Council and citizens, despite one report that Dundonians were Jacobite in sentiment in 1745.

It is perhaps worth noting at this point that there are clouds of obscurity over many of the events of the occupation. What seems to have occurred is that, once the Jacobite army was installed at Perth, a detachment of 200-300 Macdonalds of Keppoch and Clanranald were sent to proclaim James VIII at Dundee. They entered the town on 8 September, made a search for arms and ammunition and are believed to have taken two ships, mistakenly believed to have such a cargo. A week later, the *Penny London Post* or *Evening Advertiser* reported that this force was acting as the lawful government, collecting public money and taxes for which they gave receipts. David Fotheringham was duly appointed governor and Sir James Kinloch, who did not commit himself to the cause until after the battle of Prestonpans, was eventually responsible for collecting taxes laid by the Jacobites in Forfarshire. Kinloch also recruited for the 2nd battalion of the Forfarshires which remained in the district for some time to hold it for the Prince and to help unload any supplies that arrived.

The first appearance of Charles Edward's men seems to have made little impression on the town. This is not too surprising when relative numbers are considered. Two or three hundred Highlanders could hardly be expected to subdue immediately a population that may have been around 10,000. In 1755, Dr. Webster calculated that 12,474 Protestants and three Roman Catholics lived in Dundee. It is unlikely that there was a larger population ten years earlier, but there must have been many more than the 5,000 or 6,000 that Dr. Small reckoned, when he was writing his contribution to the first *Statistical Account* in 1792. Despite the presence of some Jacobite soldiers in their congregations, on 9 September the ministers of the town churches held their services and, according to reports that reached Edinburgh, bravely recommended their hearers to remain steadfast in their loyalty to the ruling monarch. None of the local records consulted except those of the United Presbytery of Dundee and Forfar and of the Dundee Kirk Session give any written evidence of the arrival of the rebel army. Not only was the Town Council discreet in 1745; Wrights, Masons, Slaters, Hammermen, Weavers, even the Guildry, nowhere indicate that the rebellion ever happened, either in 1745 or afterwards. The blanks that occur are quite consistent with the general irregularity of craftsmen's documentation, such as the Weavers' entry of Joseph Rhind as a free apprentice on 8 October, 1745, followed by a gap until 1757. Surely more significant is the total lack of comment on the rebellion or on any effects it may have had on the various trades. Thomas Haliburton, who was entered as a master wright in March, 1732, had been one of the first to join the Jacobites in Edinburgh. He served in Gask's troop of the Perthshire Horse (Strathallan's) and put his local knowledge to good use, providing 'guides and intelligence' at the end of February and in early March, 1746, for which he was paid £7-16-0 (Scots) by the Jacobite treasurer. In the Wrights' records only his entry as master appears. He was not even expelled, unlike one master who had been found guilty of stealing timber. Are we to assume that dishonesty was a worse crime than treason in the eyes of these artisans?

The ministers and elders of the Church of Scotland are less inhibited in their comments. Perhaps they had stronger feelings on the subject. The Kirk Session made no secret of its views on 'the insurrection of rebellious and wicked men', who had risen 'against the righteous King and the Protestant interest'. The Kirk Treasurer, Charles Jobson, was a prominent merchant, and his account book holds more than mere finance. One entry in 1746 leaves us in no doubts as to his sentiments. '17 January – Falkirk, shameful'. On 4 September, the United Presbytery 'because of the present dangerous situation of affairs by a most unnatural rebellion' recommended a day of fast and humiliation, which a month later they noted they had been unable to observe. They had also administered the Lord's Supper in all their parishes except Dundee, not because of the presence of the Jacobite force but because the new minister, Mr. Gellatly, had not been settled in his parish. Jacobites or no, he had clearly been established in the next month, for he was made Moderator of the Presbytery on 23 October but he was unable to attend throughout the occupation. The Presbytery meetings were moved from parish to parish during this time, but the Dundee ministers were never able to be present.

On 8 January, 1746, the clerk to the Presbytery wrote that the fast appointed to be held on 18 December by George II had been interrupted in Dundee by armed men. The Kirk Treasurer also notes this and claims that public worship had been stopped by the rebels, while the *Scots Fasti* relates that, twice, soldiers threatened to shoot John Willison if he prayed for

George II. The Kirk Session minutes put a slightly different gloss on these
incidents. According to these, the Session wondered if it would be safe to
read the proclamation about the proposed fast 'considering the town was
garrisoned by rebel clans most savage and cruel'. A week later, their clerk
reporting the next meeting tells us, not that the fast had been stopped
precisely, but that 'a Highland captain' had told them they could not pray for
George while his forces were in the town, but could pray for all Christian
kings. Willison, a prominent theologian, the oldest of the town's preachers,
refused to comply with this. Colonel Gordon, the officer responsible, then
apparently had second thoughts and 'sent his servant' to say that no kings
should be named. And at that it was *decided (sic)* to hold no public services.
Undoubtedly, the 'servant' may have been armed, but this does not tally
exactly with other versions of the incidents. The Kirk Session was meanwhile meeting regularly, and the following week recommended preaching in
private houses at baptisms.

In these troubled times, one group of Dundonians was likely to suffer
disproportionately, if there were no public services and therefore no collections and no poor fund. The church did not forget its charitable duties.
Members of the Session were asked to make door-to-door collections for the
town's poor in their respective quarters, the Nethergate, the Overgate,
Murraygate, Wellgate and the Seagate. Each week, from 18 December to 14
January, 1746, the treasurer carefully noted the sums gathered – an average
of £25-18-8½ per week. When the Jacobite soldiers left, liberal donations
were recommended by the Session to make up for the losses, and the next
collection was almost double – £50-14-2, all Scots money.

One area in which Jacobite influence was certainly felt was in the realm
of public finance. Supply was vital to them; their army was 'hungry and
rapacious', so throughout the rebellion they imposed and collected heavy
taxes in the areas under their control, as if James VIII and his regent Charles
Edward were indeed the rulers of the country. Scrupulous honesty seems to
have been the watchword among the officials concerned and receipts were
usual. This is not surprising from someone like Oliphant of Gask. In 1746,
the Dundee town treasurer, who had had to disburse some of his funds, was
duly credited by the council with £194-14-6 paid to the Jacobites. Henry
Pattullo, a Dundee merchant who became Muster-Master of the rebel army,
seized the Dundee Customs House and sold the goods he found there.
Throughout the autumn and winter of 1745-46, the Board of Customs
Collector in the town has no records of shipping leaving the harbour and, in
October and November, was able to levy taxes of only £21-1-6¾ from the
Alison and the *Elizabeth* entering the port. But ships were undoubtedly
entering and leaving throughout the period. The *Contented Margaret* took tar
to Leith from Dundee; occasionally, there were arrivals at Perth, vessels
having called in at Dundee en route, and Thomas Mathew of the Dundee
Ropery Company was paid cash for various orders of rope, including cables
for lifting a third cargo of cannon on board ship. All the taxes collected from
such cargoes, however, were going into the Jacobite purse, not to the Board

LORD GEORGE MURRAY

LIEUTENANT GENERAL OF THE JACOBITE ARMY

"From the first he showed an inherent military genius for he invented a simple form of drill that was quickly picked up by the raw recruits : he introduced discipline, he organised transport and commissariat, and he gained the confidence of the men."

JOHN CAMPBELL 4th EARL OF LOUDON, HANOVERIAN COMMANDER

"Though as an officer he with exactness discharged his duty, yet behaved with great humanity to the unfortunate."

John Cameron, Jacobite, Presbyterian preacher.

PRINCE CHARLES IN OLD AGE

"Sir what is this? You have been speaking to him about Scotland and his Highlanders.
No-one dares to speak about such things in his presence."

CLUNY MACPHERSON, 16th CHIEF

"seen passing the Kirk door on Communion Sabbath in his tartans as if for a shinty play."

Laggan Kirk Session Minutes.

THE TITULAR JAMES VIII OR III

"That honest man, my father."
Prince Charles.

Prospectus Civitatis TAODUNI ab Oriente. The Prospect of ye Town of DUNDEE, from ye East.

DUNDEE

"We did not give credit to the first accounts brought us of the beginning of the rebellion, but continued unprovided for resistance, till we were overcome by a superior force."

LORD ELCHO

"He had a greater share of both bearing and virtue than is common to those of his rank. ... As he engaged in the Rebellion from principles, so he acted his part with all the candour and spirit natural to him."

Boyce, Whig historian.

LORD PRESIDENT FORBES

"I found myself almost alone, without arms and without money or credit, provided with no means to prevent extreme folly except pen and ink, a tongue and some reputation."

of Customs officials. One of these, John Orrok, a land-waiter in Dundee, was said to have 'countenanced the rebels' but by the spring of the following year he had been cleared, at least to the satisfaction of his employers in the Customs.

The accounts of the Jacobite treasurer show that he had more dealings with private tradesmen in Perth than in Dundee, even though a small force remained in the latter town, but William Lighton, a Dundee shoemaker, made and was promptly paid for what must surely have been an unusually large order − 262 pairs of shoes at 3/2 Scots per pair. Mathew of the Ropery Company gave discount because he got cash payment. These two may have been quite sorry to see the departure of such admirable customers.

Though Dundee was not important strategically for either Jacobite or Hanoverian, only small forces being allocated to the town by the former in the autumn of 1745 and by Cumberland in the spring of the following year, and the greater part of foreign supplies being directed to Montrose, Stonehaven or Aberdeen, life was probably not too comfortable for non-Jacobites during the short occupation. After the anti-Jacobite riot on 30 October, there are signs that stricter controls were exercised. The governor gained a reputation even among his fellow-Jacobites for having 'managed in a tyrannical manner', and he cannot have enjoyed having to leave so ignominiously, if only temporarily. As we have seen, the Town Council was silent from early November and public worship in the presbyterian churches ceased in mid-December. The Council claimed that many had to flee the town for fear of their lives and property. On 5 December, 1745, the *Edinburgh Evening Courant* published a letter from an Angus gentleman 'of undoubted credit' describing Perth, Dundee and the country around as 'one scene of Horror and oppression, robberies are perpetual ... in the public street', but few concrete examples emerge. After the rebellion, the only physical damage to buildings that needed much attention seems to have been to the town hall. The ministers defied the rebels' orders in their private capacity as well as in regard to their public duty. They refused to light their windows to celebrate the arrival at Montrose of the first supplies from France and their manses were attacked by the Highlanders as a result. The aged Willison refused to leave his house to seek safety and only an appeal to one of the commanders he knew saw the withdrawal of the soldiers. Or so the *Scots Magazine* reported.

Kinloch's recruiting for the Forfarshire was presumably felt in the town as well as in the landward area but the town's sufferings, such as they were, were to be of short duration. Charles Jobson entered in his account book for 14 January, 1746 that the rebels had departed 'never to return'. One wonders how he was so sure, but he was not alone in that certainty. All contemporary comments in the town's public documents imply that the rebellion was all over bar the shouting, once the Jacobite army had retreated north of the Tay. In February, the Provost was rushing off to Montrose to pay his respects to Cumberland and, even before the battle of Culloden had been fought, the council was planning to honour him with a burgess ticket and a toast on his birthday, 15 April.

When the Council first met again on 8 February, 1746, it is rather extra-ordinary to find no mention of the stirring events of the previous few months, but Councillors realised nevertheless they must rapidly ensure Hanoverian respectability after their equivocal behaviour in the previous autumn. On 1 March, the jailor James Gibb was dismissed for behaviour that was 'not as it should have been' during the occupation. 30 July saw loyal addresses trying to excuse the town's actions to the king and Cumberland. From the accusations levied at many of the prisoners in Dundee town jail, it would seem that the authorities for a short time indiscriminately incarcer-ated anyone with the vaguest association with the rebels or with any shadow of doubt over his credentials – having first released those imprisoned by the Jacobite forces. Merchants who had opened the post bags, the tailor who seems merely to have drunk the Pretender's health and confusion to King George, the Edinburgh falconer Lewis Blair 'on suspicion' – into prison they all went in an excess of loyal zeal. Many were released by the end of the summer and most under the 1747 general pardon. By early May, there were government forces in the town and town council business began to look more like normal, except for the occasional mention of guns and the quartering of soldiers, though even in 1748 payment was made to David Jobson for work connected with the rebellion and the army.

As early as the beginning of January, the Kirk Session had happily returned to its more usual business of fornication, adultery and unclean liv-ing, but continued to show sensitivity about the conditions of the commons. The poor were so numerous that special pleas were to be made from the pulpit (16 January); there was compassion, expressed by a special collection, for the indigent wives and children of Cumberland's men who had to travel to and from the north to join their husbands and fathers (20 March). Compassion there was none, however, for the women who left with Sackville's regiment without the benefit of marriage lines and then returned when the regiment was shipped abroad from Burntisland. And in the summer of 1746, Thomas Mudie, or Moodie, a weaver, was rebuked before the Session because of having taken part in the rebellion. He had to clear himself before he could have his child baptised. His story was that he had indeed taken up arms, but only for two days! He left the gun and sword given him by Ogilvie (*sic*) at Kenny on the river Melgam, near Airlie Castle. He claimed that joining the Jacobites had 'grieved him most of anything he ever did' and such repentance persuaded the Session to let him off by doing penance before the congregation in the morning so that the baptism could take place at the afternoon service.

As for those who had remained with the Jacobite army until Culloden, most Dundonians in the Forfarshire regiment, it was believed that 'most of the private men' were back home early in May. The regiment had suffered little harm in the battle and marched in good order, first to Ruthven and then to Glen Clova where they disbanded. Like the non-commissioned, the officers from the area seem to have made their way home and some sought safety abroad. They sailed from Dundee or further north, local shipmasters giving help both willingly and involuntarily. For the greater number in the town, the excitement was nearly over. A few prisoners appeared in the town after a belated skirmish in July, and Lord Sackville gave a splendid ball in October. The town was soon back in its pre-45 stride, with few lasting scars to be found, mental or physical, and the most important aspect must be the question of why Dundonians did or did not support the Pretender. The majority, like the rest of the Lowlands, did not. There would be fewer 'fighting men' in 1745 than Webster calculated − 2495 ⅔ (*sic*) − but not so many less that the number who did take up arms or show support, like the merchants who broke open the post-bags, can be seen as anything but insignificant. Even allowing for mistakes and omission in the contemporary lists, there were not many more than 100 avowed Jacobites and only 86 carrying arms. The Forfarshire Regiment in which most locals joined is considered particularly well-documented. Such numbers do not denote strong commitment to Charles Edward's 'Rash Adventure'. Of those in the army, only 17 are described as 'volunteers', though another seven including Sir John Kinloch joined after Prestonpans, which must be considered a type of volunteering. Of the 39 who are merely said to have 'carried arms', we cannot know whether they were persuaded to join by the attractions of Ogilvie's men's smart red and black-checked uniform, by the promise of regular pay of 8d per day for a private, or even by pressure from landlords or employers. How many were like Mudie, if he told the truth?

One must not discount traditional commitment and loyalty to the Stewarts, and there are signs of this in the Dundonians concerned. Four medical men joined up and nine of the locals were officers, which is a high proportion. There were undoubted connections with the Angus gentry, most of them staunch Jacobites, which would be social, religious and familial, the Fotheringhams being an example of the last. A dozen or more merchants also gave open support, though the majority were non-combatants. But there are no obvious common denominators among those who did come out. A few can be identified as members of the episcopalian congregation that met at the Yeaman shore, including the deputy governor, Watson, and perhaps his clerk, James Rattray, a ropemaker, but James Rattray is not an uncommon Dundee name. Dr. William Rait's father was one of those listed in 1743 at a meeting of heads of families but, apart from those identified in this list by their territorial designations, the majority of the names are not distinctive enough for certainty. The two episcopalian congregations in the town, the other meeting in the Seagate, retained their separate places of worship throughout the rebellion, both using the same office − the Scottish. A few Jacobites were Freemasons − Watson again, Thomas Ogilvie, Dr. George Colville and others − but so was John, Master of Gray, Right Worshipful Master of the local lodge and he was neither episcopalian nor Jacobite. Of the twenty-nine named craftsmen, including apprentices, seven weavers, four masons, three silversmiths, three wrights, two slaters, two coopers and one each from other crafts hardly provide a good statistical base for generalisations.

The town as a whole does not seem to have been any more enamoured of the occupying Highland force than were any other Lowlanders. The Kirk Session made no comment on the 'ladies' of the town consorting with them, while they were not silent about connections with the government army, as we have seen. That may or may not be significant, but there is no evidence of the sort of popular sentiment that was expressed in Montrose, where the women wore white gowns and carried white roses through the streets, even when the Duke of Cumberland was in the district. In 1745, attitudes had changed even among some of the Forfarshire landed men with Dundee connections. Sir George Stewart of Grandtully, at whose family house James, the Old Pretender, had been a welcome guest in 1716, was specially invited by the Town Council to join public rejoicing at the Cross when news of Culloden reached the town.

One charge has been made against Jacobites in general that they lacked 'political seriousness', and at the local level the merchants involved tend to merit this description. Not one appeared in a position of authority in Dundee before 1745. None served on the Council of the Guildry or on the Town Council. David Fotheringham, the Jacobite governor, may have been eminent as a merchant, and socially as one of the Powrie family he would have a position of some standing, but he was not eminent in governing circles in the town. Henry Pattullo and his trading partner, Thomas Ogilvie, were assessors to the Dean of Guild at one point, but they were only two out of a very long list. And they may have had very good reason to hope for Jacobite success. They had been caught out smuggling tobacco on a very large scale, the seizure of 199 hogsheads confiscated at Dundee, Leith, Edinburgh, Alloa and Glasgow being the largest recorded by that date. No wonder Pattullo had been keen to break into the Dundee Customs House. Ogilvie, like the Fotheringhams a member of an Angus landed family, the son of Sir John of Inverquharity, had been substantial enough a man of business to be exporting to America. His outward goods were a miscellaneous lot, the cargo of the *James of Dundee* on one occasion including six hogsheads of bread, a cask of wright's tools, linen, sugar, candles and shoes. Pattullo appears less often on the Dundee Collector's accounts, but the entrepot nature of some of the local trade can be seen in one of his entries, the re-export of Portuguese salt to Bergen in the *John and Anne*. The other merchants cited as 'concerned' in the rebellion were in business in rather smaller ways, at least in the export/import side, dealing with the Scandinavian ports and the Low Countries. One, Alexander Stewart, victualled one of the ships in which fleeing rebels escaped.

Corporately, the town lends weight to Sir John Clerk's cynical belief that only those in poor financial shape supported Jacobitism.

In 1705, town lands had had to be sold off to satisfy creditors; in 1706-7, those elected to the Council only reluctantly accepted office, such heavy financial burdens still lay on them. These were largely the result of seventeenth century expenditure on the long lawsuit with the Maitlands over the position of Constable and the cost of fortifying the town, though the poor trading conditions of the time could not have helped. By the time of the 1715, there was little improvement. In 1711, 'visitors' from the Convention of Royal Burghs, i.e. delegates from other burghs sent to inquire into a town's affairs, reported that the whole revenue of Dundee was 'exhausted' by unavoidable expense of stipends, schoolmasters' salaries, public burdens. There were still massive debts, the whole town was 'very ruinous' and there was not income available for essential repairs to the harbour and tolbooth. The visitors' recommendation of a twelve year grant of £50 per annum was nullified by the objections from Aberdeen, Glasgow and Dumfries and it was 1724, following further 'visits', before any Convention funds reached the town; then the Town Council received £40 sterling.

By mid-century, there are signs that the town was throwing off the depression of the previous century. Physical growth must have been visible, for in 1748 the Town Council was negotiating to feu land for building on both sides of the road to Dudhope. A new water-supply had been provided in 1743 and while money was borrowed to pay for this, borrowing can be interpreted as either a sign of poverty or as proof that the council felt the cost was bearable and a worthwhile investment. Debts had still to be serviced and Parliament allowed two pennies Scots on each pint of ale brewed, brought in or tapped in the town from 25 March, 1731 towards this, but also for enlarging the harbour, paving the streets, building a new town hall. Designed by William Adam, the hall stood from 1734 (though not completely paid up for some years thereafter) until the 1920s, and with the other schemes must raise the question as to whether a truly depressed community would have been interested in such expenditure.

Industrially, there were changes. Though the old textile industry of making plaids had collapsed since the Union, by the 1730s Dundee could be described as the centre of 'coarse cheap linen production', and the pressure of business in the stampmasters' offices, Dundee included, was such that it was impossible to stamp every piece. The Council negotiated with the Board of Trustees for Manufactures and Fisheries for help in setting up a local bleachfield to lower costs, with the Guildry prepared to allow £250 towards it. Richard Holden, an Irishman, was duly established a few miles out of town at Baldovie. He used kelp as a bleaching agent which produced a rather yellowish cloth, but he remained for many years and by 1739 his costs 'with encouragement' were ½d – 4d per yard. James Cox had set up in Lochee before 1741, osnaburgs were being spun in the town from 1742 and according to the *OSA*, coloured thread manufacture must certainly have begun by the 1740s. Admittedly, not all the linen produced was being spun, woven or bleached within the town's liberties, but the general activity engendered, the import of flax and the export of cloth, the fact that the Guildry was prepared to subsidise Holden, all point to some degree of prosperity, even though it was not to be compared with developments in the industry at the rival port, Perth, further up the Tay.

The town authorities were not initially over-enthusiastic about the industry. They refused the Board of Trustees' offer to help set up a spinning school in 1729 on the grounds that no money was available for such a purpose and, in the early 1730s, emphasised that only with the Trustees' aid could a bleachfield be provided. Nor was much private capital invested in linen until nearer the end of the century. On the other hand, one must bear in mind that the Council was dominated by merchants, not tradesmen or manufacturers, and that after the victory at Culloden, they were magically able to find £500 to celebrate George II's birthday out of official income that was nominally much the same as it had been earlier in the century. It may have been the will and the vision that were lacking in 1729, not the finance.

Though not all sources of the town's income could be immediately farmed out at the annual October roups, in one area there was a definite increase. In 1718, 1,105 merks, c. £736 Scots, was the bid for the Petty Customs; in 1740, there were sufficient offers above the town's upset price to warrant a rerouping and, significantly, Helen Wood, who had been tacksman for some years previously, valued her investment enough to make the highest bid again at £1,296. In 1744, £1,636 was offered and in October, 1745, astonishingly, Gilbert Thomas was prepared to offer £1,700 and to give his bond for this amount. At a time when inflation was negligible if existing at all, this increase is surely indicative of increasing commercial activity in the town. The amount of shipping belonging to the port also demonstrates growing trade. In 1706, 22 vessels were registered in Dundee; by 1730, the number had doubled and the increase continued, the *OSA* recording 116 in January 1792.

The Guildry's income multiplied too during the thirty years between 1715 and 1745. In 1717-8, £1,799-6-2 Scots was the total charge; by 1734-35, Charles Jobson, their treasurer at the time, had collected over £6,180 and though that dropped in 1737-38 to just over £5,115, the 1745-46 charge and discharge amounted to £7,151-16-8, despite the rebellion.

There was more money about, if only from increased membership and/or fees. Expansion in building also may be adduced from one section of the Wrights' records. Wrights included joiners, carpenters, cabinet makers, glaziers, plasterers and occasionally painters. From 1700 to 1721, they registered only 77 journeymen in employment by masters; from 1720 to 1740, 243 names appear.

When we consider such evidence of economic growth, perhaps we may begin to believe that the Town Council actually meant what they said when they wrote to the king of 'the gradual increase of our trade and manufactures and the security with which we enjoyed the reasonable profits arising from these'. The operative words are, of course, 'gradual' and 'reasonable'. The increase in population, trade and in income cannot be compared with the massive growth of the next century and a half. Nevertheless, for perhaps the greater number of those engaged in commerce, crafts, manufactures, there were tangible signs of hard-won, increasing prosperity. Understandably, there seems to have been little desire in Dundee to put this at risk for the doubtful benefits that might arise from the return of an autocratic, Roman Catholic dynasty, supported mainly by foreigners and by Highlanders, just as alien, whose representative in 1745 showed himself a worthy heir of his forefathers.

SOURCES/BIBLIOGRAPHY

PRIMARY SOURCES

DUNDEE DISTRICT ARCHIVES
> Dundee Town Council Minutes
> Dundee Town Charters
> Dundee Kirk Session Minutes
> Dundee Kirk Treasurers' Accounts
> Minutes of the United Presbyteries of Dundee and Forfar
> Records of the United Trades of Dundee, the Dundee Mason, Wright and Slater
> Trades

DUNDEE UNIVERSITY LIBRARY
> Microfilm of the Collector of Customs Accounts, Dundee, 1742-1830
> Records of the Diocese of Brechin

NATIONAL LIBRARY OF SCOTLAND
> Receipts of Laurence Oliphant of Gask
> Yester Papers

PRIVATE SOURCES
> I should like to express my gratitude to Mr. H.S. Fothringham of Granttully
> Castle, Aberfeldy for much useful information about the family of Fotheringham of
> Powrie.
> I am grateful to the Mason, Wright and Slater Trades of Dundee for allowing
> me access to their Lockit Books.

UNPUBLISHED SOURCES
> W. Christie: *History of the Episcopal Church in the Diocese of Brechin*
> (Unpublished Ph.D. thesis, University of Dundee)
> 1968) Enid Gauldie: *Scottish Bleachfields*, 1718-1862 (Unpublished B.Phil. thesis,
> University of St. Andrews, 1966)

SECONDARY SOURCES

> *Caledonian Mercury*
> *Edinburgh Evening Courant*
> *Penny London Post*
> *Scots Magazine*
> *Old Statistical Account*
> Andrew Jervise: *Memorials of Angus and the Mearns* (Edinburgh, 1885)
> David, Lord Elcho: *A Short Account of the Affairs of Scotland in the Years 1744,
> 1745, 1746* (James Thin, 1973)
> J.G. Kyd (ed): *Scottish Population Statistics* (Edinburgh, 1975)
> Bruce Lenman: *The Jacobite Risings in Britain*, 1689-1746 (Eyre Methuen, 1980)
> A. Livingstone, C. Aikman, B. Stuart Hart (eds) *Muster Roll of Prince Charles
> Edward Stuart's Army* (Aberdeen University Press, 1894)

Alexander Mackintosh: *Forfarshire or Lord Ogilvy's Regiment* (Inverness, 1914)

Rev. Walter MacLeod (ed): *A List of Persons concerned in the Rebellion* (Scottish History Society, Edinburgh, 1890)

J.D. Marwick (ed): *Records of the Convention of the Royal Burghs of Scotland* (Edinburgh, 1885)

R.W. & Jean Munro: *The Scrimgeours* (Scrimgeour Clan Association, 1980)

David Murray: *The York Building Company* (Glasgow, 1883)

Hew Scott: *Fasti Ecclesiae Scoticanae* (Edinburgh 1925)

Sir Bruce Gordon Seton & Jean Gordon Arnot (eds): *Prisoners of the Forty-Five* (Scottish History Society, Edinburgh, 1928)

9

HOUSES DIVIDED
by
Ian Grimble

Ian Grimble was born in Hong-Kong in 1921 of colonial
Scottish parentage. He was a Williams History Exhibitioner at
Balliol college, Oxford, where he graduated. As an Officer in the
Intelligence Corps 1943-6, he served in India. After the war he
worked in the House of Commons Library 1947-55, and as a
B.B.C. Producer 1955-59, setting up the first VHF local radio
to be established in the British Isles, in the north of Scotland.
He attended Aberdeen University 1959-62, working on a Ph.D.
thesis about Gaelic Society in the north of Scotland, the basis
for *The Trial of Patrick Sellar* (1962), *Chief of Mackay* (1965)
and *The World of Rob Donn* (1979). Other books include *Scottish
Clans and Tartans* (1973), *Highland Man* (1980), *Clans and
Chiefs* (1980), *The Sea Wolf: the Life of Admiral Cochrane* (1978),
Scottish Islands (1985), and *Robert Burns* (1986). Dr. Grimble is
a frequent broadcaster in radio and television on historical and
literary subjects, generally relating to Scotland. He is a Fellow
of the Royal Historical Society, and Honorary Member of the
Clan Mackay Society.

THE KINSLEY EDITION of Robert Burns's poetry still
preserves the original footnote to 'The lovely lass of Inverness.' It tells that
the battle of Culloden was joined between 'the Highland Clans, fighting
under Prince Charles Stuart, against the English army commanded by the
Duke of Cumberland.' David Morier's contemporary painting of the battle,
seen by thousands of visitors to the palace of Holyroodhouse in which it
hangs, presents the same picture. It depicts kilted Highlanders falling

beneath the bayonets of what appear to be English soldiers. Neither gives the slightest impression that there were approximately the same numbers of Gaels fighting on each side in the uprising of 1745.

The conflict involved the legitimate Stewart sovereign, excluded from the throne by Act of Parliament because he was a Catholic, in favour of the Protestant house of Hanover. But although religion was consequently a fundamental issue, by no means all the Jacobites were Catholics or every Protestant a Hanoverian in his sympathy. Prince Charles raised his standard in Glenshiel and it was a predominantly Highland host that marched into the Lowlands. This aroused the same kind of antagonism to his cause as the Lord of the Isles did when he approached Aberdeen in 1411, and Montrose when he brought a Gaelic army into the Border country in 1646. Hostility between Highlander and Lowlander, exacerbated by the language barrier, still exercised a potent influence on public attitudes. Yet there were Jacobite Lowlanders and Hanoverian Highlanders.

In fact this last civil war in the British Isles cannot be explained simply as a confrontation between Scots and English, Catholics and Protestants, or Highlanders and Lowlanders, even if their frictions contributed to the alignments of the '45. They did not even unite entire clans or families in the opposing camps. Within families, people were influenced to varying degrees by inherited attitudes, matured during the religious and political conflicts of the previous century. To a certain extent the '45 has the appearance of an epilogue to a long drama, in which descendants re-enacted the parts of their forebears, though not always in corresponding roles.

This is well illustrated by the behaviour of two great families which dominated opposite sides of Scotland where the country swells to its widest extent, the MacLeods of the Hebrides and the Forbeses of the North-East.

The Forbes response to the religious changes which followed the Reformation in Scotland is remarkable for its variety and its seriousness. The family had much property to lose, surrounding its network of castles, Pitsligo and Corse, Craigievar, Tolquhon and castle Forbes. In their devout adherence to almost every conceivable shade of belief they ran repeated risks of losing their inheritance. During the reign of James VI two successive heirs to the ancient barony of Forbes renounced all their secular rights to become Capuchin friars in the Catholic Spanish Netherlands. Here the second of them was said to have converted upwards of 300 Scottish soldiers, sent to fight for the Calvinist Dutch in their war against Spain. Ten years after his death in 1606 his kinsman John Forbes, of the branch of Craigievar, arrived to help reverse this process. He had been convicted of treason and banished for opposing the royal policy of replacing the authority of the Assemblies of the Church with that of bishops, and so came as Pastor to the British congregation of Middleburg.

While the family were exporting their rival convictions in this way, other members were proclaiming them at home. Patrick Forbes of Corse castle accepted a bishopric reluctantly from James VI, and opposed Charles I's high church liturgy. His son John became Professor of Divinity at Aberdeen, opposed the National Covenant, and was driven into exile during the great rebellion. Another Forbes became Charles I's first Bishop of Edinburgh, but died before this could embroil him in the strife that followed.

During the civil war the Forbes castles were menaced and beseiged, their owners as diverse in their military as in their religious allegiances. One of the most bizarre and successful of them was Arthur, eldest son of Sir Arthur Forbes of Corse castle. He fought with Montrose until he was captured in 1645, survived two years of captivity in Edinburgh castle, joined the exiled court of Charles II, and received large grants of land in Ireland after the Restoration. There he became Commander-in-Chief, although he was a devout Presbyterian. He was created Earl of Granard, welcomed William of Orange in the revolution of 1688, and died at Castle Forbes in 1696. His Chief, the 12th Lord Forbes, made the same political choice and lived to support the Union of 1707.

In the far north lived a branch of the sept of Tolquhon castle, Duncan Forbes of Culloden and Ferintosh. He too was active in securing the expulsion of the Catholic James VII, as a result of which his property was ravaged by the Jacobites. He was compensated with a licence to distil whisky at Ferintosh.

But the clan solidarity in favour of a Presbyterian national church and a Protestant succession to the throne failed to withstand the advent of George I from Hanover in 1714. The most colourful of its champions of a divine right of kings was Alexander, 4th Lord Forbes of Pitsligo. His forbear had been ennobled by Charles I, then retired to a timely death like Bishop Forbes of Edinburgh, before any dire consequences could befall him. His family continued to enjoy the former priory lands of Moneymusk which the Reformation had brought them, and the castle of Pitsligo. But the 4th Lord had for his mother a daughter of John Erskine, 9th Earl of Mar. Her brother the 10th Earl did support William of Orange, but her nephew the 11th Earl raised the Jacobite standard in the Braes of Mar in 1715, and his cousin Alexander of Pitsligo joined him.

Compared to the Earl Marischal and others, Lord Forbes of Pitsligo was extremely fortunate. Although he was compelled to flee abroad after the failure of the uprising, he was not attainted, and returned to enjoy his patrimony in 1720. He immersed himself in philosophy and published an interesting, reflective book of *Thoughts Concerning Man's Condition* in 1732 which was printed a hundred years later. Perhaps the reputation of his name in Hanoverian circles had helped to mitigate his treatment. It cannot have appeared likely that he would leave his seclusion again in the Jacobite cause.

At Culloden House, his remote kinsman Duncan Forbes had died in 1704. The distilling of whisky did not occupy his thoughts entirely. He was an enthusiastic genealogist, who also committed to paper his thoughts on bringing peace and prosperity to the Highlands. But his two sons were evidently no strangers to the amenities of Ferintosh. When they were sent to Inverness grammar school they earned a joint reputation as the greatest boozers in the north. Others of their neighbourhood and household appear to have followed their example. At the funeral of their mother in 1716 the mourners became so drunk that the corpse was found to be missing when they reached the burial ground. But Duncan the younger son had adopted more temperate habits by 1725.

In that year his skill as a lawyer was recognised by his appointment to the Office of Lord Advocate. In 1734 he succeeded to the estate of Culloden on the death of his brother and three years later he reached the supreme office of Lord President of the Court of Session. Already he had displayed his father's concern for the welfare of the Highlands, so perilously close to his doorstep. During the 1715 uprising the Mackintosh Chief had come to his home with a Jacobite force, demanding all its arms and ammunition. In the absence of her menfolk, Mrs Forbes had organised such a determined resistance that Mackintosh had ridden away to join the Earl of Mar, leaving her unmolested. After the defeat of this uprising Duncan Forbes protested against the illegality of trying Jacobite prisoners at Carlisle in England. Although the letter he addressed to Robert Walpole the First Minister appealing against the government's harsh treatment was sent anonymously, Duncan's known humanity exposed him to the charge of Jacobite sympathies, a slur that was to besmirch him for the rest of his life.

Sometimes accusations of this sort were circulated by political rivals, and unscrupulous means were sought to justify them. For instance, in 1717 the Duke of Montrose tried to blackmail Rob Roy into bringing false witness against the 2nd Duke of Argyll, incriminating him in treasonable communication with the Jacobites. Duncan Forbes would have been relatively easy to trap, since he remained in contact with the disaffected deliberately in the hope of dissuading them from further rebellion. His policy paid handsome dividends to the government but proved extremely damaging to himself.

He took steps that could be genuinely misconstrued. In 1734, the year of his brother's death, he supported a nephew as candidate for the parliamentary constituency of Ross. The electors consisted of a small number of freeholders, of whom the most influential were MacKenzies. Their Jacobite Chief, the Earl of Seaforth, was living in exile in Paris when Duncan Forbes wrote to him, asking him to direct the MacKenzie electors to vote for the Forbes candidate. This clan, too, was a house divided. The Jacobite Seaforth's son Lord Fortrose was active on the Hanoverian side; the opposite to the arrangement in the Gordon family, whose Duke was a Hanoverian while his son Lord Lewis Gordon was a Jacobite.

Some were hedging their bets, and almost all might have been convicted of treason, whichever side won, if their correspondence were to fall into the wrong hands. But Duncan Forbes never wavered in his allegiance as so many did around him. He was as staunch in his loyalties as his close associates the 2nd Duke of Argyll and the 3rd Duke who succeeded him at his death in 1743. A particular concern of all these men was what might happen in the Hebrides if the Stewart standard were to be raised again.

The different islands presented their particular problems. In Mull the Macleans had been ousted by the Campbells from their castles of Duart and

Aros, and their Chief was a Jacobite exile. But many of the Maclean tacksmen remained in Mull as well as in neighbouring Coll and Tiree. There were also members of the same order of the clan hierarchy in the Presbyterian ministry. Prominent among these was John Maclean, known as Maighstir Seathan, a good Gaelic poet, Minister of Kilninian, and a prosperous tacksman. In 1737 Lord President Forbes came to Mull to act gratuitously on behalf of the Duke of Argyll in promoting a reorganisation of society in the island. Their object was to rescue the inhabitants from 'the tyranny of tacksmen, of freeing them from the oppression of services and Herezelds, and of encouraging them to improve their farms by giving them a sort of property in their ground for 19 years by leases.'

In Islay a Campbell administration implemented just such a policy during the 18th century, and turned an island that was amongst the most poverty-stricken at its beginning into the most improved and prosperous by its end. But while Duncan Forbes' humanitarian motives in Mull are not in doubt, there were obviously sound political grounds for attempting to cut the wings of the Maclean gentry in the island. As for the attitude of the subtenantry, examples of oppressive services demanded by the tacksmen can be found throughout the Highlands and islands. But after the Chiefs had become anglicised absentees, the tacksmen class provided both a cultural and an economic bulwark in the communities in which they resided. The poet-Minister Maighstir Seathan is a notable example of the amenities that this class provided, with his promotion of schools, pastoral activities and passionate defence of his menaced Gaelic language and culture. At Culloden, which lies outside the Highlands, Lord President Forbes had evidently not become sufficiently acquainted with the value of such a man to his society, and he would not have been likely to learn more in Edinburgh. This most conciliatory of men incurred the hostility of one whose co-operation would have served him well, and he returned from Mull in 1737, disappointed by his reception there. 'To my very great surprise, every creature, from the highest to the lowest, seemed to undervalue the leases proposed.'

When the 1745 uprising occured, the Maclean Chief returned to join it, and many of his clansmen rose in the Jacobite cause. But Maighstir Seathan remained as staunch a Hanoverian as Forbes could have wished. After Culloden he sat with the Presbytery of Mull in Aros, where Maclean chiefs had pronounced the law in earlier times and Duncan Forbes had come to promote his new order. There the Revd. John Maclean and his brethren castigated the Revd. Duncan MacPherson for his part in 'the late wicked and unnatural rebellion.'

Forbes was more successful in Skye. Here Norman MacLeod of MacLeod had been born in 1706 and inherited the chiefship in the same year. His family had been among the most conspicuous survivors of the era in which the MacDonalds of Islay had been dispossessed and the sons of Lord Forbes became Capuchin friars. This was largely the achievement of Sir Roderick MacLeod, probably the ablest Chief of his clan. He too embraced the Catholic faith, yet he succeeded in preserving his patrimony at a time when the MacLeods of Lewis lost theirs to the MacKenzies, and even retained the esteem of James VI who regarded his Hebridean subjects as utterly barbarous. During the remainder of the 17th century Dunvegan became the principal centre of Gaelic music, poetry and learning. But by the end of it Roderick Morison, the Blind Harper, was lamenting that the MacLeod chiefs had degenerated into spendthrift absentees, and such was Norman MacLeod, whom Lord President Forbes took such pains to lure into the Hanoverian camp.

One of MacLeod's closest friends was Sir Alexander MacDonald of Sleat, who was five years younger than himself and had also inherited the chiefship of his clan as a child. He enjoyed this rank because the MacDonalds of Islay were dispossessed. There had not been much more to inherit at the outset, since MacDonald's uncle had joined the Jacobites in 1715 and been forfeited after the suppression of the uprising. But his lands were recovered and he received a charter to them in 1727.

MacLeod was allied to MacDonald by marriage with his first cousin Janet of Sleat, but the couple quarrelled and in 1733 she left him and went to live extravagantly in Edinburgh. Lord President Forbes exerted his influence to prevent a rift between the two young tycoons of Skye, to such effect that MacLeod wrote to his wife: 'I hope, my dear, we shall soon meet with a fixed resolution to pardon one another's failings and to be happy and agreeable as long as we both live.' She returned to Dunvegan, where she remained until her death.

In 1740 both MacDonald and MacLeod were on a list of supposed Jacobite supporters that was submitted to the Pretender in Rome. Their inclusion may have been no more than wishful thinking, and certainly MacDonald registered a protest when he found out. But MacLeod cultivated a close acquaintance with his cousin Lord Lovat, potentially dangerous for one of his somewhat unstable and erratic nature. Forbes provided other company for MacLeod by securing his election as Member of Parliament for Inverness-shire in 1741. At Westminster he became known as a member of 'the Duke of Argyll's gang.'

Such was the situation when the Prince landed in the Hebrides on the 2nd July 1745. It was MacLeod who informed Lord President Forbes in Edinburgh, and he had delayed writing for over a month, which appears odd. Forbes was over sixty years old by this time, with only two more years to live, but he rode north with speed and energy. 'I found myself almost alone, without arms and without money or credit, provided with no means to prevent extreme folly except pen and ink, a tongue and some reputation.' Despite all his representations to the government, no preparations had been made to deal with such an emergency. The totally incompetent Scottish Secretary of State John Hay, 4th Marquess of Tweeddale, wrote to Forbes promising that every payment he made in arming the north would be reimbursed, an undertaking that was dishonoured. Forbes was to write later: 'had arms and ammunition come when they were first called for, before the unexpected successes blew up folly to madness, I could have answered it with my head that no man from the North should have joined the original force of rebels that passed the Forth.'

MacLeod had assured Forbes on the 3rd August that both he and MacDonald had rejected the overtures of the Jacobites. 'Sir Alexander MacDonald and I not only gave no sort of countenance to these people but we used all the influence we had with our neighbours to follow the same prudent method.' Forbes summoned MacLeod to Inverness, and it appears that during his absence MacDonald planned to raise 1000 of his clansmen for the Prince. While he was discussing this undertaking with MacLeod of Raasay and others, letters arrived from Forbes and MacLeod of MacLeod. After he had read them, MacDonald left the conspirators abruptly, for which he was regarded ever after as a turncoat.

The MacDonalds for Clanranald supported Prince Charles, and so did the MacLeods of Raasay. The sept of Raasay made an issue of their descent from the MacLeods of Lewis, and would not recognise the incumbent of Dunvegan as their Chief. Dr. Johnson was to discover this when he assumed otherwise and was obliged to publish a correction of what he had written on the subject. On the other hand MacLeod of Bernera belonged to the Dunvegan branch, yet he too joined the Jacobites. As for the top men of both names, the Jacobites did not despair of rallying them to the cause, especially after their initial successes. The Duke of Atholl wrote to them in September: 'His Royal Highness having constituted me Commander-in-Chief of his Majesty's forces benorth the river Forth, do hereby desire you'll raise all your men in arms, and with the utmost expedition march with me to join his Royal Highness.' By this time the government had provided Forbes with blank commissions to distribute among the loyal clans at his discretion, although he possessed all too little else apart from his personal influence. So far as MacLeod and MacDonald were concerned (though not Lord Lovat) this proved effective.

While Lord President Forbes concentrated his attention on the west, his cousin of Pitsligo reflected on the cause of divine right to the east of him. 'I thought, I weighed, and I weighed again.' He was even more elderly than Duncan of Culloden, 67 years of age, yet he forsook his library, rode off on his horse, and raised a force of 100 cavalry from amongst the gentry of Aberdeenshire. When these had assembled, he took off his hat as he reviewed them, raised it to heaven and declared: 'O Lord Thou knowest that our cause is just. March, gentlemen.'

Another Forbes whose Jacobite sympathies were to earn him equal renown was Robert, son of a schoolmaster of Rayne in Aberdeenshire. Duncan the genealogist might have had difficulty in discovering his place in the family tree, since pedigrees generally follow property and are generally less attentive to the younger sons of younger sons who disappear into the professions. Robert Forbes became an Episcopalian clergyman after leaving Marischal College, and in September 1745 he was arrested near Stirling with two of his brethren, on suspicion that he intended to join the rebels. Fortunately for posterity (and probably for himself also) he was not released until May 1746, the month after Culloden. So he lived to become a Bishop, and to compile the testimony of Jacobites in ten volumes of manuscript which has been published under the title of *The Lyon in Mourning.*

It is this collection which tells how Sir Alexander MacDonald of Sleat was conspiring with MacLeod of Raasay when the letters arrived from Lord President Forbes and MacLeod which changed his mind. They had no such effect on the Laird of Raasay or his nephew Malcolm MacLeod who was present in the company. These raised no less than 100 men in their little island, whom Malcolm led with outstanding gallantry at Culloden.

The rival allegiances led to curious consequences, not all of them un-happy, after the Jacobite defeat. Prince Charles fled to the Outer Hebrides, to find that there was no ship to carry him away, while Hanoverian troops were searching for him there. Flora MacDonald's step-father was one of these, yet he gave her a pass to sail to Skye with her servant 'Betty Burke', although it is hardly credible that he did not know he was aiding the Prince to escape. Flora conducted him to the home of Sir Alexander MacDonald, to find that the Chief's wife was entertaining Hanoverian soldiers when she arrived. The two women organised the Prince's safe departure almost before their very eyes. The Prince was perhaps safest among people who would not be suspected of harbouring him, although they would not betray him.

Unfortunately Malcolm MacLeod rowed him across the sound of Raasay to his island, a notorious nest of Jacobites too small to afford a safe asylum and already occupied by soldiers in search of him. After two miser-able nights in a hut, consoled by a bottle of brandy, Charles Edward allowed the gallant young Captain Malcolm to row him back to Skye before returning to take care of his wife. A week later he was arrested by Hanoverian MacLeods from Skye. 'Donald MacLeod the lieutenant said he was very sorry for my misfortune. I told him there was not any name in Scotland would have taken me prisoner but theirselves.' Malcolm MacLeod was carried a prisoner to London, but he did not suffer the hardships of the prison hulks at Tilbury. He remained under house arrest while he awaited trial, and although some of his own companions in arms were sentenced to transportation, no witness could be found to bring evidence against him despite the conspicuous part he had played at Culloden. He was released under the general amnesty of 1747, when Flora MacDonald chose him as her escort on their long journey home to the Hebrides.

Dreadful atrocities had occured there during their absence, committed for the most part by Lowland Scots. Malcolm MacLeod had himself wit-nessed the appalling treatment of prisoners aboard the sloop of war *Furnace*, whose Captain he described as 'that cruel, barbarous man, John Ferguson of Aberdeenshire.' When General John Campbell of Mamore learnt of his villainies he was credited with threatening to nail him by the ear to one of his own masts. John MacCodrum the Hebridean poet composed a savage poem about him, 'the venomous boar that would not grant mercy, who showed his hand in slaughter and murder.'

The Raasay Chief's son deposed that Captain Ferguson 'ordered

Lieutenant Dalrymple ashore to execute his vengeance against the island, who burnt Raasay's good house to ashes, as also the whole houses of the island, excepting two small villages that escaped their sight.' Some of their men raped a blind girl, others flogged a man to death. The terror lasted until September, when Prince Charles was known to have escaped from the Hebrides. By this time, according to an eye-witness, 'the whole island of Raasay has been plundered and pillaged to the utmost degree, every house and hut being levelled with the ground; and there was not left in the whole island a four-footed beast, a hen or a chicken.' In addition, every boat had been removed or destroyed, so that the islanders could neither fish nor cross the sound for supplies.

MacLeod of Bernera's home was spared the fate of MacLeod of Raasay's when Mrs MacLeod shamed Captain Ferguson by her lavish hospitality, though her island was ravaged. Nor could she be dispossessed, since her husband was merely a tacksman of MacLeod of MacLeod who had supported the Hanoverian cause. MacLeod of Raasay was not forfeited because he had conveyed his property to his son before he joined the rebels, and it does appear that the process of healing and reconstruction was helped, here as elsewhere, by the very divisions which had contributed to the Jacobite defeat. Raasay house had been rebuilt by the time Johnson and Boswell paid their visit in 1773. Malcolm MacLeod, by now 62 years of age, rowed them across the sound as he had rowed Prince Charles, wielding an oar himself. He sang to his guests the Gaelic incitement to rise for the Prince, *Tha tighinn fodham éiridh.* He was a piper and composer of pibroch as well as a singer, one of the people whom the travellers had been most eager to meet, and whom they described in admiring detail.

As for Clan Forbes, the government's treatment of the Lord President was as disgraceful in its own way as any of the atrocities committed against the Jacobites. To no single man did the Hanoverians owe so much as to Duncan of Culloden: people had received a dukedom for less. Yet his attempt to alleviate the sufferings of the defeated led only to Cumberland's jibe, 'that old woman talked to me about humanity'. The money he had defrayed on the government's behalf was not repaid to him in full, and instead of honours he received abuse. The depression this caused is said to have hastened his death in 1747.

The 4th Lord Forbes of Pitsligo proved more resilient. He did not escape forfeiture this time as he had done in 1715, nor leave the country as he had done on the former occasion. He made his home in a cave under one of the arches of a bridge in a remote part of the moors of Pitsligo, from which he would emerge disguised as a beggar. On one occasion he received a coin from a soldier of one of the search parties scouring the country for him. When his estates were seized after the Act of Attainder of 1748, he contested the forfeiture on the grounds that the Act had misnamed him Lord Pitsligo, rather than Lord Forbes of Pitsligo. The Court of Session upheld his appeal in 1749, but the House of Lords reversed this judgement in the following year.

Nevertheless, the hunt for him relaxed, so that it was possible for him to live with his son at Auchiries under the pseudonym of Mr Brown. His safety remained precarious, however. On one occasion a search party was observed approaching the house, so Mr Brown was hidden behind the wainscotting at the back of a bed in which an old woman lay. The soldiers stroked her chin to make sure she was not a man, while she exploded in a violent fit of coughing to drown the noise of Mr Brown's asthmatic breathing behind the woodwork. The last Lord Forbes of Pitsligo lived on well into his eighties, before he died in December 1762. What was left of his estate passed to collateral heirs who planted New Pitsligo in the age of improvement, while his old castle crumbled into ruin.

The issue that divided his family, and so many others, originated in one that divided the royal house itself. The two young cousins who confronted each other at Culloden were pursuing a quarrel that filtered down to the meanest of those who they claimed as their subjects. One of the fatalities of the situation in those days was that members of royal families had nothing to occupy them except the profession of arms, unless they were actually sitting on a throne. Prince Charles found nothing to do after his defeat except to drink himself to death. The Duke of Cumberland was given military command as a young man although he soon proved that he possessed no talent whatever as a soldier. Culloden was the only battle he ever won, and it was one that it would have been impossible to lose. His only real claim to fame is that he was the most savage flogger of his own men of anyone who has ever held command in the British army.

As for those who served one or the other of these two not very edifying royal youths, there were all too many who still took it for granted that political, dynastic and religious issues might justifiably be decided by violence. Sympathy has often been expressed for their dependents, compelled to fight on one side or the other without being asked for their opinions, or whether they believed in the use of force. Such sympathy must be weighed against the evidence of more recent times. Now that the majority of people possess a freedom to speak and act such as was denied to their forbears, it is possible to observe how widely diffused are the aggressive instincts of our carniverous, combative, hunting species.

In the Jacobite era the voices of the lesser folk were rarely heard: today anyone can proclaim their opinions, whether they contain a grain of sense or not. It is only a minority of families of well-to-do people of that age whose divisions we can study. Today it can be seen that principles and passions divide most families in varying degrees, and the descendant of a peasant may be just as apt to promote his prejudices by force as any prince in the days of old.

10

JACOBITES AT HEART
An Account of
The Independent Companies
by
Alasdair MacLean

Alasdair MacLean was born on Raasay in 1918.

He graduated in Medicine from St. Andrews University. After several hospital appointments and a period of wartime service in the R.A.M.C. he took up general practice in South Uist in 1950. Being a Gaelic speaker and sharing a family interest in oral tradition he took the opportunity of absorbing some of the rich folklore of the island.

In this connection he became aware of the importance in local tradition of Neil Maceachen, a shadowy figure who appeared briefly on the historical scene as the manservant who accompanied Flora MacDonald and Bonnie Prince Charlie on the famous voyage over the sea to Skye. After 30 years of research into oral and written sources he was able to build up a picture of this South Uist man who was successively a student priest, French soldier, and Jacobite secret agent. This research resulted in the publication in 1982 of *A MacDonald for the Prince* and stimulated an interest in several, little-researched aspects of the '45 rising, including the ambivalent position of the Independent Companies of Militia raised by government to assist in the suppression of the rebellion.

This study indicates that they were largely ineffective, and offers possible reasons for that situation.

Alasdair MacLean is now retired and living on Skye.

THE POPULAR IMPRESSION of the Jacobite Rebellion of 1745 tends to be expressed in terms of 'the Highlanders against the Redcoats'. The fact is, however, that at various times during the years 1745 and 1746, there were nearly as many Highlanders mobilised in the Hanoverian interest as there were under the banner of Prince Charles Edward Stewart.

Unlike their compatriots in the Jacobite forces, who were essentially the same stock, frequently close blood relations, the Independent Companies won no dramatic victories and suffered no honourable defeats and left no appreciable imprint on history, and it is interesting to speculate on why this was so.

The Independent Companies, which had originally been raised in 1725 as part of General Wade's process of pacification of the Highlands had, in 1743, been amalgamated to form a regiment of the line, the Highland Regiment later the 42nd (Black Watch). In 1745 Lord John Murray had succeeded as titular 'Colonel'. The same year it was decided to raise three additional companies of the Regiment. Because of the success of the first Highland Regiment it was also decided to raise a second one whose 'Colonel' was to be John Campbell, 4th Earl of Loudon. These companies and this Regiment were incomplete at the outbreak of the Rebellion.

Prince Charles Edward landed on Eriskay at the end of July, 1745, and raised his standard at Glenfinnan on 19th August. Subsequently Sir John Cope, commanding the Royal Army in Scotland, having avoided battle with the Prince's forces advancing over the pass of Corrieyairick, marched on to Inverness, leaving the road to Edinburgh open to the Jacobites. Cope was obliged to follow as best he could, taking with him the skeleton elements of Lord John Murray's and Lord Loudon's companies that he could find in Inverness. Thus the North of Scotland was stripped of any forces that could be used to contain the Rebellion.

The Earl of Stair proposed therefore that a number of blank commissions for companies be issued to Duncan Forbes of Culloden, the Lord President of the Court of Session, to be distributed among the well affected clans as 'the Lord President shall think proper'.

So the elderly Forbes, having returned to Inverness from Edinburgh on the 13th August 1745, immediately set about exerting his considerable political influence with the various Highland chiefs, in order to secure their loyalty to the Government.

Also in August Major General Campbell, cousin and heir of the 3rd Duke of Argyll, asked his Commander in Chief's permission to return to Scotland in order to organise Argyll and raise men there for the Government service. A comparatively junior General, he had had long military service, and his friendly relationship with the King and his knowledge of the strategic importance of Central Scotland, ensured the granting of his request. He wrote on the 25th September ' . . . His Majesty intends to send me to Scotland, to command, under Marshal Wade, in the West of Scotland and in the Highlands'.

That same week Cope's army sustained a crushing defeat at Prestonpans.

It is an indication of the state of preparation of Murray's and Loudon's new companies that a nominal four companies of Loudon's and one of Murray's could muster only one hundred and eighty five men, and they were virtually all made prisoner. Of the Earl of Loudon's officers Captains Alexander Mackay, son of Lord Reay, and John Stuart, son of the Earl of Moray, were among the prisoners. Despite giving their parole, most of them later rejoined the Government forces, however Ross yr. of Pitcalnie crossed over to the Jacobite side to the distress of his grand uncle Lord President Forbes.

But the Earl of Loudon escaped capture at Prestonpans. Handsome, dashing, and a favourite of the Duke of Cumberland, he was at forty-one the youngest General in the Army. He arrived in Inverness on 11th October to take command of the troops between Inverness and Fort William, which at that stage totalled only about 150 men.

The Lord President had since 13th September been allocating commissions for Captain, Lieutenant and Ensign for Independent Companies of 4 serjeants, 4 corporals, a piper, and 100 men each. His task was not made easier by the susceptibilities of certain magnates. Ludovick Grant of Grant felt that his family should have been given more than the one company which was offered, and declined to raise a second when asked. Lord Lovat refused a company for his second son, and the Earl of Cromartie refused a similar offer for his son Lord Macleod. The reasons behind the refusal of both these nobles emerged later. As the Lord President was awaiting arms and money to pay them, he could not mobilise the companies, but the arrival of Loudon on the sloop 'Saltash' carrying both arms and money enabled Forbes to call them forward.

In Argyll similar delays were being experienced. General Campbell, in London, reported to the Secretary for War at the end of October, that the King had ordered him to raise 'eight Independent Companies each of 100 men with the proper officers; and likewise to arm 16 such companies more, without the charge of commissioned officers, who are to serve without pay and are to be raised from the Duke of Argyll's and the Earl of Breadalbanes' Contreys.' Difficulties of administration and supply, however, delayed his departure to an exasperating degree, and although the General was ultimately able to sail he was held up by bad weather and it was the 22nd December before he arrived in Inverary.

By this time the Jacobite forces retreating from Derby were expected to occupy Glasgow. General Guest had been pressing for 1,600 to 2,000 Argyll militia, which the General's son, Lt. Col. Campbell of Loudon's Regiment had been organising in his father's absence, to be sent to Stirling, albeit without proper arms, clothing, or equipment. General Campbell was thus immediately embroiled in countless administrative problems.

Two men, very different in training, were thus involved in the same task, in Inverness and Inverary, the lawyer and the soldier. Their task was to organise the preparation of Highland auxilliaries to support the regular forces of the London Government. But they each brought to bear the same meticulous attention to detail, and in a short time they had set up formidable organisations in difficult conditions of supply and communication.

By March 1746 General Campbell had 2776 men under arms. It should be noted that the Independent Companies were usually designated by the territorial designations of the captains, almost all Campbells in the case of the Argyll units.

In addition to eighteen companies of 100 men each, established by Forbes, from the 'loyal' clans of the shires of Inverness, Ross and Suther-land, units of irregular militia were raised at various times at his or Lord Loudon's request to serve for a specific purpose and period. For convenience all these units, whether detached companies of regular regiments, formal Independent Companies or irregular militia, will hereafter be referred to as independent companies, as their function and personnel were frequently interchangeable.

It must be remembered that the functions envisaged for the Independent Companies were, at their inception, threefold. They were first, to prevent Jacobites in their neighbourhood from joining in the rebellion, secondly they were expected to occupy lands vacated by the Jacobites in the course of their campaigns, and thirdly, to march where ever and when ever a need for them arose. How successful the Companies were in reaching these objectives is difficult to quantify. It was, however, in the third requirement, which was in effect to go into action in support of or instead of regular forces, that they failed signally.

The Macleods of Skye were said to have worn white cockades when leaving the island to foster the impression among men that they were going to join the Prince. Some may have lacked motivation, and the idea of possibly having to fight against their friends and relations was repugnant to all. Sir Alexander Macdonald expressed the dilemma when, in September 1745, he said that his gentlemen felt a delicacy in coming out to fight their friends and relations, 'however ready to hack and hew Frenchmen'. Lord Fortrose, whose title Earl of Seaforth had been forfeited in 1716, also had difficulty in finding officers for his companies. 'Some want resolution, some honour, and some are free of both'. The Earl of Sutherland had difficulty in raising men for a second company, less than six being volunteers.

It is true that what contemporary evidence we have of pro Jacobite or pro Hanoverian sentiment is mainly from the literate and upper or officer stratum of society. What is invariably more difficult to assess is the feeling of the ordinary man in the ranks, who after all, makes the decision to fight or run. It is Duncan Bán Macintyre, an illiterate monoglot Gael from the Breadalbane country, who makes the most explicit statement of the attitude of an ordinary soldier in a Highland Independent Company. Duncan was serving in Carwhin's company, raised by Lord Glenorchy, heir to the Campbell Earl of Breadalbane. In fact, he was serving as a substitute for one Fletcher on a promise of payment. His motivation would therefore be no higher than that of most mercenaries, but he was present at the Battle of Falkirk and left two metric accounts of the action, which were so strongly pro Jacobite that one of them could not be published during Duncan's lifetime.

It is reasonably certain that Duncan was not the only pro Jacobite in the Company. He and his companions took to their heels at the first suggestion of a Jacobite charge. It is clear that Duncan found his position distasteful, but he also says 'Rinn e cuideachadh d'ar naimhdibh gu robh dith chomman- daidh oirne . . .' (it gave our foes assistance that our leadership was wanting) and again ' . . . Cha d'fhuair sinn focal commandaidh . . . ach comas sgaoilidh feadh an t-saoghail . . .' (we did not get a word of command . . . but liberty to scatter everywhere). In short Duncan demonstrates poor motivation and poor command structure in his Independent Company, and it will be interesting to consider whether one or other of these factors apply to the other actions in which the companies were involved.

It was the Macleods along with the Munroes and the Inverness Company who had had the doubtful distinction of being first 'blooded'. By the beginning of December 1745 Lord Loudon had 13 Independent com- panies under command at Inverness, as well as units of his own Regiment. He had been observing the tortuous movements of Lord Lovat who had finally decided to throw in his weight with the Jacobites and, when he could no longer disguise the fact that the Frasers had moved, blamed his son as responsible, being beyond his control.

The Earl of Cromartie had quietly led our many Mackenzies in the Jacobite interest also.

On the 10th December, Lord Loudon marched out to Lord Lovat's Castle, Dounie, with 800 men; 100 of his own Regiment, two Companies of Sutherlands, one each of Munro's, Grant's, and Mackay's, and two Companies of Lord Fortrose's men. His object was to get the best guarantees possible of Lovat's future good behaviour, which he decided to ensure by bringing Lovat back into Inverness. On the same day the 10th, the Laird of Macleod was ordered to march towards Aberdeen in accordance with the original remit of the companies, to prevent the Jacobites recruiting and to occupy that city which, it was believed, the Jacobites had left. He had with him 400 men of his own people and a Company of Assynt men under Hugh Macleod of Geanies.

Macleod of Macleod's neighbour in Skye, Sir Alexander Macdonald, had declared himself unfit for high command and that his pride would not allow him to accept a lesser. But Macleod, who had admitted that he had no military experience either, had had command thrust on him, for Forbes was insistent that either he or Sir Alexander should accompany the men from Skye. Macleod was assured that Lord Loudon would join him in a day or so, when the business of Lord Lovat had been settled. The settlement proved far from simple, and on the 13th December Munro of Culcairn, an experienced officer, was sent to support Macleod. Munro had with him his own company and one raised by the town of Inverness.

Having crossed the Spey on 15th December, Macleod wrote to the President Forbes, reporting that Ludovick Grant of Grant had collected about 500 men and was, apparently on his own initiative, marching east to support Macleod and was expected in Keith the following day and

Strathbogie the next. Macleod informed the President that he would consequently require to change his own route and march to Cullen and Banff,
'where we are vastly wanted'. There he would await orders and hoped
Culcairn would join him; '. . . I am so little a military man' and requiring his
advice.

On the 17th President Forbes replied with some commonsense advice.
He suggested that Macleod should seek out information concerning possible
arms dumps for rebel forces in his neighbourhood in order to disperse the
men and secure the arms. If not otherwise impeded he should march straight
to Aberdeen, leaving a party at Strathbogie. Perhaps if the Grants would
agree to remain a few days they could undertake that duty. He emphasised
that Aberdeen was in much need of relief and that the Jacobite 'posse' there
was mainly of pressed men and very weak.

It was thus important that Macleod should quickly get to Aberdeen, as
the Jacobites, hearing of its occupation, would probably detach troops from
Perth to retake it, thus weakening their forces in the South. Forbes added
that Loudon would be 'quickly up to sustain him'.

In a postscript Forbes said that Lord Loudon was unwilling to pay the
Grants and it was doubtful whether they would advance. Despite this, in a
brief accompanying note Loudon ordered that Macleod should march
straight to Aberdeen, without leaving a party at Strathbogie, unless Grant
wished to do so, in order to protect his own interests. It was reasonable for
Macleod to accept that Grant was to accompany him to Aberdeen. Loudon's
letter to Grant two days previously had hardly been more specific, but Grant
equally reasonably, interpreted its intention as directly opposite to
Macleod's interpretation. Loudon's letter had been very vague: He could not
order Grant to go back to Strathspey, as he had not ordered him to go
forward, but he would be as well pleased if he did go back. He could not pay
the men, as there were sufficient troops 'upon the Establishment' for the
purpose on hand. He could not supply arms although he understood that the
arms of Grant's militia were 'certainly not extremely good'. Grant, writing
to Macleod on 25th December, apologised for not marching with him but
said that he had 'not been encouraged to do so' – a masterly understatement.

On the 20th Macleod was obliged to make a forced march from Banff to
Old Meldrum, where on the following day he received intelligence that
French Picquets (companies of men selected from Irish Regiments in the
French service) had arrived in Aberdeen. He decided to join Culcairn at
Inverurie, and there await the arrival of Lord Loudon, as he had been
instructed.

What Macleod did not know was that Lord Lovat had escaped from
surveillance at Inverness and that Lord Loudon had marched West with his
own Regiment and five Independent Companies, to chase a wily old man
who knew full well where to avoid capture in his own hills. If there was any
point to that exercise, it was a political one and it could have been much
better left to the Lord President. As it was, Macleod, without military
experience and with completely raw troops, was being sacrificed as a pawn

in a doubtful strategy, very badly managed. It is clear, also, that Macleod's intelligence service was bad. There was nothing lacking, however, about the Jacobite intelligence of Macleod's movements.

On the 23rd December, Lord Lewis Gordon marched out of Aberdeen with about 1,000 Jacobite troops, including Lord John Drummond's French. His force advanced in two divisions, one of which crossed the Don, the other the River Urie, and invested the town of Inverurie. Macleod, taken by surprise, made a token resistance, perhaps assisted by the fact that the two Jacobite parties were at one point firing on each other in the moonlight. Three and a half of his companies, quartered outside the town, ran away at the first fire and did not halt until they reached Elgin, and some not even then. Macleod retired to Elgin leaving 70 men killed, wounded, or captured. Writing from Elgin he reported that he had only 70 men left in each of his four Companies, adding, surprisingly, that he had not 'abated one bit of my spirit'. He marched back to Forres, whence he wrote on 29th December that, as a result of continuing desertions, he had only 200 men left of his four Companies. By 2nd January, Sir Alexander was able to tell Macleod that some of them were already back in Skye.

At Inverary General Campbell wrote to General Hawley on 15th January, that his son Lieut. Col. Campbell was on his way to join Hawley with 800 militia (12 Companies), and three companies of military (Lord Loudon's Regiment). In fact there was also with him a company of Lord John Murray's Regiment. The Argyll men arrived at Falkirk on the morning of the battle, the 17th January, and a brief note from young Campbell informed his father the following day that the dragoons had behaved badly and that the militia, though not engaged, had lost half by desertion.

The story of the débâcle of Falkirk is well known. Hawley, who was contemptuous of the Jacobites, arrived too late on the field to dispose his troops properly. The Campbell Companies were vaguely instructed to take position at the bottom of the hill (Falkirk Muir) out of sight of the enemy, and were overrun by Cobham's dragoons as they recoiled from their encounter with the Jacobites on the hill crest.

Lieut. Col. Campbell (in Queensferry on 20th January) did not criticise the most responsible officer of all, General Hawley, but he said he was distressed by the want of officers who knew their duty. He believed that, out of 800 militia, he had no more than 350 left. He put all this down to the care-lessness and ignorance of his officers. His father agreed with him, as will be seen later, but as already noted Duncan Bán Macintyre, an erstwhile private in Carwhin's Company, added another dimension to the opinions of the Colonel and General.

Following the victory at Falkirk the Jacobite General Lord George Murray and several Highland Chiefs, including Lochiel and the Master of Lovat, meeting at Falkirk, advised the Prince that they should retire to the Highlands. There they should take and reduce all the forts, and by spring they would be able to collect 10,000 Highlanders in order to continue the campaign.

On the 16th February, Loudon in Inverness learned on reliable authority that Prince Charles, with a small guard, was spending the night in the house of Macintosh of Macintosh at Moy. His hostess 'Colonel Anne' had raised about 200 men of the Clan Chattan confederacy for the Prince's service, despite the fact that her husband Aeneas, the Chief, was Captain of the Company of Lord John Murray's Regiment stationed at Inverness, a mere twelve miles away. Loudon's opportunity to capture the Prince, and, hopefully, to end the Rebellion, was too good to miss.

To maintain absolute secrecy, Lord Loudon called together his officers at 8p.m. and told them that he had intelligence that an attack on the town was projected and that, although he personally did not believe it, it was necessary for them to be on guard, and he asked them to stand to at eleven at night until he should lead them out of Inverness. He had, in the meantime, thrown a guard round the town to stop any information leaking out. He did not even let the Lord President know what he was about. News, however, did get out and there are many explanations offered for that.

Captain Malcolm Macleod quoted the Prince as saying that the warning came to Moy from Aeneas Macintosh of Macintosh himself, which is most likely, as he was one of the few in the secret, and it was natural that he should want to protect his wife. Accounts recorded by the Jacobite Bishop Forbes and published in the *Lyon in Mourning* tell how the blacksmith of Moy was sent out with four men and intercepted Loudon in the dark. He called out orders to create the illusion that he had a strong defensive force and, firing his musket, killed Macleod's piper, the illustrious Donald Ban MacCrimmon, and routed Loudon's army.

Lord Loudon's own account, which is corroborated by others, is even less flattering to his own troops. Some three miles from Moy Hall he sent off a detachment of thirty men to seal off a short cut along which intelligence of his cautious approach might reach the house. The detachment opened fire on what they thought were four men and threw the main body, a mile away, into such confusion that five companies ran away while the remainder, whom Loudon managed to hold together, were all set to return the fire. Indeed some guns were discharged accidentally, killing the piper who was at Lord Loudon's side. Loudon still had the best part of one thousand men but, having dithered on the ground for an hour, decided that he had lost the element of surprise and returned to Inverness.

Having described how his scheme could have put an end to the rebellion, Loudon goes on '... if it had pleased God that the accident had not happened in the March ... and, had I men that I durst trust would follow me, I could strike another (blow) yet. It is a cruel situation to have Names of Numbers, that you dare not fight.' Loudon may have been throwing doubt on the loyalty of his soldiers, but if not his attack on their military potential ignored the fact that, apart from a political label, his men were no different from those from whom they had run away.

Lord Loudon's attitude is in marked contrast to that of his namesake, General Campbell of Mamore, who, even after the experience of Falkirk, was able to stake his reputation on his men. Writing to Hawley, on 27th January, he said that some of their officers did not do their duty. To the Duke of Argyll he wrote two days later, that the men were good but that the officers were such as the Deputy Lieutenants chose to name. He continued that the mistake was from the heart and not the head, indicating that the appointments had been made for social rather than military considerations.

There is no doubt that some of Loudon's officers were also appointed for the same reasons. Lord Reay persuaded Forbes to grant a commission to his grandson, Hugh Mackay yr. of Bighouse, who was only thirteen years old. The boy and his father were both named Hugh and there is some confusion about which of them was commanding Lord Reay's second company at the beginning of March 1746. Loudon was very lenient with his officers, however; explaining how his five rear companies had gone missing, he said that the fifth company from the rear, a Mackenzie one, '. . . went off entirely from their officers. The Officer, who led the fourth, a very good man, but very short sighted, did not perceive They were running, in the Darke marched after Them, which carried two more Companies after Him . . .' Any officer who did not know he was running away from firing had to be deaf as well as blind. Munro of Culcairn, highly rated by Loudon as an officer, had also run away.

Because of his flight from shadows at Moy, Loudon was in no frame of mind to defend Inverness, and on the 18th, he marched his men out of Inverness and across the Firth by Kessock, closely pursued by the Jacobites who had quickly discovered his intentions. He was accompanied by Lord President Forbes, who went to his own estate at Ferintosh. Loudon's Regiment and the Independent Companies, with the exception of the Grants and Rosses, who had been left as a token garrison at Inverness, lay that night along the North shore of the Beauly Firth. The already demoralised Mackenzies, holding the right flank nearest to their own country, deserted to a man. Next morning Lord Loudon decided to continue his retreat across the Cromarty Firth.

This was as a result of the threat posed by the advance of the Jacobite Earl of Kilmarnock who had crossed the Beauly river on the 21st February and was closely followed by the Earl of Cromartie with additional Jacobite troops.

Loudon then continued his retreat across the Dornoch Firth into Sutherland, taking up a position on the north shore where he collected all the boats he could find on both sides. Thrice he recrossed into Ross-shire, retiring smartly whenever danger threatened and justifying each move on strategic grounds or merely failing to report them. He offered to take ship to join the advancing forces of the Duke of Cumberland, but declined when ordered to do so. The pattern of retreat without joining action could only lead to demoralisation among his troops and indignation among observers. John Maule, the M.P. for Aberdeen Boroughs wrote . . . 'Loudon's campaign is incomprehensible . . . the whole plan is ill laid and worse executed and makes people here believe we are all Jacobites together.'

By the 15th February, there were 1,200 Argyll men with the Hanoverian army. Sir Thomas Agnew, the tough and eccentric Lieutenant Colonel of the Scots Fusiliers, was now ordered to occupy Blair Castle with 500 regulars, with 200 more in Castle Menzies (Weem) to guard the Bridge of Tay. He was to be supported by Argyll militia in Rannoch and Atholl.

Seven companies of 60 men were involved: Knockbuy with four in Atholl, Glenure with two in Rannoch and Southall with one at Balquidder and the West end of Loch Earn. Knockbuy was in fact to guard the military road from Stirling to Dalnacardoch, joining the road north from Blair Atholl. The other companies were to protect the access to that road from the West by Loch Rannoch and Loch Earn. But Knockbuy's detailed orders, allegedly as captured in his baggage, introduce a sinister new dimension into the remit of the Independent Companies. They were issued on 20th February at Nairn House, 5 miles from Perth:

> 'It is the Duke of Cumberland's orders that you take post according to the above list. You are to have command of the several Companies. Such of the rebels as may be found in arms, you are to take Prisoner and if any of them make resistance, you are to attack them, provided their numbers do not exceed yours. *And it is his Royal Highness's orders that you give them no quarters.*'

Lord George Murray the Jacobite General, who was meantime in Inverness, was distressed by reports coming from his native Atholl of repressive measures adopted by its new occupiers, of men being taken prisoner for complicity in the Rebellion, and of houses of those involved being burned or occupied as were Castle Menzies, Blairfetty, Kynichan, and Lude. He wrote to Macpherson of Cluny, who had remained in Badenoch, that he intended to make a raid through Cluny's country into Atholl. Cluny seized the passes on his Southern marches in order to prevent any leakage of information about the projected raid in which he, Cluny, intended to engage. On 10th March, Lord George arrived at Dalnaspidal, and his force was divided up into small parties, each made up of Atholl and Badenoch men and ordered to make synchronous attacks on positions at Bunrannoch, Kynichan, Blairfetty, Faskally, Bridge of Tilt, the Inn of Blair and Lude. These attacks were duly carried out before daybreak, sometimes after a march of 30 miles in hail and snow, on about thirty posts with complete success, with the exception that the party at Peter McGlashan's inn at Blair Atholl were able to escape into the Castle.

A triumphant Cluny writing to Lochiel on 17th March, as it was all happening, his enthusiasn slightly exceeding his accuracy, told how these attacks had been completely successful. They had put a tolerable guard on the Pass of Killicrankie, seized, killed, wounded or taken prisoner every man and officer on the different commands, and 'not one of the commanders had smelt the design'. At 6p.m. he repeated that the Bunrannoch attack had been successful, they now had prisoner 400 Campbells and 16 officers, including

Knockbuy and the 'famous Barcaldine cousins'. But Knockbuy was not a prisoner. Glenure was the son of Patrick Campbell fourth of Barcaldine and a daughter of Sir Ewen Cameron, and thus, he, Lochiel, and Cluny were cousins. Glenure was not a prisoner either, but his younger brother, Allan, an officer in Lord John Murray's Regiment, may have been captured.

A letter from Taymouth, written on 18th March, was General Campbell's first inkling of the disaster: Knockbuy and Glenure, it said, had been unjustifiably absent from their posts when they were over-run. The General was furious and declared that they should both be court-marshalled as they had King's Commissions. (Colin Campbell of Glenure, 'the Red Fox', was later the victim of the Appin murder, for which James Stewart of the Glens was wrongfully executed in 1752.)

Having dispatched some of his companies to Atholl, Colonel Campbell marched North with his remaining companies, in advance of the Duke of Cumberland's main force. His route was by Angus, and on the last day of February he left Aberdeen, moving from Strathbogie a week later to pursue a Jacobite force under Colonel John Roy Stuart to Huntly.

But another set-back was suffered by the Independent Companies on 20th March. Alexander Campbell, brother of Barcaldine and Glenure, had assembled a force with the purpose of intercepting small parties of hussars, which Lord John Drummond was daily sending back across the Spey, to reconnoitre the movements of Cumberland's forces between Fochabers and Keith. Captain Campbell's party was spotted near Fochabers and observed by the Jacobites to retire to Keith. Here they requested Colonel Campbell's permission to remain, and that reinforcements be sent them. Both requests were refused but the reply was not received by Captain Campbell, who lodged his men to sleep in the church, leaving a guard of twenty men in the school.

In the meantime, Lord John Drummond sent out a composite party of 50 picked men of John Roy Stewart's Regiment, 20 to 30 hussars and 16 French service troops, all under the Command of Major Nicholas Glasgoe of Lally's French/Irish Regiment. They marched towards Keith, but short of the town they made a diversion, crossing the River Isla at the Mill of Keith, and approached the town from the East, as if coming from Strathbogie. Having thus satisfied the Campbell sentinel, they were able to overcome him, and without any warning they attacked the guard in the school at one o'clock in the morning. The guard made some resistance but asked for quarter after four men had been killed. In the church Alexander Campbell was unable to get to his weapons, and was badly wounded and left for dead, although he did recover. The Jacobites lost one French service man. Major Glasgoe was back in Fochabers by daybreak with 50 Campbells and their officers as prisoners, as well as 21 of Kingston's Horse with their mounts. This unfortunate affair was as much due to the inexperience of an officer and bad staff work as to the brilliant tactics of Major Glasgoe.

By a strange coincidence, on the very day that Lord John Drummond's men distinguished themselves at Keith, his brother the Duke of Perth masterminded another brilliant tactical stroke on the shores of the Dornoch Firth.

The Earl of Cromartie had been appointed Commander in Chief of the Jacobite forces North of the Beauly, where he was engaged in the thankless task of trying to corner Lord Loudon and his forces. When Loudon re-crossed into Ross on 28th February Prince Charles sent the Clanranald Regiment, the Glengarry, the Stewarts and the Frasers to join Cromartie at Kinkell before eight o'clock the following morning. The Earl of Loudon returned smartly to Dornoch.

Half-way through March, Loudon once more decided to cross over into Ross. But his courage quickly failed him when he discovered that Cromartie's force was again marching against him. He also, probably, at that point received the Duke's order for Loudon to join him at Peterhead, as the advance from Aberdeen was being delayed. Nevertheless Lord Loudon returned to Sutherland, bringing down on him the criticism of Cumberland.

But Cumberland's delayed march also gave the Jacobites leisure at last to dispose of Lord Loudon. The Duke of Perth was sent to direct that operation, although the Earl of Cromartie remained in nominal command.

Perth was full of enthusiasm. He informed Cromartie 'for your encouragement' that Loudon's men had been calling over to the Frasers that they had only rye to eat and begging for meal, which showed that they would not long tolerate these conditions. He added that Loudon's men, guarding the boats, were ready to desert to him, but that the oars were locked away. Conversations across the water, possible at low tide, would certainly be overheard. They were of great value to the Duke of Perth, but someone on Loudon's side ought also to have been aware of what was going on. There is no firm evidence that Lord Loudon was.

But meanwhile the Prince had ordered the boats necessary for the Duke of Perth's scheme to sail from the Moray coast. These arrived late on the evening of the 19th, and were dragged down the sands of Tain by Perth's men and launched the following morning, to make the attack under cover of a fog that had persisted some days.

The clearest account we have of the Battle of Dornoch is that given by an unamed volunteer who was with Lord Loudon's Regiment.

> 'Lord Loudon was gone . . . 16 miles to visit the quarters
> upon the River Shin . . . Upon the alarm, the Major beat to
> arms and immediately got together about 120 of the
> Regiment, the rest being 3 miles distant, guarding the ships
> that had the money and arms aboard, then laying in the little
> firth of Ferry Oons . . .'

Major Mackenzie then marched to the place of landing, expecting to be joined by the Mackays to see if it was possible to beat off the Jacobites. On the way they learned that 800 had landed in the first wave, of which 300 immediately marched up to Overskibo. (Such was the quality of the Duke of Perth's intelligence). They intended to seize the Lord President, who had been there with a guard of 60 men commanded by his son, but the bird had flown.

Loudon's Regiment marched on and found themselves within a few yards of the remainder of the landing party. Other troops were in the process of landing and, as the 40 Mackays guarding the boats had retired without firing a shot, Loudon's Regiment decided to retire similarly. They retreated to Dornoch and, having dumped some ammunition, made for the Little Ferry which might have delayed the pursuit. However, a panic set in and they decided to ask for terms; officers who had previously been prisoners at Prestonpans were given the option of escaping. With them, Lord Charles Gordon, the young Laird of Macleod and the relater, crossed the Little Ferry as the guard on the ships had already done. Captain Inglis of the store ship had been warned, put the military chest aboard a small boat, and escaped to sea. The volunteer saw the other officers and men fleeing in some disorder up Loch Fleet, but, being a realist, went to Dunrobin and warned the Earl of Sutherland and others of what had happened, and, with them, was able to put to sea in a small boat. They were picked up by the sloop *Vulture*.

Lord Loudon's own account to General Campbell shows that he was much nearer, but certainly not in command of the situation. He had left to inspect the posts at seven o'clock but had only gone three miles when the alarm was raised. He galloped back to the shore but could see nothing because of the fog, and found no one but scattered groups of Mackays without their officers. Trying to collect the Independent Companies as he retreated westwards he also tried to contact his own Regiment with instructions to secure the military chest and join him to make a stand on the River Shin, but he had been unable to confirm whether his instructions were received. He crossed the Shin, and going by Strathoykell and Lochcarron, escaped to Skye.

The Duke of Cumberland was savage in his criticism.

> 'His Majesty must have observed how negligently these Highlanders who are with us do their duty; as well as by the surprise of the posts upon the Hills, as the last affair that happened at Keith, and I have further proof of this, which is of much more consequence. His Majesty will see that Lord Loudon's people suffered themselves to be surprised at Dornick ... it looks as if Lord Loudon's and the Lord President's army would be entirely dispersed ... I own that I never expected much assistance from them.'

Lord Loudon was not without his protagonists. Lord President Forbes was loyal if slightly inaccurate. But Loudon had had the best part of 2,000 men in a position which could have resisted an attack from three times that number, according to the opinion of Captain Porter of the *Speedwell*. The Duke of Perth had 1,800 men, but Loudon's did not fire a single shot at them.

Leadership had certainly been lacking, and the Mackays, who had been making offers across the water to desert, probably did desert when they were abandoned by their officers, as Lord Loudon says. Curiously, the author of the Book of Mackay makes a similar charge against the first Sutherland company, who deserted to a man. The loyalty of their Captain, Chief of the Clan Gunn, was suspected. It was also said that most of the soldiers of Loudon's Regiment who were captured (mainly Macleods) joined the Jacobites.

Another disincentive to fight on the part of the Independent Companies is also highlighted at the Battle of Dornoch. The Chevalier Johnston refers to the agony of mind of Donald Macdonald of Scotus who feared he would meet in battle his own son, an officer in Loudon's Regiment, and his relief when he accepted his surrender. There were Macintoshes in the Jacobite party, to which their Chief, Capt. Macintosh of Macintosh surrendered. It is also unlikely that Major Mackenzie, the grandfather of a future Earl of Seaforth, would relish fighting the Mackenzies in Cromartie's force.

Lord Loudon's aversion to engaging the enemy is difficult to explain. It would be unjust to accuse him of physical cowardice, but he was clearly prey to the crippling indecision which was summed up in a later remark: 'Lord Loudon was always on horseback but never advancing'.

The Battle of Dornoch spelt the end of Lord Loudon's force as a factor in the outcome of the 1745 Rebellion. Indeed, it may be said that the role ended two months before the date of the Battle of Culloden, when he retreated into Sutherland. It was thus that only disorganised bands restored to Loudon's independent companies any semblance of credit.

The renamed Jacobite sloop *Prince Charles* was returning from France with supplies, including £13,000, when she was spotted in the Moray Firth by the *Sheerness*, which pursued her round the north end of Scotland. In the running battle 36 of her men were killed and the *Prince Charles* was forced to run aground in the Melness Bay. The remnants of Mackay companies and some of Lord Loudon's Regiment, who had escaped from Dornoch were, as it happened, at Lord Reay's House of Tongue just opposite. The castaways, a mixed bag of 20 French service officers and 120 soldiers and crew, were attacked and forced to surrender by a party led by Lord Reay's Steward and Captains Alexander Mackay and John Macleod of Lord Loudon's Regiment, as they were being guided towards Lord Cromartie's men in East Sutherland, by a sympathetic Mackay.

It is not clear where the Mackays found the courage which had been so lacking at Dornoch six days previously, but they were on their own doorstep and there was an attractive smell of money in the air, which must have proved a motive. This is clear from the haggling which followed the apportionment of the spoils.

After the bloodless victory at Dornoch, the Duke of Perth, having realised that it was pointless to follow Loudon, returned to Inverness, leaving Lord Cromartie to collect men, money, and meal in Sutherland and Caithness. He had indifferent success in the attempt. About the 13th of April, his force was recalled to Inverness in the face of Cumberland's advance. He halted the rearguard of his force at Golspie, and made the cardinal mistake of leaving his men, when he and his officers went to Dunrobin Castle to make his compliments to his neighbour (albeit political opponent) the Countess of Sutherland.

Ensign John Mackay of Mudale of a Sutherland independent company, seized the opportunity to attack Cromartie's men and chased them to the Little Ferry across Loch Fleet. There some 40 were killed or drowned and 178 taken prisoner. Cromartie, his son and 18 officers were similarly captured in the Castle, on the day before the Battle of Culloden.

At the Battle of Culloden, on the 16th April, the only Highlanders engaged in the Hanoverian service were the ten companies under Lieutenant Colonel Campbell. They were disposed on either wing of the royal army and, under the eye of the Duke of Cumberland, they behaved well. Their most significant contribution was to throw down the park walls to allow the dragoons to attack the Jacobite right wing in the flank. Of the Campbell company commanders, Balliemore was killed and Achnaba was mortally wounded. Col. Campbell was congratulated on the field by the Duke, and thereby some of the stains incurred at Falkirk, Keith and Atholl were erased.

The victory at Culloden also launched the independent companies into the process of completing the crushing of the embers of rebellion, a task for which they had little stomach despite the promptings of the Hanoverian Butcher Cumberland and the Dutch Albemarle, who succeeded him as Commander in Chief. The Duke of Argyll had urged moderation on the militia. 'Leave devastation to the Regular forces ... the Militia to burn houses and possibly to murder women and children in the scuffle, I should be very tender of.' In the main, Loudon's men followed the same principle. There were exceptions of course: Capt. Campbell of Skipness was a sadist, and Lieut. Allan Macdonald of Knock in Skye merely avid for money.

Culloden also liberated Lord Loudon and his companies from their suspended animation in Skye. Loudon lost no time in becoming courtier again, and brought from Skye to Inverness 500 newly raised militia who were armed and immediately sent back. Two of these companies were sent to South Uist, and the captains, Alexander Macleod of Ullinish and Hugh Macdonald of Armadale, contributed materially and deliberately to the escape of the fugitive Prince Charles from that Island.

The independent companies and militia were disbanded within six months of the battle, Lord Loudon's Regiment was brought up to strength with drafts of the independent companies and sent to Flanders in 1747, and disbanded in Perth in 1748.

Lord John Murray's Regiment lives on as the Royal Highland Regiment, the Black Watch.

Lord Loudon was appointed Commander in Chief of the British forces in America in 1756, and dismissed in the following year. Loudon's protagonists suggest that Pitt the Elder, the Prime Minister, was jealous of the Duke of Cumberland and starved his protégé of men and materials, and that may well be true, but it is also likely that Pitt knew something of Loudon's record.

This then, was the tragedy of the Highlanders who suffered and died in the service of King George in 1745 and 1746, and it may be summed up in the three words of John Maule, the member of Parliament. Some of them were, no doubt, 'Jacobites at Heart', but others fought less than well, because they were badly led, and their London masters considered they all were 'Jacobites at Heart'.

(This is a shortened version of a much more comprehensive paper on the Independent companies prepared by Dr MacLean.)

BIBLIOGRAPHY

PUBLISHED MATERIAL

Argyll in the Forty Five	*Sir J. Ferguson*	*London 1951*
Book of Mackay	*Rev. Angus Mackay*	*Edinburgh 1906 (BoM)*
Book of Dunvegan	*R.C. Macleod*	*Aberdeen 1939 (BoD)*
Chiefs of Grant	*Sir William Fraser*	*1883 (C of G)*
Chronicles of the Families of Atholl and Braudalbane	*Collected and Arranged by 7th Duke*	*Privately printed in Edinburgh 1908*
Culloden Papers	*Duncan Forbes*	*1815*
Dornoch Cathedral and Parish	*C.D. Bentick*	*Inverness 1926 (Dornoch)*
Earls of Cromartie	*Sir William Fraser*	*2 vols 1876*
Highland Independent Companies	*Mackay Scobie − Printed in the 'Journal of Army Historical Research'*	*1941 (H.I.C.)*
Highland Songs of the Forty Five	*ed. J.L. Campbell*	
Historical Geography of the Clans, with Narrative of the Highland Campaigns	*W. Kirk Dickson*	*3rd edn. (Hist Geog).*
History of the Rise, Progress and Extinction of the late Rebellion in Britain 1745-1746	*Dougald Graham*	*8th edn. Edinburgh 1808 (Dougald Graham)*
History of the Rebellion	*Chambers*	*7th edn. Edinburgh 1869 (Chambers)*
Itinerary of Prince Charles Edward Stewart	*W.B. Blaikie*	*1897 (Itinerary)*
Life and Work of the Rt. Hon. Duncan Forbes of Culloden		*London 1818 (Forbes)*

Loudon in North America	*S. Pargellis.*	*1933*
Lyon in Mourning	*Robert Forbes – ed. Henry Paton*	*Scottish History Society 1975 (Lyon)*
Macdonald for the Prince	*Maclean*	*Stornoway 1982*
Macintoshes and Clan Chattan	*A.M. Macintosh*	*Edinburgh 1903 M&C.C.*
Memoir of the Forty Five	*the Chevalier de Johnstone*	*Folio Soc. Ed. 1958 (Chev. Johnstone)*
More Culloden Papers	*ed.Duncan Warrand*	*Vols. iv-v 1929-30(M.C.P.)*
Origins of the '45	*W.B. Blaikie*	*1916 (Origins)*
Sar Obair. Beauties of Gaelic Poetry	*Edinburgh 1904(S.O.)*	
Scots Magazine	*Feb – May 1746*	
Sutherland Book	*Sir William Fraser*	*8 vols, 1892 (BoS)*
Transactions of the Gaelic society of Inverness	*(T.G.S.I.)*	
Sketches of the Character, Manners and Present State of the Highland of Scotland with details of the Military Service of the Highland Regiments	*Stewart*	

UNPUBLISHED MATERIAL

Campbell of Mamore Papers	*N.L.S. 8733-35*	*National Library Edinburgh*
Cumberland Papers	*Royal Archives Windsor Microfilm*	*St Andrew's University (Cumb P)*
Loudon Papers	*Huntington Library*	*San Marino California (LP)*
Macdonald Papers	*Scottish Record Office*	*Edinburgh G.D. 221*
Macleod of Geanies Papers	*N.L.S. 19296*	*National Library Edinburgh*
Cumberland Papers	*Royal archives*	*(microfilm in St. Andrews University Library)*

11

'THE SUMMER'S HUNTING':
Historiography of Charles Edward's escape

*How, down the years, the story of the
Prince's escape from the Highlands emerged*

by

John S. Gibson

John S. Gibson was born in 1923, the son of a Renfrewshire schoolmaster. He was educated at Paisley Grammar School, and read history at Glasgow University, this being interrupted by war service which took him to the Far East as a Commando subaltern. He joined the Scottish Office in 1947, serving there until his retirement in 1983.

Has written *Ships of the '45: the Rescue of the Young Pretender*; Hutchinson, 1967.
Deacon Brodie: Father to Jekyll and Hyde; Paul Harris, 1977.
The Thistle and the Crown: a History of the Scottish Office, HMSO, 1985
Playing the Scottish card: The Franco-Jacobite Invasion of 1708. Edinburgh, 1988.

In 1985 he also presented the Scottish Office Centenary Exhibition in Edinburgh.

'I'd heartily wish that some capable personne woul'd set the Prince's history in the form and light it merits.'

THIS IS COLONEL John William O'Sullivan writing to King

James at Rome about the '45 and Charles Edward's summer-long ordeal in the highlands and islands after the catastrophe of Culloden. Near to two and a half centuries later we might well echo the Colonel's sentiment. Here is one of the great adventure stories of all time. It was of international importance; as played out in the wet west highland summer of 1746, then and for long after the talk of the courts of Europe. It unites in valour the highlanders who protected the Prince with the French and Irish who rescued him. For the most part it even reflects well on the intrepid British Navy seeking him with frigate and sloop in stormy waters. Down the years it has taken the attention of a procession of historians. It has delighted literary eminences from James Boswell to Eric Linklater. And yet, still it awaits adequate presentation.

The main reason for this is the piecemeal way in which the story has come to light, from the very first fanciful accounts gleaned from Jacobite refugees, right down to the present day. Now at last we have it all, as much as we can hope to know; and the too familiar tale of brave Prince escaping the clutches of cruel enemy with the help of steadfast highlanders becomes something much more subtle, truer to the heights and depths of human nature; something much more *highland.*

Throughout the summer of 1746 the whiggish *Scots Magazine* carried reports of the search for the Prince as it happened, such as a letter in July from 'an officer at Fort Augustus' (which may or may not have been authentic) reporting that 'the Pretender has been chased this fortnight past from one island to another, sometimes dressed as a highlander, sometimes as a woman. We hang or shoot everyone that is known to conceal him, burn their houses and take their cattle.' Within months of this, the first narrative '*translated from a manuscript privately handed about at the Court of Versailles*' made its appearance in London during that winter of Hanoverian jubilation. It was a garbled version of the highly-coloured accounts given by O'Sullivan to eager listeners at the French court, Charles Edward the hero of the hour. Significantly, this narrative of the Prince's adventures is somewhere within hailing distance of the truth up to the point in June where the sick O'Sullivan had to part company with the Prince, as the search closed in on them on Uist. Thereafter it is mere invention by the literary hack who put it together. And throughout the story is draped in a Virgilian toga; speeches by Charles Edward such as:

> 'You must not, you shall not, my dear Sullivan, die and leave me here in these wretched circumstances. Forbid it Gracious Heaven . . .'

To press home comparison with the *Aeneid* it bore the title *Ascanius*, and translations quickly appeared in Spanish and Italian as well as in French.

That the true story of the Prince's highland adventures ever began to be preserved owes everything, ironically enough, to King George's ministers in their anxiety to quash Jacobitism once and for all. In the July of 1746, in what he termed 'the summer's hunting', Major General John Campbell of Mamore with ships and troops had followed the Prince's track from Uist to Skye and on to the mainland of Inverness-shire. One by one he had Charles Edward's Hebridean protectors picked up and shipped to the Thames for state punishment – for some, perhaps even death. Of these, old Lady Clanranald, Flora MacDonald who was already a celebrity, Malcolm MacLeod from Raasay who had delivered the Prince to the McKinnons of Skye, and the aged Laird of McKinnon who had brought him back to the mainland, all were committed to the private prisons in London run by those court officials, the 'messengers'. It chanced that with them was confined another prisoner of the '45, a middle aged English physician and Jacobite, Dr John Burton of York. He won their trust and took down their story from their lips. Released as they all were in the summer of 1746 – King George's ministers having commendably had second thoughts about retribution – Burton came to Edinburgh before the end of the year to seek out other narratives by the Prince's saviours, now that the hangings were over and the general amnesty in force.

Near Edinburgh another frustrated Jacobite was Robert Forbes, a Scottish Episcopalian priest. In travelling to join the Prince's standard in the summer of 1745 he had been so unwise as to pass under the Union flag flying above Stirling Castle, and so was locked up for the duration of the rising. On release, he had begun to collect the scaffold speeches of Jacobite martyrs. Then, in the summer of 1747, there came into his hands a copy of Burton's narrative. This pointed him to his life's work.

By now Forbes was living in the house in Leith of the elderly and intensely Jacobite Lady Bruce, a meeting place for those still well-affected to the Cause. He was there one July day in 1747 when Lady Bruce entertained on his release from Edinburgh Castle Alexander MacDonald of Kingsburgh, in whose house on Skye the fugitive Prince had spent a memorable night a year past. Forbes read to them the short narrative which Burton had put together from his fellow captives in London, and Kingsburgh talked freely of the consternation at the midnight arrival of 'Betty Bourk'. All this Forbes noted down.

That summer in Edinburgh copies were being handed round of other narratives by the Prince's protectors. There was one by the Hispanic Irishman, Captain Felix O'Neil, first written on playing cards during his incarceration in the Castle. There was another by the erstwhile itinerant preacher, John Cameron; by 1747 he had gone to France, but a year before he had been one of Lochiel's fugitive posse in the braes of Lochaber. There was Edward Burke's story, he who had acted as servant to Charles Edward and his companions in misfortune through the May and June of 1746. His biggest 'catch' was, however, Malcolm MacLeod of the Raasay family, newly released from imprisonment in London. 'Leith, Friday's evening, 6 o'clock, August 7th 1747', Forbes recorded, 'in the house of James MacDonald, joiner, Captain Malcolm MacLeod, second cousin to Malcolm MacLeod, Laird of Raaze, gave the following account . . .' Consider Forbes's careful method; a week later the Captain from Skye and the Jacobite joiner dined at Lady Bruce's, and Forbes read over to them the narrative he had compiled. At another meeting ten days later, as MacLeod was making ready for his return to the north, Forbes asked him to seek out more narratives, particularly from one Captain John McKinnon who, like the old laird his uncle, had also played a gallant part. He also asked MacLeod 'to try if Armadale [Hugh MacDonald of Armadale, Flora's step-father and captain in the militia which had supposedly been hunting the Prince on Uist] would vouchsafe me a written account of his part of the management.' This was thin ice; not surprisingly there was no response.

But, at the instigation of MacDonald of Kingsburgh, there now called on Forbes Captain Donald Roy MacDonald who likewise had swerved from his allegiance to the pro-government chief of the Skye MacDonalds. Despite his still painful wounds from Culloden, Donald Roy had played a distinguished part in ensuring the Prince's safety on Skye.

With Donald Roy, the well-read gentleman from the Hebrides (as with the illiterate Ned Burke), Forbes quickly established good *rapport*. His memorable account of the Prince's parting from his friends in the little inn at Portree comes alive when you read it today because Forbes, as intermediary, was so clearly himself reliving the fear, suspense, and high emotion of that evening.

That winter there also came to the Citadel of Leith the distinguished son of Clan Donald known to posterity as Alasdair MacMhaighster Alasdair, the outstanding Gaelic poet of his time. He had served as a captain in the Clanranald Regiment, and his purpose was to give Forbes the narrative he had compiled with young Clanranald and the heroic MacDonald of Glenaladale. This included Glenaladale's own account of the days of desperate danger among the braes of Morar and the mountains of Knoydart as he took the Prince northward to seek word of ships from France. It was a comprehensive narrative of the Prince's flight from the April to September of 1746 which the gentlemen of Clan Donald now offered – though it rather gave the impression that they unaided, had brought him safely through!

A little earlier that winter Dr Burton himself had come to Edinburgh with publication on his mind. Soon he was in touch with Forbes who seems to have let him copy the several narratives he, Forbes, had by now amassed, even though he deplored the proposal to publish. Burton was not to be deterred. The outcome was the appearance in London in 1749 of the *Genuine and True Journal of the most miraculous escape of the Young Chevalier ... by an Englishman*.

Said its preface:

> 'The following relation, or Journal of the young Chevalier's Escape was at first wrote out of curiosity; which I was induced to do by having so many opportunities of conversing with the chief of the parties who were instrumental in conducting and assisting him in his escape .... . Part was

taken from those carried Prisoners to London, and the rest
from those in Scotland.'

The anonymous author, ie Burton, continued:

> 'This much I thought proper to premise in order to convince
> the Reader that this relation is genuine and not composed of
> a very few facts, and the rest made up of Falsities and
> Fiction, the work of a fruitful brain; like those pamphlets
> entitled *Ascanius* . . .'

No mention in all this of the Revd. Robert Forbes. This would be his
wish, for it was still Forbes's ardent hope that Charles Edward would make
another attempt for the Stuart cause. Cluny MacPherson remained at large
in the mountains of Badenoch with his rebel henchmen (and what was left of
the Loch Arkaig treasure). Even two years later, one of the Jacobite *côterie* at
Leith would be flung into prison for having published a map of Charles
Edward's expedition. Nonetheless, Forbes's generosity to Burton is surprising, until you recognise that Burton had access, as Forbes had not – to Flora
MacDonald. While Burton was in Edinburgh he had taken from her a much
fuller account of the part she had played, and this he let Forbes copy. This
purported to be the whole truth with Felix O'Neil now safely back in France
as the author of the escape to Skye. Forbes was suspicious. 'Hapening to
mention several questions that were fit to be proposed to Miss MacDonald',
he noted, 'the Doctor desired me to give them to him in writing, for that he
would endeavour to procure direct answers to them.' As in his message to
Kingsburgh, Forbes now sought to elicit the true role in the affair of Hugh
MacDonald of Sleat. Had her step-father contrived the Prince's escape to
Skye, he asked? In reply Flora spoke of other things. Had he ever met the
Prince? Yes, she replied, wilfully missing the point; in the Sepetember of
1745 when he happened to be in Arisaig as the Prince first landed!

The following March of 1748 the long sought meeting with Flora
MacDonald took place. Again Forbes asked about the step-father's role ;
again he was fobbed off, Flora speaking instead of her servant Neil
MacEachain and the 'minor' part he had played. Forbes had to be content
with this, though Flora, as we will see, would not forget Forbes and the
narratives he was amassing in secrecy.

On its appearance in 1749 'printed for B.A. near Charing Cross', the
Most Miraculous Escape was well received by the Edinburgh Jacobites, so
Forbes tells us. But Forbes himself clung to his disapproval ; it was a much
more detailed history he had in mind to produce when the king enjoyed his
own again. As was customary in these days the run would be only of a few
hundred copies, and being paper-backed they would soon wear out. No
doubt the Edinburgh book trade would be shy of offending 'the people
above' by keeping it in stock. The upshot was that when in 1773 James
Boswell set out on his famous tour to the Hebrides he seems to have been
unaware of Burton's work of a quarter of a century before. But then, the

younger Boswell's thoughts had been all for Corsica, not at all for *Tearlach*. Yet Boswell's apparent ignorance of the earlier work is baffling (even though it seems to be confirmed by the inscription by his younger son, made somewhere around 1820, on a copy of Burton's book now in the National Library of Scotland); by the 1760's the *Most Miraculous Escape* may have been out of print, but another London bookseller was bringing out another quite full narrative of the Prince's escape which lifted extensively from Burton and ran to three editions.

When it came to publication of his own *Journal of a Tour to the Hebrides with Samuel Johnson LLD*, Boswell rightly judged the readiness of the public of the 1780s to learn more about the 'wanderings of the grandson of King James II' as in deference to the House of Hanover he designated Charles Edward in his narrative of the latter's brief sojourn in Skye and Raasay. But there was more to this brief historical narrative than literary flair. As Boswell had informed the chief of the MacDonalds in Skye – tactlessly, since Sir Alexander was edgy about the ambiguous stance his forebear had taken in the '45 and heartily wished that Flora MacDonald be forgotten – his 'only errand into Skye was to visit the Pretender's conductress', and he 'deemed every moment as lost that was not spent in her company'.

At Flora MacDonald's married home at Kingsburgh, with its memories of the night the fugitive Prince spent there, Boswell and Johnson were given a highland welcome but little that was new, and nothing about the story behind Charles Edward's perilous crossing to Skye twenty-seven summers past. However, on Raasay Boswell had already met the valiant Malcolm MacLeod who had so impressed Bishop Forbes. There was an immediate bond of liking between the Edinburgh advocate and the handsome old highlander; and from this came both some memorable passages in *Hebrides* and a string of lively anecdotes for Boswell's narrative of Charles Edward's adventures.

'Here I stop', wrote Boswell in ending this narrative with the Prince's perilous crossing to the mainland from the McKinnon country of Skye, 'having received no further authentic information of his fatigues and perils before he escaped to France'. Apart from what he might have made of Burton's book had he known of it, throughout his week on Raasay there had been available to Boswell a source of 'authentic information' in the high-spirited presence of another Jacobite, Alexander MacLeod, who had been aide-de-camp, and much more than a decorative one, to the Prince throughout the '45. He had accompanied his royal master in the flight from Culloden; and the narrative of the 1760's of the Prince's escape mentioned above says, probably on his own testimony, that it was he who forced Charles Edward from the field of battle. MacLeod would know what fears of treachery swirled in the Prince's mind on that day, and this was something which Boswell did not even suspect. He had also other information to impart which would surely have fascinated Boswell, for he had assisted the rescue attempts from France of that summer – of which more later – which played such a crucial part in the Prince's eventual escape. Nor would 'Sandie' MacLeod have been reluctant to talk; he spoke freely enough to Boswell and Johnson.

But despite the huge success of *Hebrides* and the interest in the Prince's highland adventures which it stimulated, the tour of 1773 was first and foremost about the display to the Hebrideans of Dr Johnson's intellectual prowess. MacLeod's 'excessive flow of spirits', says Boswell, was a distraction to the otherwise attentive company; his 'loud rattling, romping' made Johnson irritable. In the antipathy which he felt for the former aide-de-camp Boswell lost a unique opportunity; Sandie MacLeod — while he could move freely in the Hebrides was still nominally a fugitive and could not appear in Edinburgh.

In the matter of missed opportunities, worse was to follow. When Flora MacDonald recounted to her visitors as much as she was prepared to say about June 1746, Dr Johnson, says Boswell, told her that 'all this should be written down'. To this she replied that 'Bishop Forbes at Leith had it'. Boswell would surely know of Forbes, but he did not follow Flora's lead. Then, when the Journal was being made ready for publication ten years later, her reference to Bishop Forbes was edited out. So it was that a further half-century was to pass before there came to light Forbes's life-work which, in allusion to Scotland's heraldic beast, he had entitled *The Lyon in Mourning*.

With its thirty individual narratives of the Prince's escape 'The Lyon' was to become the main quarry for what we know of this epilogue to the '45. What was Forbes's own contribution? While scrupulous in accuracy, and though he relived the narratives as he compiled them, Forbes lacked the spark of genius that animates Boswell's. Take, for example, the night on Skye when the Prince and Malcolm MacLeod sought shelter at the house of the latter's brother-in-law in McKinnon country. Bemired to the knees as they both were, MacLeod asked the old servant woman to wash his companion's legs — the Prince posing as MacLeod's servant. Forbes's vision of the crone's reply was:

> 'No such thing, although I wash the master's feet I am not obliged to wash the servant's.'

Boswell, hearing the same anecdote from Malcolm MacLeod had the wit to preserve the translation of her very words as they were told to him:

> 'Though I wash *your* father's son's feet, why should I wash *his* father's son's feet.'

But, this said, there are two major points to make about *The Lyon*. The first is Forbes's honesty.

In 1761 he made the final addition to his collection of narratives when he found Captain John McKinnon (in whose house the above little comedy had been enacted) lying crippled and penniless in the Royal Infirmary of Edinburgh. Captain John it was who had taken the Prince from Skye to the mainland, there to entrust him once more to Clan Donald. McKinnon was vehement in his assertion to Forbes that, in the search by sea and land closing in on Morar and Arisaig in these fearful July days of 1746, some gentlemen of Clanranald, including the chief himself and young Clanranald, would not take the Prince back into their protection. Forbes seems to have accepted the truth of this version of events from the dying cripple, though it was out of accord with the heroic picture of the highlanders he wished to present, and he embodied it in *The Lyon*.

The second point to make about *The Lyon* – whether or not the Prince's adventures enthrall you – is the unique window it opens on that long vanished society of clanned gentry ferociously proud of their good name, and of simple clansmen of astonishing fortitude. As to this last, consider what it says of Euan McVee. He was one of Lochiel's men captured by government troops in the August of 1746 while on his way from Loch Broom to Lochaber as messenger to the Prince with news of the fourth rescue mission come from France that summer. Starving, cold, and bleeding from the 'one hundred good lashes' which General Blakeney had prescribed for him, McVee died in the Inverness Tolbooth having given nothing away. The Rev James Hay, an Inverness minister who visited McVee in his wretchedness, told Forbes of the highlander's last hours. In his native tongue McVee had said to his reverend visitor

> 'Let them do their worst. It signifies nothing what they can do to me in respect of what could be done to those from whom I came and to whom I was going ... Their deaths would be a great loss but mine will be none.'

It is in a hundred such insights to the ways of the old highlands that *The Lyon* has its imperishable importance.

By the end of the eighteenth century Burton's *Most Miraculous Escape* was long forgotten; the ten black leather-bound volumes of *The Lyon* lay somewhere in Scotland, their very existence unsuspected, Bishop Forbes long dead; and while Boswell's lively narrative in his *Hebrides* had sharpened interest, it covered only seven days out of Charles Edward's six months on the run. However, John Home, doyen of the literati, was known to be compiling a history of the '45 in which so many years past he had played his own small part. Great expectations were dashed on the publication in 1802 of Home's *History of the Rebellion in Scotland in the year 1745*. How, in toadying to the House of Hanover, he came to omit any mention of the barbarities by the Royal army on Drumossie Muir is another story; he had had plenty of informants thereanent. But, like Boswell, he was unaware of Burton's book as he was of *The Lyon*. Though he was able to incorporate Cluny MacPherson's narrative of the Prince's sojourn in the former's hide-out on the slopes of Ben Alder, his account of the highland odyssey is thin. Thirty years on, the same want of authentic information afflicted Sir Walter Scott, passing lightly over the Prince's escape in writing his great contribution to Scottish historiography, *The Tales of a Grandfather*. Perhaps he felt that his young protégé Robert Chambers had already given as complete a

narrative as was possible in his history of the '45. Or it may have been that
Sir Walter simply was unfamiliar with the northern highlands − unlike
James Boswell who had noted in his journal of his tour 'We were shewn the
land of Moidart . . . that stirred my mind'.

So to the discovery of *The Lyon* by the same Robert Chambers in the
year of Sir Walter's death. It turned up in the library of a country house in
Lanarkshire. Chambers was quick to see its importance. In *Jacobite Memoirs
of the Forty-Five* he now presented its key narratives from out of the detritus
of Jacobitiana in Forbes's ten little volumes; and in 1840 he followed it with
a completely revised (and still enthralling) *History of the Rebellion*.

Chambers was as much taken by Bishop Forbes's narratives in *The Lyon*
of the cruelties perpetrated on 'Drumossie Day' as by those on the Prince's
escape. 'Now wae to thee thou cruel lord [meaning Duke!] a bluidy man I
trow thou be', Burns had written on visiting the battlefield. He spoke for
popular memory; here in *The Lyon* was the proof that it had not lied.
Curiously, the indignation stirred up in Scotland of the 1840's by Chambers'
presentation of these Culloden narratives now served to strengthen the
appeal of those others in *The Lyon* describing the Prince's subsequent
adventures. The public was, perhaps, ready to see in Culloden the presage
of the social catastrophe of the Clearances now afflicting the north from
Strathtay to Strathnaver, and to turn in nostalgia to the seemingly simple
heroics of Charles Edward's adventure. At last the whole story of these
seemed to be told. Robert Chambers thought so. There was now, he said,
'sufficient information to satisfy all reasonable curiosity upon the subject'.
He was soon proved wrong.

The year of publication of Chambers' revised history of the '45 also saw
the appearance of so much as survived of the memoirs of Neil MacEachain.
Flora MacDonald had persisted in describing him as her 'servant' in
narrating the story of her historic voyage to Skye with Charles Edward, but
in fact he had been the Prince's closest *aide* in his sojourn in the Hebrides.
These memoirs gave a very different picture of events; the Prince irascible
and in constant fear of betrayal; MacEachain himself, not Captain Felix
O'Neil, seemingly the veritable adjutant of the Prince's escape to the Isle of
Skye; Flora's step-father the master-mind, though as an officer in King
George's highland militia ostensibly active in the search for the Prince.
MacEachain's manuscript had been brought to light by, of all people, a
Parisian barber into whose hands it had chanced to come. But though its
authenticity was clear it was only published in a magazine and did not shake
the romantic view of the Prince sustained by *The Lyon*. It was also incomplete, lacking an account of MacEachain's part in Charles Edward's
eventual rescue in the September of 1746.

For another reason Chambers' would-be definitive account of the
Prince's escape could not be the last word. The story could not be unravelled
from the various, often conflicting accounts without an intimate knowledge
of the geography − the changing background of glen and mountain, of the
islands and their surrounding seas. This unravelling did not come until the

publication in the 1890s by the newly formed Scottish History Society of the full text of *The Lyon* and Dr Walter Biggar Blaikie's splendid *Itinerary of Prince Charles Edward Stuart,* which accounted in detail for every day the Prince spent from landing in Moidart in 1745 to his final embarkation in the late September of 1746. To this wealth of material now made freely available to Jacobite scholars there were added the papers of the Earl of Albemarle, who had been in overall command of the search for the Prince. As published by Aberdeen's New Spalding Club, here was the view from the other side of the hill; the despatches from the ships in the Minch, the army detachments in the hills, the government spies everywhere, to Albemarle at Fort Augustus and the Lord Justice Clerk at Edinburgh. Here too was the artlessly vivid report by a Glasgow shipmaster of the Prince's embarkation from Loch nan Uamh on the 19th of September 1746, as he saw it happen.

There should by now have been a thorough revision of the story of the great escape, the more so in that Professor Sanford Terry of Aberdeen had brilliantly woven the various accounts of the '45 and the Prince's adventures into a continuous narrative. Instead there was an outrageously bad 'biography' of Flora MacDonald by a highland cleric, and the fourth volume of W Drummond Norrie's *Life and Adventures of Charles Edward Stuart.* Norrie did indeed write with an awareness of the misty mountains and the glittering waters, for he had trudged or sailed every mile. But his work was shot through with the lachrymose view of the Prince which was currently all too popular.

> 'The gallant but reckless Prince ... had played for a crown, and the glittering bauble had slipped from his grasp, but in its place he had won, what was far better, the deep and lasting affection of the Highland people ...'

And so on, and so on.

The twentieth century was to see a steady reversal of this romantic view of the Prince in the Highlands, though echoes of Drummond Norrie would not be lacking and still reverberate. The change began with the publication in 1907 of the narrative of Lord Elcho of the '45 so long kept (more or less) secret at Gosford. In the preface the editor, Sir Evan Charteris, had given an extract from Elcho's private journal which was blunt about the state of mind in which the Prince began his adventures after the disaster of Culloden – the information which Sandie MacLeod of Muiravonside might well have imparted to Boswell.

Sir Walter Scott had learned that there was a tradition in the Wemyss family that Elcho's parting words to his royal master on that occasion had been – 'There you go for a damned cowardly Italian'. He also had access to the Elcho narrative (though not to the more explicit journal) but he apparently felt it politic to half-throw a veil over the story when he wrote the *Tales of a Grandfather* two years later. Further evidence that Charles believed himself to have been betrayed came with the publication of the memoirs of the Chevalier Johnstone and of Maxwell of Kirkconnel, one of Elcho's officers; but throughout the Victorian years the alternative legend (so dear to latter-day Jacobites) held sway, that had he had his way the Prince would have charged into the mêlée, and so to an honourable death.

Elcho's private journal had been clear about the Prince's poor behaviour:

> 'The Prince as soon as he saw the left of the army yielding and in retreat lost his head and fled with the utmost speed and without even trying to rally any of his scattered host.'

When Elcho made up with the Prince by the Water of Nairn:

> 'I found him in a deplorable state ... he believed that all his disaster was caused by treason and appeared to be afraid of the Scotch as a whole, thinking that they would be capable of giving him up to the Duke to obtain peace and the 30,000 £ sterling that the King had offered for his head ...'

But Sir Evan Charteris had given only a few extracts from Elcho's Journal. It was difficult to assess their credibility, and all too easy for later Jacobite champions such as Sir Compton Mackenzie to see Elcho's strictures as the venom of a disappointed man. However, in the 1930s those formidable Jacobite historians Alister and Henrietta Tayler made the biggest coup since Robert Chambers unearthed *The Lyon in Mourning.* Though they had been little used by Jacobite historians in the past, the Royal Archives at Windsor had held since 1807 the papers of the Jacobite Court at Rome. Among these the Taylers now found O'Sullivan's report to King James at Rome. Here in the portly Irishman's inelegant English was his vivid account of the '45 from its beginning to its end, including the Prince's flight to the Hebrides and the desperate June days in South Uist and Benbecula. O'Sullivan's narrative revealed that fear of treachery had indeed been uppermost in Charles Edward's mind after Culloden; ten days after the battle he had insisted on precipitately sailing to the Outer Hebrides through the rising storm, being persuaded that Coll MacDonell of Barrisdale, his battalion of Knoydart braves still intact, was on the point of handing him over to the Duke of Cumberland.

The Taylers had also unearthed at Windsor the short narrative of his adventures which the Prince had dictated on the voyage back to France in the big St Malo privateer *L'Heureux.* Since O'Sullivan's narrative had ended with an account, albeit sadly jumbled, of what the Prince had told him of his adventures in the later summer of 1746, it was now possible from both of these to begin to see the Highland odyssey through Charles Edward's suspicious eyes. On Benbecula in April (when Clanranald personally came to his aid) the islanders had been 'so cautious and timorous as not to assist him'. The guide who led him and his companions astray among the bogs of southern Lewis did so 'by ignorance or malice'. The faithful Donald MacLeod of Gaultergill, whom Bishop Forbes so revered, was remembered only as the man sent on ahead to Stornoway to find a ship who 'indiscreetly blabbed for whom it was which spoiled the whole'. And what had the Prince to say about the romantic peak of his adventures, his deliverance from danger by Flora MacDonald and her friends on the Isle of Skye? He was, it appears, consumed with anger at Lady Margaret MacDonald, wife to the (Hanoverian) chief of Clan Donald in Skye, for not having come in person to meet him, though Lady Margaret − as the Prince well knew − had put herself and her family at huge risk even by arranging the Prince's passage through Skye. Such were the ways of a Stewart Prince.

It was, however, the threat posed by Barrisdale, the fair-haired giant, and his Knoydart men, which throughout was uppermost in the Prince's mind. As the summer progressed, the rumours of Barrisdale's defection had intensified. By mid-June the Prince had learned that Barrisdale had entered into some arrangements with Albemarle at Fort Augustus, bartering for his freedom an undertaking to catch the Prince. Barrisdale's descendants, touchy about the good name of Clan Donald, would maintain that he was only making a pretence of acting to orders from Fort Augustus, and that the rumours were all mere Cameron slander rooted in their old rivalries in the business of cattle lifting. But for the fugitive Prince, who knew not whom to trust, fear of treachery could be as great a danger as treachery itself; and when in September he eventually sailed to France, the Camerons rightly ensured that Barrisdale accompanied him − in irons, a French prison his destination − while his several score of followers seeking passage to France were dumped ashore.

That fear of Barrisdale was indeed the Prince's obsession could have been seen by historians of the '45 (but was not) from the middle of last century, when the memoirs of Louis XV's court were published by his elderly courtier, the Duc de Luynes. De Luynes had shared in the stir at Fontainebleau on Charles Edward's return from Scotland and his long audience with the King; and he reported at length what the Prince had to say about the worst days of the whole six months ordeal in the hills of Knoydart. Said de Luynes:

> 'They were surrounded with patrols searching for them. These passed so close that they could hear them speak, and the patrols were led by a highland chief who was a traitor. This man knew all the ways through the mountains, and it was this which so greatly aggravated the Prince's difficulties in remaining concealed. While the patrols were all around him, he heard them say 'we will surely find him for we known just where he is . . .'

Perhaps the Prince was improving on events, just as he had touched up the story of his horse being shot under him at Culloden − but here, surely, is his authentic voice.

And the identity of this traitor chief?

'His name is Magdanel', said de Luynes, 'He has another name which no one can tell me,' added the bewildered Duke, foxed by the Scottish 'territorial designation'. And from this one sees that the nightmare of Charles Edward's enforced return to the mainland from Skye and Raasay in the first days of July lay not only in the ships of the navy along the coast and the cordon of troops among the hills, but in that Knoydart to which he had come was Barrisdale's country. With de Luynes in mind, one may also turn back to Boswell's narrative and see the reason for the Prince's reluctance to leave Skye for the mainland as Malcolm MacLeod described it, and the identity of 'the person in Knoydart of whom he had suspicions', (Note Boswell's tactful avoidance of naming him; Barrisdale's son was still lairding it in Knoydart.) Also illuminated is the Prince's admission to Malcolm MacLeod, likewise recorded by Boswell these twenty-seven years after, that while he had no fear of the red coats he 'was somewhat afraid of the highlanders who were against him'.

So there it is. The Prince's perception of his highland adventures seems to have accorded little with the legend of highland loyalty which adorns his name. How could it have been otherwise? To his bitter disappointment and anger more than half of the clans had ignored his summons to rise for the Stewart cause. Of these the MacLeods and MacDonalds of Skye, ostensibly Jacobite right up to the autumn of 1745, had along with Seaforth's people, the MacKays, the Grants, and all Clan Campbell raised militia in King George's service. Add to this the delusion, which he carried to the tomb, that his highland general had betrayed him at Culloden. In the long years after the '45, until maudlin old age took over, he does not seem ever to have spoken of the fidelity of his highlanders. Others did so: not he.

However, this more realistic, somewhat anti-romantic view of the Prince in the heather has not percolated through to the popular histories. Eric Linklater and Moray MacLaren still hold their shelf space in the bookshops. Any work from their pens could not be less than sparklingly readable, but ignoring as they did the new sources for an understanding of all that was involved in the Prince's escape, his own view of events in particular, it is a case of 'Hamlet without the soliloquies'. Nor, more generally in regard to the '45, did Lord Elcho's sweeping condemnation of the Prince's conduct receive the attention it merited when Henrietta Tayler presented the full text of Elcho's Journal for the period of the rising. This was done in a Roxburgh Club publication, and very few libraries hold these. It was also unfortunate that Miss Tayler allowed her passionate Jacobite sympathies unfairly to impugn Elcho's credibility. And so, two hundred years after the bonnie Prince's death, Scotland has still not quite been able to make up her mind about him.

If the familiar, heroic view of the Prince's highland adventures was now becoming – what shall I say? – more complicated, it was a very real privilege for me twenty years ago to be able to bring to light the unambiguously heroic tale of the six commando-style attempts from France in that summer of 1746 to rescue the Prince. (*Ships of the '45: The Rescue of the Young Pretender*, John S. Gibson: Hutchinson, 1967). These narratives had lain hidden in the national archives in Paris, suppressed at first by considerations of state and then forgotten. They shewed how the six attempts fitted together, the success of the two big ships which came into Loch nan Uamh in September being built out of the seeming failure of the five, earlier rescue attempts.

It was equally clear that Charles Edward's 'wanderings', as the earlier historians from Boswell on had dubbed his adventures, were in fact a sustained search for the rescue ships from France which he knew must come.

But if, like Robert Chambers, I too had thought that I had written the last word, then I too was wrong. A visit to Paris in the 1970s elicited the missing report of the second rescue mission, written as the little *Lévrier Volant* heaved about in the Minch: and Alasdair MacLean, then the GP in South Uist, brought to attention the vivid island tradition of the arrival there of the third rescue attempt, two days after Flora MacDonald had whisked the Prince over the sea to Skye. Dr MacLean then went on to match Hebridean tradition more generally with the written record of the Prince's sojourn there (*A MacDonald for the Prince*, Alasdair MacLean: Acair, 1982). Here he has shown that it was a widespread outwitting of authority by the MacLeod gentry as well as by those of Clan Donald that made possible the last farewell at Loch nan Uamh, this and the management of the affair up to the end by the intrepid Neil MacEachain. To crown it all, Alasdair MacLean was able to reveal how for long after the '45 Flora MacDonald was doubly the Hebridean heroine because she was also a mistress of deception. But that is too good a story to be compressed into a paragraph.

The burning of the Jacobite glens from the middle of May 1746 is seen today as, like Culloden, a blot on the honour of British arms. What is to be said about this, as seen from 'the other side of the hill?' There is this; that the Duke, in the weeks following the battle ponderous as Montgomery in the follow-up to Alamein, could not know that the '45 was over. Nor indeed was it. Clan Donald and those other regiments which had not closed with the redcoat ranks had quitted the field in some sort of order, and had been allowed to do so. The accession of Clan MacPherson from their Perthshire duties and Barrisdale's force from the north could have gone far to make up for the Culloden losses, as some leaders of the Highland army saw. A full four weeks after the battle a strong 'rebel' force under the leadership of Lochiel came together in the hills of Lochaber; and sloops of the navy met armed resistance in Moidart and Knoydart. Even much later that summer the fugitive Lochgarry would talk wildly of renewing the fight, while Commodore Smith with his force of frigates at Tobermory was all the time sharply aware of the danger that the Duc d'Anville with the Brest squadron might be coming his way.

By mid-May, as he marched his army to Fort Augustus, all this added up to an urgent need in the minds of Cumberland and Albemarle, assented to by as staunch a highland gentleman as Major-General Campbell of Mamore, to deter any further rising by distressing the Jacobite glens. It seemed their only option, given that the Duke felt that he could not safely rely on his redcoats in any prolonged campaign among the hills (some of the harrying was in fact carried out by the clans in King George's pay); and that for Private Thomas Atkins the high hills, the terrifying mists and the rain filled him with a 'hypochondriacal melancholy', as an observer put it.

There may well have been more to it than this. In the Stuart Papers at Windsor there is a curious letter of 1748 to old King James at Rome from the Jacobite exile, Drummond of Balhaldy, announcing the death in France of his kinsman Lochiel; and this letter asserts that shortly after Culloden the Duke of Cumberland contrived to send a message to Lochiel, still under arms in the hills of Lochaber with what had survived of the Clan Cameron regiment. This message extended the prospect of amnesty if Lochiel would lay down his arms forthwith and persuade other highland chiefs to do likewise. Jacobite scholarship has never paid attention to this letter; Balhaldy was such a liar. But very recently a truly remarkable document has come to light in the Archives of France in Paris – so Alice Wemyss, who made the discovery kindly allows me to say – which seems startlingly to corroborate Balhaldy's claim. This is a copy of a submission of April 1747 to Louis XV, apparently from the Duke of Perth who had been Lord John Drummond of the '45. It states that such an offer was indeed made by Cumberland to Lochiel after Culloden, and that Lochiel spurned it since he felt sure that Charles Edward (whom he thought had by then made his escape) would return to the Highlands with French help, as he had promised to do.

As has been mentioned above, instead of accepting amnesty in the mid-May of 1746 Lochiel, lame from his wounds though he was, did muster several hundreds of his clan with Barrisdale's and Lochgarry's men to keep up the fight against the Duke's army then moving down the Great Glen to Fort Augustus.

This blowing of the embers of the '45 came to nothing; and it was followed immediately by the savaging of the glens by Royal troops. Cumberland, his patience – such as it was – at an end, may indeed have felt this sort of brutality was his only option if he were to be free soon to resume his search for military glory in Flanders, the real theatre of the war.

Lochiel it seems had made an appalling miscalculation, and the Jacobite glens paid the price. Explicable too becomes the devastating self-reproach in a letter of Lochiel's in the Stewart papers, written in January, 1747. In this he speaks of the Highlanders as 'the people I have undone', and that he is haunted by 'the reproach of their Blood'.

The past is dark and cavernous as the bottom of the Minch. For anyone who is at all interested in history this epilogue to the rising, of the Prince's escape from the Highlands, like the '45 itself, has special significance precisely in that it has been so well researched. Here almost uniquely in our country's history, what was done at a time of heightened feeling and fearsome danger, and why it was done, can be discerned in vivid illumination. Here is a rare case-study of people under stress.

But the '45 is still with us for another reason. It raises an eternal issue. Faced with the challenge to do what you feel your God requires of you – what *do* you do? What do you do when you recognise, as did Lord George Murray ... or Euan MacVey ... that the price of so doing is ruin and death? As we look back down the ages we recognise that their plight can be ours.

(I am grateful to Dr Donaldson of the National Library of Scotland for guidance on 18th-century publishing, and to David Daiches for making available his rare narrative of the Prince's escape.)

12

'TO SECURE OUR LIBERTIES'
by
Lesley Scott-Moncrieff

Lesley Scott-Moncrieff is a daughter of writers George and Ann
Scott-Moncrieff. She grew up in various parts of the Highlands
– Badenoch, Lochaber, and the Isle of Eigg. In Edinburgh she
worked as a journalist, wrote for the B.B.C. and is author of
Scotland's Eastern Coast. She is married to a civil engineer.
They have eight children and in peripatetic life have lived in
Fife, Easter Ross, Kintail, and East Lothian.

' "I think any individual is obliged by the laws of God and
man to do their best to contribute to what is just and right
... Upon the whole I am satisfied there is much greater
need of a Revolution now to secure our liberties and save
Britain from utter destruction than there was at the last –
even if the King's right were not in question".' (Letter from
Lord George Murray to his children.)

WHEN LORD GEORGE joined the Jacobites at Perth it is
recorded that there was much surprise and rejoicing among them, for though
he had kept his political principles quiet for many years he was
well-respected.

He was a friend of the Lord President and the Lord Advocate: he was an
excellent farmer and administrator of his brother's and his wife's family
estates: though personally often 'pinched for money' in all his letters he
shows primary concern for the Atholl men. He read the French and Italian

newspapers and kept abreast with the continental wars and politics. He was a staunch Presbyterian, a cosmopolitan Scot, but he was also a Highlander and it is significant that the only two officers who knew him well before the rising were Keppoch and Cluny.

But it is a supreme irony that Lord George, who got on well with the rest of his officers young and old and who all his life was sympathetic to the young, yet could not develop a sympathetic bond with the Prince he had given up all to serve. It is impossible to avoid the conclusion that for various reasons, chiefly jealousy, the brilliant and capable but rather evil youth John Murray of Broughton, the Prince's Secretary, and less culpably those muddlesome men O'Sullivan and Sheridan, poisoned Charles against his best officer from the start. Lord George was by far the most brilliant among them; without him the Jacobite army would have been cut to pieces quite early on. It is just possible that the young Charles had an intuitive edge on Lord George, but they were rarely able to work in harmony.

There was also a disparity of vision between them. To Lord George and most of the Scottish army the re-establishing of a Scottish Parliament was a priority, and if the English refused to rise for the Stewart Cause and the French were indecisive in their help, then to hold Scotland alone, or at least establish it for the Stewarts, was a distinctly preferred option. Charles never saw this, let alone understood it.

Lord George's life had much in common with the Prince's, only the parts were in different order. In 1715 he had gone off to join Mar's Jacobite rising and then been attaindered and exiled: he had landed in the West Highlands and fought again at Glenshiel where he was the only officer wounded. After nine months hiding in the Highlands he had gone into years of penniless exile on the Continent. In Rome James had treated him like a son and Lord George had grown to love and admire this wise and Christian man, with his democratic ideals of monarchy, who paid for him to go to the Paris Academy. When his own fierce old Whig father lay dying Lord George had returned home, President Forbes wording an oath he could in conscience sign.

By contrast, James VIII had found Charles at fifteen 'wonderfully thoughtless for one of his age'. Aeneas MacDonald his Paris banker, who later accompanied him to Scotland, noted that he seemed to have been badly educated, while according to Lord Elcho he seemed 'to know very little of geography, politics, or law of his country'. Modern experts have recently concluded that Charles was almost certainly dyslexic. But he was undoubtedly strong and courageous and he carried with him the wonderful charisma and hope of youth.

By 1745 Lord George was twice the age of the Prince, for whom the battles, Highland hiding, Continental exile, and the claims of a dying father all lay in the future.

At Perth the Prince, retaining the Supreme Command himself, appointed Lord George Murray and the Duke of Perth as his Lieutenant Generals. Lord George and his fellow officers trained and drilled the disparate groups of clansmen into an army, very few of whom had ever been in battle before, for the days of clan warfare were over. He impressed on the Prince the importance of an army being properly provendered, and had knapsacks made for all the men to carry meal in and bread carts made for the march.

His constant care and that of his fellow officers for the troops under their command is in outstanding contrast to the grim approach of most of the English commanders of their day, apart from Ligonier: Wade and Cumberland considered health and welfare as pampering, and regarded their troops as largely the scum of the earth. Is it possible that there was some connection between the brutalization that took place before Culloden and the brutality which took place afterwards?

In a characteristic letter to his wife Lord George, on leaving Perth, writes:

> 'I'm sorry I have taken off all your horse, but I do not like to oppress the poor people by taking their's : for whatever excuse we may have for our baggage, we have none for taking them to Ride.'

But he had good reason to be pleased with his new troops when they went to seek the dragoons stationed at Linlithgow (who fled.)

> 'A thousand men went, about one in the morning, which I commanded the whole way and I was much satisfied to find the men could march in such order; and upon any emergency were perfectly obedient, though when no enemy was near, they were not so regular.'

It has to be emphasised that the Jacobite leaders never saw their rising as a civil war. For this reason they were good to their prisoners and took great care of the enemy wounded. Mercy was Charles's most outstanding quality, at least to his foes. He would never even execute a spy, for they too were his father's subjects.

It was all a matter of *political* differences. For instance, after the capture of Edinburgh the Jacobite officers dined cheerfully with the Provost and Whig civic dignitaries. This dichotomy seems to have been commonly understood north of the border but not south. Perhaps the very much crueller English system of criminal justice had long since induced an awful carefulness.

Edinburgh had capitulated without a shot being fired, though with much indecision and heart-searching beforehand. But as Lord Elcho recalled bitterly of the citizenry, 'Not one of the mob that were so fond of seeing the Prince ever asked to enlist in his service', and this was very nearly true.

Cope and his army having landed at Dunbar, on the 20th September Charles led his troops by the west side of Walleyford and up Faa'side Hill, then entering the road at Dolphinstone marched up the Birsley Brae, halted and formed his army.

The story of the Battle of Prestonpans is well known, and of how the youth Robert Anderson came to Lord George as he lay sleeping in a field of cut peas with the Prince and several of the chiefs lying near him, and woke and told him he knew of a place where they might easily pass the morass without being seen by the enemy. Lord George hesitated not a moment, Charles listened, called Lochiel and the others into council, and the whole army came down, not a whisper among them, until they were all on the march through the morass in the darkness and the mist.

The horror of the dragoons can be imagined as the mist rose, and what they at first took to be a hedge turned out to be a moving one, and they realised the Jacobite army was upon them with broadswords, and even scythes and knives tied to sticks in the case of the ill-armed MacGregors, giving them no time to prime and fire their cumbersome muskets.

The armies were equally matched, having about 2,500 men each, and if few of Cope's poor men had ever fought in battle before, neither had most of the Highlanders. The battle lasted about twenty minutes and Cope was totally routed. The dragoons fled to all the airts . . . west to Edinburgh, east to Dunbar, Cope and his officers galloping up over the Birsley Brae, and south to Selkirk and from thence to Berwick, where he was probably not the first to bring the news of his defeat.

Lord George wrote to his brother:

> 'I can now tell you for certain there can never be 500 men assembled of Mr Copp's armie again, perhaps scarce half. Our loss may be about 36 kill'd and 50 wounded; their's, 600 killed, as many wounded, and we have actually from 16 to 18 hundred prisoners, of which above 80 officers . . .'

As James Johnstone pointed out, the political significance of the victory at Prestonpans was that it rendered:

> 'the Prince entirely master of the kingdom of Scotland, where there remained no more English troops, except the garrisons in the Castles of Stirling and Edinburgh, all the towns in Scotland having been obliged to acknowledge the Prince under the title of Regent of the Kingdom.'

The Prince having refused an offer made by the French to ship all the prisoners to France, Lord George, who had spent the night after the battle sleeping by the prisoners and attending to the wounded, organised the transfer of the ordinary prisoners to Logierait and provisions of meal and mutton, and for guarding them – 'though there be no arms but Lochaber axes it will suffice'. Sixty officers were sent north to Perth, and he wrote to his wife to provide dinner for them when they passed Tullibardine. The Jacobite leaders hoped that many would change allegiance, and some did. But manpower was needed to guard and conduct the prisoners, and at the last, when Jacobite officers and men were being hanged, drawn, and quartered at Carlisle, had the Hanoverian prisoners been in French hands an exchange could have been made and the Jacobite lives saved.

The sure hand of Lord George had been felt throughout this first manoeuvre, for he had led the army in person, as he was to do at Clifton, Falkirk, and Culloden. It would have been at Holyrood that Maxwell of Kirkconnell first shrewdly observed how:

> 'Secretary Murray from the beginning aimed at the direction and management of everything and was almost the only personal acquaintance of the Prince in Scotland. . . . Lord George was the man the Secretary dreaded most as a rival . . . The Prince had the highest opinion of the Secretary and knew little of Lord George. Naturally affable, fond of knowing everything for himself and willing to listen to everybody, he was eternally beset by those who had surprised his confidence.'

But apart from his Secretary it was the Irish and French officers whom Charles turned to most, who knew nothing of the country or the enemy, and who as foreigners stood to lose nothing should they be captured or the cause lost. Naturally they looked for a Stewart-controlled Britain, regardless of a Scottish option.

However Kirkconnell did admire Charles's ability to keep 'tolerable decorum' among his adherents during the councils of war which were held daily during the month long sojourn at Edinburgh. The Prince's desire to march immediately after Prestonpans to follow up with another victory over Wade who was stationed at Newcastle with an English army and 6,000 recalcitrant Dutch mercenaries, was over-ruled by Lord George and others on the grounds that they had only about 2,500 fighting men.

At a subsequent council Lord George and his supporters were over-ruled in their preferred option to stay in Edinburgh and hold Scotland alone. James Johnstone, A.D.C. to Lord George and later to the Prince, recorded that:

> 'Some of the Chiefs said to him that it was to make him King of Scotland that they had taken up arms in exposing themselves to perish on the scaffold, with confiscation of their goods, but that they had nothing to do with England. In the meantime the Prince pretended to have received letters from many English Lords, assuring him that he would find them on the frontiers of England, under arms, ready to join him with a considerable corps of English; the Chiefs of the Clans allowed themselves to be brought about, and consented in the end to his proposition, after much debate.'

Frank Mac Lynn has pointed out that this decision was only carried by one vote, and had John Roy Stuart (who was a Colonel, but only subsequently on the Council) been present, it could not have been carried. On such cliff-hangers does every turn in the story of the '45 depend.

Towards the end of October, formal alliance between the French King and Prince Charles Edward, and the immediate embarkation of Lord John Drummond at the head of the Scots Royals, meant that the French could insist on the withdrawal of the 6,000 Dutch troops from English soil.

Yet at almost the same time the arrival in France of George Kelly, envoy from Prince Charles to the French Ministers, probably tipped the scales the other way. Kelly, who could tell a good story, gave a vastly exaggerated description of the Prince at the head of an army 12,000 to 15,000 strong, intending to encourage the immediate embarkation of the French invasion. But this seems to have had the effect of delaying it: the Jacobite army must have sounded invincible on its own.

In fact the army numbered about 5,000 when it set out for Carlisle, Charles marching the whole way at the head of the Highland half. The taking of Carlisle, which was very much due to the efforts of the Duke of Perth and Lord George Murray, was followed by the Prince's contemptuous treatment of Lord George, who then resigned. Forthright protest from officers and men and the Duke of Perth (who asked to be made second-in command to Lord George) averted disaster.

Lord George was tactless and overworked: it was said of him that during the whole campaign he did the work of three men. The Prince on the other hand was thoughtless and too influenced by his advisers.

It is difficult not to see them like the figures in *The Thrie Estates,* or other morality plays, in the human guise of Flattery (Sheridan), Vanity (O'Sullivan), Deceit (John Murray), with Sloth or Incompetence (John Hay of Restalrig) hovering about in the wings until the *dies irae, dies illa* of Culloden. These are of course temptations that beset us all, only more noted in Princes, and crucial in campaigns. With such friends, Charles had no need of enemies, but he was thoughtless and perverse enough to remain under their tutelage.

So long as the Jacobite army remained in Scotland the Hanoverians were well able to keep cognisance of them through their spy network, but as soon as they started to march they moved so rapidly ... despite appalling weather, that after Carlisle the government had great trouble keeping track of them. The expedient of blowing up bridges to prevent their advance of course made no impression on the Highlanders who were used to fording rivers. By Penrith, Kendal, Lancaster, Preston, Wigan, and Manchester they marched.

The Whig Lord Cobham wrote 'I don't know who has the command of these people's affairs in the military, but this I can assert that they have not committed one mistake since they came into the kingdom.'

But as a whole the English cared neither about the House of Hanover nor the Stewarts, and hardly any joined the Jacobite army. Charles's assurances of English Jacobite help now showed themselves as proof of either his gullibility, or wishful thinking or worse. Because of having to divide the army the officers saw less of each other during the march, and the Duke of Perth, whose thin arms had so surprised the Highlanders when he led them in digging the trenches for the siege of Carlisle, and whose health was so poor that after each day's merciless duty he had to sit up all night to keep breathing, was not able to continue his rôle as peace-keeper. For this and for other reasons by the time the Council of War had met at Derby there was little chance of Charles and Lord George thinking along the same lines or working intuitively together.

Morale was high in the whole army and the men were well fed, in good fettle, and high in hopes as they were within 200 miles of London. Yet the decision taken by the officers was one of caution : no support at all for their cause had been evinced by the English : they were not to know that London was in a state of panic : Lord George feared that if they advanced his army would be crushed in a pincer-like movement by two giant English armies, and felt that he could not justify such a risk. MacLynn, in *The Jacobite Army in England*, describes what was possibly a deciding factor in the vote : the introduction of a man named Bradstreet, claiming to be a Jacobite, who assured the Council that Cumberland was encamped at Northampton with 9,000 men. 'Observe that there were not nine men at Northampton to oppose them, let alone nine thousand', exulted Bradstreet later. He was of course a spy.

The vote went against Charles ... 'The Prince heard all these arguments with the greatest impatience, fell into a passion and gave most of the Gentlemen that had spoke very abusive language, and said they had a mind to betray him.'

If the Prince's morale was broken, that of his troops was severely shaken. MacLynn has also pointed out that the Oxfordshire Jacobites were ready to rise and the Welsh were already on their way ... but the Highland host were never to know this. It was decided to withold the news from them until the army was on the march, and when they realised an hour or two later that their direction was not part of a manoeuvre but actually a retreat their distress was palpable. They felt that whereas there had been at least a chance of success, now defeat was almost certain. It need not have been so.

If the winter march south had been bad, the return was ghastly. Yet a contemporary Whig writer commented on the restraint with which the invaders 'conducted themselves in a country abounding with plunder. No violence was offered, no outrage committed, and they were effectively restrained from the exercise of rapine. Notwithstanding the excessive cold, the hunger, the fatigue to which they had been exposed, they left behind no sick and lost very few stragglers; but retired with deliberation and carried off their cannon in the face of the enemy.' One of the reasons for so few stragglers was that the English country-folk, now that they saw the army in retreat, had taken to cutting the throats of any who were sick or who were slow.

The Prince had declared that 'in future I shall summon no more councils, since I am accountable to nobody for my actions but to God and my father and therefore I shall no longer either ask or accept advice', and from then on was almost as good as his word. This effectively released him from the guidance of his senior Scottish officers. Whereas on the way south he had always risen early before his army, he now slept late, and at a time when haste was all-important he deliberately kept them waiting for him. To punish Lord George he put him in charge of all the baggage and cannon, with the orders that nothing whatsoever was to be left behind. In effect, Charles was sulking.

This refusal to co-operate was evident on the night of the skirmish at Clifton. Held back by the wretched baggage, Lord George and a few troops (Cluny's and Glenbucket's) became trapped at the village of Clifton and separated from the rest of the army: Cumberland's advance guard was just behind them and, Lord George realised, was ready to harry them as they left the village. So he sent word forward to the Prince telling him he was about to take rear-guard action and asking him also to send back 1,000 soldiers, as he reckoned that they could take on Cumberland's army from an advantageous position the next day. This the Prince refused to do, and also forbade him to take any action.

Lord George, realising that a skirmish was essential if they were to survive, placed Cluny's men behind dykes as the first of Cumberland's dragoons entered Clifton. The fighting took place in the dark only relieved by fitful moonlight, the dragoons were beaten back and pursued by the Highlanders, the unfortunate men being hindered in flight by their great boots. The aged Glenbucket, being too old for such action, had lent Lord George his good targe and waited on his horse at the end of the High Street for news of the outcome. Lord George, in the teeth of darkness and bullets, had led the onslaught as usual. On their catching up with the rest of the army the Prince was pleased, but an opportunity to take Cumberland at a disadvantage, which was never again to present itself, had been thrown away.

Even worse was Charles's decision to leave Carlisle garrisoned by the Manchester Regiment. The Scottish officers were appalled and pleaded with their now autocratic leader in vain. No council was held: Charles was determined to leave evidence that he would return, though the officers and men realised very well that Carlisle could not be held and that the regiment was probably doomed. It was a foretaste of things to come.

The Esk was forded on December 20th: it was in a raging spate and the officers, Charles amongst them, set their horses in the river downstream while the infantry crossed lest any be swept away, and Charles saved at least one lad's life by catching him by the hair and holding on to him and calling for help in Gaelic. In physical action he was never remiss.

The army divided and marched to Glasgow by two different routes: here the Prince reviewed his whole army on Glasgow Green: in spite of hardships and perils of the march not more than forty men had been lost.

Meanwhile General Hawley's Hanoverian army had reached Edinburgh. They advanced to meet the Highland army, burning Linlithgow Palace on the way, and camped about Falkirk. Lord George at the head of the Highlanders chose his time and his position and advanced towards the

Carron river; at this point Hawley was being lavishly (and purposefully) entertained to lunch in Callander House by Lady Kilmarnock. His officers knew that the Highland army was on the move, and sent to him for permission to take to arms. He angrily dismissed them.

By the time General Hawley had galloped up to his waiting army, hatless and with every sign of having wined and dined too well, the Highland army had gained the advantage of position and reached the crest of Falkirk Hill when Hawley's dragoons were only half way up, and climbing into driving wind and sleet. Utter rout followed.

Partly because there was no command of the left wing of the Highland army and partly because of the gathering darkness, this was not followed up in a decisive way: it was decided by Lord George they should at least take Falkirk, but on their arrival the Jacobite army found that Hawley's soldiers had already withdrawn. Prince Charles was served their Commander's supper.

The victory could probably have been followed up the next day, and many of his officers were exasperated at the change from the Prince's former decisiveness: still no councils were held and the Prince retired to Bannockburn House, keeping with him the Athollmen so that they were without their commanding officer, Lord George, a source of considerable frustration to them and him. Discipline was no longer what it had been now that countermanding orders were coming from the top : the Highland army was also upset by the accidental death of young Glengarry.

Meanwhile the news reached them that Hawley was 'court-martialling his men for the faults of their commanders.' The gallows which he had boastfully erected before leaving Edinburgh for hanging Highlanders were put to use on some of his own men, and he wrote in his dispatches that he had had thirty-two men shot for fleeing at Falkirk.

The Jacobite withdrawal to the Highlands was by no means the end of the heroic tale. In the north they took Inverness, Fort Augustus, and Ruthven. Despite the exigencies of a terrible February march up the east coast, Lord George and the Atholl men and Cluny with his men made an outstanding foray into Atholl country and took thirty government posts in one night. It was at one of these posts that Lord George found a letter referring to Cumberland's order to his men to give Jacobites no quarter.

Lord George even laid siege to the family seat of Blair Castle where he had grown up, and which was held by Government forces, lobbing red-hot lead to set fire to the roof, 'a work I was not over-fond of'.

Now the 6,000 unwilling Dutch troops had been replaced by 6,000 Hessians under the command of Cumberland's brother-in-law, the Prince of Hesse. The Hessians were not far from Pitlochry, and as Lord George recounted:

> 'One morning we took one of their Hussars . . . . As he said he did not expect any quarter (for Hussars seldom gave it) he was surprised when he found himself so well treated. I sent

him back to the Prince of Hesse, desiring to know if he
intended to have a cartel settled : but I had no answer. The
Swede asked me if he must return. I told him not, except the
Prince of Hesse sent him. He went away very well pleased.'

Lord George probably never knew the sequel to this story: Cumberland
scorned the proposal to exchange prisoners: the Prince of Hesse then
declared that he had no interest in the quarrel between Stewart and Hanover
and did not intend to fight men as he said 'so desperate in their misery',
and withdrew his forces. So at Culloden Cumberland was minus not only
the Dutch but the 6,000 Hessians as well.

Before Blair Castle could be taken, Lord George and his forces were
recalled to the North-East by Charles. Cumberland and the Hanoverian
troops were advancing steadily and the Prince was determined to make a
stand. Now the plan of Lord George and the other officers had been to retire
to the hills and conduct a campaign of guerrilla warfare against the
Hanoverian troops, which they had shown themselves very capable of doing
despite their exhausted state. They were on their own ground and among
friends, and there is no reason to suppose they could not have held the North.
But O'Sullivan had no experience of that sort of warfare and did not
understand it, like others amongst the Irishmen whom, as James Johnstone
wrote at the time:

> 'the Prince had adopted as his own counsellors on all
> occasions, men of the most limited capacities, great confusion
> of ideas, very bad counsellors, and altogether ignorant of the
> nature and resources of the country and the character of the
> Highlanders.'

Perhaps most crucially, the Prince could not now bear to be seen
retreating in the face of his cousin Cumberland's forces.

During the Athollmen's absence on the foray, Secretary Murray had
been taken ill and never recovered sufficiently to rejoin the campaign, and
the provisioning of the Highland army fell to the task of the totally incompetent Hay of Restalrig. Lord George in his account afterwards pays tribute
to his old enemy John Murray, declaring that had he still been in charge the
Highland army would never have gone hungry as it did.

As it was, the night march which was to conduct a surprise attack on
Cumberland's forces as they lay at Nairn did not come off because they
reached their goal only by daybreak : the old accustomed speed was not
possible due to the exhaustion and hunger of the men. Having retreated to
Culloden, at dawn the Highland officers once more begged the Prince and
his advisers to take to the hills, or at least to find a better battle-site. The
Prince was adamant that he would take his stand there once and for all. He
then gave O'Sullivan complete charge of choosing the battle-site and
disposing of the troops, and he had forty-eight hours in which to do it. As
Lord George commented bitterly, he showed his ability. The dead flat

site beside a long dyke in front of a marsh could not have been more abysmal.

Culloden, the final battle and its aftermath, are too well known to re-tell in detail. The starving Jacobites were out-numbered two to one by the well-supplied Hanoverians : fearful slaughter was caused by the Hanoverian artillery while the Prince dallied in futility : the heroic death charge by about a third of the Highland army was followed by the massacre of the wretched wounded on the battlefield and elsewhere.

Three days after the battle, at their temporary refuge in the deserted castle at Invergarry, O'Neill and O'Sullivan persuaded Charles that all was lost; they were wrongly convinced that even Lochiel was dead, along with so many others, and that the Prince's only hope was to escape to France. Charles then sent word of this intention to Lord George at Ruthven, bidding every man to look to himself and saying that he now needed the monies intended for the army for his own needs.

Lord George then wrote his famous letter of indignation, for which Charles never forgave him. This letter is still more understandable when we realise that Lord George was not at the head of a stricken band of survivors but that the Highland army which had re-assembled at Ruthven was already between two and three thousand strong, and had very definite plans for harassing the Hanoverian troops and so pressing the government to come to more favourable terms. They now 'took a melancholy leave of each other' and so dispersed.

All this was as we know followed by unspeakable cruelties to the Jacobite prisoners in the prison ships and hulks, illegal trials, hangings, drawings and quarterings, and other executions at Carlisle and London, while the glens were turned into human deserts by Cumberland's orders, with brutality to men, women, and children alike.

Slowly the shocking realisation must have come home to Charles. 'Surely that man who calls himself the Duke, and pretends to be so great a Duke, cannot be guilty of such cruelties ? I cannot believe them.' But he was forced to believe them among the smoking ruins of Raasay.

One suspects that on the whole Charles responded to the discipline of circumstance far better on the run in the Highlands that he did at any other time in his life. He is brave and humorous in the face of danger and discomfort, and more obedient to the robber band in a cave in Glenmoristan than he had been to his Council in Holyrood Palace. Splashing behind Malcolm MacLeod through the bogs of Skye, he puts the wistful question, 'MacLeod, do you not think that God Almighty has made this person of mine for doing some good yet?' But he answers his own large query with a very precise ambition : 'I hope in God, MacLeod, to walk the streets of London with this philabeg.'

His subsequent years in exile are the unhappy story of a disappointed man. Others paid the price with better grace. Most impressive is Lord George who had lost not a putative but a real kingdom of wife and children, friends and home-land. Yet in all his letters there is sorrow but not bitterness, nor does he criticise his Prince, who refused ever to see him again. Had the

Prince borne the character of almost any of his Scots officers − Perth, Ogilvie, Elcho, Lord George, Balmerino, Pitsligo, Lochiel, Cluny, Ardshiel, or indeed of so many who fought under them − his reputation would have rested fairly. 'I believe there never were any troops that have made such vast marches, out so early, always dark before incamping, often scrimpt for provisions . . . and yet in high spirets.' One thinks particularly of Ewan MacVey and Roderick MacKenzie who not in the heat of battle but in cold blood gave their lives to save Charles and his messengers.

Had he even been able to share the aspirations of so many who fought with him he might have remained in possession of one kingdom, for to quote finally Duncan MacNeill:

> 'It is contrary to facts and to reason to speculate whether the Scots had lost courage; the fact stands out clearly that the Scots had no interest in England or in the English Ruling Dynasty; they had not desired to put James on the English throne; they had consented to enter England in order to encourage and protect an English Rising, but when it became evident that England was not going to rise they proposed to return to Scotland and attend to the affairs of their native land'.

13

ANNALS OF
A HIGHLAND PARISH
SINCE THE '45
by
Neil Usher

Neil Usher, now in his eighties, was born in Scotland in 1903 where he has lived most of his life.

He was for ten years, interrupted by war-service, resident tenant farmer in Breakachy and for the following ten the same in Aberarder.

During part of this time he was County Councillor and Clerk to the Laggan Kirk Session.

The next ten years he and his wife were occupying Mains of Culachy at Fort Augustus where for some of the time he with officials inspected and assessed farms in the Airds and Lochaber districts for grants under the Hill Farming Act.

THE GREAT MACAULAY often prefaced his polemics with 'as every schoolboy knows'. Well of course every schoolboy did not know. Let us hope however that every Badenoch[1] Highlander knows the story of Cluny of the '45.

For others − Cluny Macpherson, the 14th chief of the clan, had after persistent lobbying gained a commission from the Government in Lord Loudon's Government Regiment of Highlanders[2] shortly before Prince Charles Edward's army descended the Corrieyairack to Garvamore; Cluny was then 'kidnapped' and joined the Prince and 'brought out' most of his clan. He was therefore in Government eyes not only a rebel but a deserter and traitor.

The clan regiment arrived too late to fight at the battle of Prestonpans, but marched to and from Derby, and, during the retreat, distinguished itself at the skirmish of Clifton where some dismounted dragoons, bogged down in mud by their heavy thigh boots, were killed. The clan fought again at Falkirk and was then to put to guard the Badenoch passes, to harry Government sympathisers in Atholl and disrupt communications, so was absent from Culloden; although its neighbours in Clan Chattan,[3] (Macintoshes, Shaws, MacBeans and MacGillivrays) took part in that terrible death-charge which broke through Barrel's and Munro's regiments and died before the musketry of fellow Scots of the Scots Fusiliers and Sempill's. Remnants of the Jacobite army reached Ruthven Barracks at Kingussie, on the advice of Lord George Murray, who was the only competent commander. Subsequent orders came from the Prince, ordering them to disband and save themselves as best they could. It is well known that Cluny spent nine years in hiding with some hair-breadth escapes before finally reaching France. Some of the details of his Highland stay are well known, others of himself and his family less so, and later events in Laggan less so again.

When the soldiers reached Cluny, Lady Cluny hid the newly born son and heir to the chieftainship in a kiln at the home farm; he was afterwards known as Duncan or Cluny of the Kiln. She watched their home being burned down from across the Spey at Breakachy, the house of a principal tacksman[4] and relation, while Cluny did the same from the limb of a tree. Lady Cluny then escaped to France with their son. Cluny hid in several places – one of them a cave high up on the face of Creag Dhu, the kind of sacred mountain of Clan Mhuirich, another an underground cellar at the beautiful Cluny Dower House of Dalchully, where he had a hair-breadth escape when caught above ground by a mounted officer, who might have been Lord Loudon the commander of the Government Highland militia. Cluny, posing as a ghillie, ran to hold the gentleman's horse and was tipped for his pains. His most famous hiding place was 'Cluny's Cage', a strange kind of bivouac contraption on the South face of Ben Alder above Loch Ericht. Here he entertained for a while the Prince himself during his 'flight in the heather', the wounded Lochiel, and Colonel Roy Stewart. Finally, much assisted and succoured by a brave young son of Breakachy, he escaped to France where he died at Dunkirk in 1756.

Euan MacPherson of Cluny must have been a man of intelligence, ability, and courage. He was evidently high in the esteem of the best Jacobite leaders, and, as was to be amply proved later, in the loyalty of his people. During his nine years in hiding among them in Laggan, with a price on his head, he paid out part of a large bullion shipment by the French to alleviate losses suffered by Jacobite adherents, in conditions of difficulty and danger for all concerned.

During the early revengeful fury of the Government, Laggan seems to have got off relatively lightly, perhaps because of Kirk intercession for good but misguided Presbyterians, and because Lord Loudon, as also his fellow Campbell, General Sir John of Mamore, were humane men. There is no evidence of their highland soldiers committing atrocities, despite the express wishes of Cumberland and of Albemarle and of Generals Hawley and Bland and so willingly carried out by the pitiless sadists commanding other Government troops.

When a general amnesty was declared, Lady Cluny returned with her son and lived quietly in a humble dwelling at Cluny.

In 1756 an event took place which was to change the attitudes and life style of many Highlanders for generations to come. At the outbreak of the Seven years' War, Parliament, under the guidance of William Pitt the Elder, the Prime Minister, enacted measures for the recruitment of Highlanders into the British Army, which was deemed to be more satisfactory than having to scour the prisons for cannon fodder, or the costly hiring of mercenaries from German Protestant Princes. To paraphrase General Wolfe, himself present at Culloden, they were bold, hardy, and there were plenty of them to replace casualties.

The young Lovat, son of the double-dyed rascal who ended his life on Tower Hill, was first in the field in 'working his passage' for recovery of the clan lands, which would then become his personal estates, by raising Fraser's Highlanders of which he was made Colonel. There was a tremendous rush of recruits from Laggan since young Cluny was his cousin. The war was unpopular and the Government desperately needed a victory and heroes to go with it. This they got at Quebec, where Fraser's Highlanders greatly distinguished themselves, the dead Wolfe became a national hero, and local heroes were provided for Laggan also, including Sergeant MacPherson of Laggan, romantically depicted with the dying General in his arms. He later gained a commission and was famous locally as the Captain of Blaragie after the name of his restored tack. This regiment was disbanded in Canada where some men settled on grants of land, others returned home and we hear the recurring theme of half-pay officers, sons of tacksmen, who regained occupation of the family tack. So we hear of the Captain of Blaragie, a splendid extrovert character, and others such as the jolly old Bard of Strathmashie, who had been 'out' and had fought at Clifton, despite which his tack had been restored. He seems to have spent his declining years in bacchanalian ceilidhs and in bardic compositions 'unfit for delicate ears'. Yet another was Parson Robert MacPherson, late chaplain to Fraser's Highlanders at Quebec, where he received a citation for gallantry 'for encouraging the young officers when they appeared to be apprehensive and for his tender care of the wounded'. He was a rather larger than life character, much built up as a local hero, and, one judges, suffering from swelled head as the result.

This widespread enthusiasm for taking King George's shilling may seem surprising, but it is scarcely so. Many of the young chiefs were engaged as recruiting officers, getting a bounty of so much for each man who joined the colours, and often obtaining an officer's commission for themselves. Thus it was with young Keppoch,[5] whose father had been killed at Culloden. He received a colonel's commission in a Highland Regiment and became an active and successful recruiter. There were also very large numbers of tacksmen's sons, proud young gentlemen of long pedigree for whom visions of glory, a fine uniform, being fed and kept, and adventure overseas must have proved irresistible, while prospects at home seemed dull and bleak and likely to become bleaker, for after the American War of Independence and the customary disbandment of regiments and retiral on half-pay of their officers it became ever more apparent that great and, as was to be proved, irreversible changes were taking place. These were 'the (Agricultural) Improvements', and with these came the sheep.

To revert to Parson Robert: the Cluny lands and those of other rebel chiefs were being administered by the Commission for the Sequestrated Estates, an appointed body of lowland gentlemen, charged with this unenviable task. By this time Cluny had been gazetted colonel, though he must have been quite young, and had successfully raised a second battalion of Frasers. The Commissioners, acting as the interim heritors,[6] placed Parson Robert in charge of religious oversight of part of the parish, and with more dubious legality started a process for the eviction of the Macdonald brothers from the important holdings of Aberarder and Tullochrome in order to lease these to the parson. The Macdonalds had been tacksmen of Keppoch's, and as such they and their people had been implicated in the '45; many of them must, moreover, have been Roman Catholics. This process for eviction was undertaken, one guesses, partly as a public reward for Parson Robert and partly with the pressure of the Lovat and Cluny interest in the background.

Ranald Macdonald of Aberarder had helped the Prince when he appeared down Coire Arder in rags on his way to Cluny's Cage, and had given him 'a short coat and plaid'.[7] Since then he had become a successful and highly respected dealer in black cattle, a prestigious occupation for minor Highland gentlemen at that time. Both brothers were said to have been well liked in the district. They made a spirited fight against the eviction order taking their case to the supreme court in London where they lost. We may suspect that political influence, much more common in the 18th century than now, may have 'leant on' the English justiciary.

So Parson Robert got his tenancy and the Macdonalds retired to small holdings at Garvamore. A daughter of Ranald married Colonel Macdonell of Glengarry, 2nd Foot Guards, who defended Hougomont at the battle of Waterloo in 1815. The only record of the parsons's pastoral activities were of mass baptisms conducted thus: when he was told that a suffcient number of infants had accumulated to make the ceremony worthwhile he ordered the mothers plus babies to assemble on the bank of a convenient burn at a stated time, where, cutting a hefty birch branch for himself, (for he seems to have been a huge man) he sloshed water at them from the opposite bank. Otherwise he made a mess of farming, spent time at ceilidhs with the bawdy old Bard of Strathmashie and the Captain of Blaragie, and was fleeced by lawyers by raising actions for eviction against poor Macdonald 'small tenants' who by now would have little more rights than squatters. I remember a Macdonald, post-man at Kinlochlaggan, who had been born in a croft-house in Tullochrome, by this time of course little more than a heap of stones: a descendant of 'Keppoch's People'.

Few tears can be shed for the parson when it is learned that he had to quit his by now large holdings and died 'in a state of indigence in Perth'.

After the rebellion, in 1747 all hereditary jurisdictions, with their rights of 'pit and gallows', had been abolished and replaced by professional Sheriffs all over Scotland.[8] By the 1760's Lovat had recovered his lands from the Commissioners for the Forfeited Estates and the same happened to Duncan of the Kiln some years later. He must surely have made a small fortune out of his military career and recruiting activities, for he soon began to build the present Cluny Castle, having as his architect Robert Adam, who did not come cheap. He retired from the army, but soon got bored, rejoined, commanded several different regiments, and died full of military honours as 'a General Officer at the Horse Guards'.[9] He had leased Cluny to an 'improver' who carried out Spey drainage and much embellishment of the castle and policies.

In 1775 the Revered James Grant was 'placed' as parish minister by the 'interest' of His Grace Alexander Duke of Gordon – 'the Cock of the North' – by this time principal heritor in the parish. The Duke showed during the remainder of his life extraordinary interest in and practical benevolence for the people of Laggan. Mr Grant seems to have been a good and kindly man and an excellent parish minister. He had previously been Barrack Chaplain at Ruthven and travelling missionary. Shortly after arriving in Laggan he married Miss MacVicar, daughter of the Barrack Master at Fort Augustus, and later the celebrated blue-stocking lady of the Manse, Mrs Grant of Laggan. The first dressed stone slate-roofed parish church was built during his ministry. In the First Statistical Account of 1791, the human population is recorded as 1803 and sheep as 20,000.

By 1790, the first Border flock-masters with their Lintons, now called Black Face sheep, were arriving. The first were the Teviotdale Sintons to Aberarder, who occupied it for several generations as a highly respected family, together with their shepherds. We read of George Scott, shepherd, compearing before the Kirk Session and being offered the alternative fines of 10/- if he would marry the lady or £1 if he would not. The cad elected for the latter. I myself knew a Gaelic speaking shepherd with the Border name of Elliot, and likewise a Gaelic speaking crofter family on Brae Lochaber with the Lowland name of Rankin.

As the sheep came in, rents soared and the tacksmen and their sons were unable to cope. Working capital, pastoral expertise and unremitting 'hard darg' were needed. All these the hardy Borderers could supply. Of the first the tacksmen had little, having lived hitherto on a more or less subsistence economy. Of the second they had little either and despised the sheep. While of the last they laughed at the Borderers, themselves no mean adventurers, in particular for carrying peats for their women, for taking their knitting with them 'to the hill', and for milking cows.

In the 1790's there seems to have been a good deal of hardship and unrest, for Mrs Grant mentions in one of her letters that 'roups are all the rage and all talk is of emigration to Australia'. This was a planned, assisted emigration scheme to South Australia which actually took place. We may suspect the benevolent hand of the Duke in this. Now for all we know there may be more MacPhersons and Cattanachs in the Adelaide telephone book than in the whole of the Badenoch Directory.

Regular parish relief, collected of course from the parishioners, was distributed by the Kirk Session, as regularly minuted, and always with a sum 'for the Roman Catholic Poor'. Perhaps owing to the good start made by kind Mr Grant there has not been the slightest animosity between Presbyterians and Catholics in the parish right up to the present day. Kindly he must have been, for in a Kirk Session Minute 'N and N compeared for the sin of . . .' – one guess only. 'After admonition by the Moderator' (that was all) 'the female panel promised to be more careful in future'. As minuted this scarcely sounds like wholehearted contrition!

Some employment must have been given by the driving west of 'the Subscription Road' from Newtonmore; when this reached Laggan and the Spey was bridged, a tremendous beano was held with the top brass present. The subscribers were the Duke of Gordon, Macintosh, and the then young Cluny MacPherson. The road, supervised by the great Telford, continued by fits and starts as subscriptions came in until it finally reached Spean Bridge.

The grandson of Cluny of the '45 had now succeeded to the chieftainship. He lived a long life of apparently ceaseless activity, maintaining all the exterior trappings of the head of a clan. He appears as a young man as *MacPherson* in McIan's print.

During the whole of this time of change there were no clearances as in the other parts of the Highlands, and the only evidence of evictions is that of the 'small tenants' from Brae Laggan in favour of Parson Robert. This may have been due to the benevolence of the Duke of Gordon and, to give him his due, to Euan Cluny who was determined to keep up the old Highland style, on his own terms of course.

But the tacksmen and their sons had gone, providing a galaxy of distinguished soldiers serving in every part of the expanding British Empire. Two Cluny MacPhersons won Victoria Crosses at the storming of Lucknow in the Indian Mutiny. More and more of them however were inclined to retire to Cheltenham or 'Ooty' (Ootacamund, a Hill Station in South India), though until very recently many retired officers of the Cameron Highlanders and Lovat Scouts lived in the environs of Inverness. 'The people' of course provided what must have appeared as an endless stream of brave and willing soldiers for a hundred and fifty years, until at the outbreak of the Second World War the stream became a trickle for so few of 'the people' were left.

Nor was all sweetness and light on the pastoral front, for the Reverend Donald Cameron, the parish minister, writing in the Second Statistical Account of 1845[10] says, 'There are but three Heritors in the Parish, the

Duke of Gordon, Mr Baillie' (a shadowy figure, presumably of the Dochfour family) 'and Cluny MacPherson'. 'His Grace is as a father to the people for beneficence and condescension'; then as a side-swipe at Cluny, 'If others behaved in a similar fashion this would indeed be a happier country'. Again in the Kirk Session minutes there is a complaint that Cluny has not paid his barley teind – a serious matter for the poor minister's stipend. Grumbles on the same matter are repeated several times, until open warfare is declared. Inserted in the Session Minute is an excerpt from the Minutes of the Presbytery of Abertarff in an attempt made by Laggan Kirk Session to have Cluny excommunicated. The principal misdemeanour was that 'Cluny MacPherson was seen passing the Kirk door on Communion Sabbath in his tartans as if for a shinty play'. But there was a turncoat among the 'cloud of witnesses', for Duncan MacPherson in Balgown (a small tenant) deponed that he had found Cluny 'a very civil pleasant gentleman'. Poor Duncan obviously had visions of himself and family being flung out on their necks if he had said anything else. Alas, for the inquisitive there is no more. Instead there are four or five pages carefully blacked out, some pages torn out, some blank pages and then another minister, from which the inference is that Cluny won. There must have been faults on both sides in view of the known track records of both men.

About now 'Old Euan', as Cluny was later called, must have begun to feel financially embarrassed in his efforts to keep up with the better-heeled Joneses. Cluny, like other Highland Chiefs of the time, was pitching the proceeds of his rugged strath against those of the broad acres of Scottish and English magnates. He had purchased a commission for his heir in the 3rd (Scots Fusiliers) Foot Guards, and this had proved exceedingly costly for the young gentleman proved an adept, if at nothing else, in losing large sums at the card tables. Legend has it that in 1848 Cluny was making an all-out attempt to try to sell Ardverikie to Queen Victoria and her Consort, as the Duke of Gordon had died and any feudal superiority[11] had thereby lapsed. The purpose of the following exercise is never mentioned but it must have been fairly obvious to all. The Royal family were invited to Ardverikie. Every presentable male likely to come within eyeshot of the Royals was persuaded or coerced into MacPherson plaid, and all possible pipers coralled, and all posted at suitable vantage points to impress the visitors. Alas, the visit was plagued by ill-luck. They were three days late in arriving owing to a hold-up of the royal yacht. It rained and never stopped raining during the visit, which was spent in a small and therefore cramped 'Shooting Box' leased by the Marquess of Abercorn. Sadly, Albert did not shoot a stag. Sadly, when a very young Lord Claud Hamilton was presented to the visitors, he stood on his head exposing his nether parts. Sadly, when taken out, given a scolding and returned to apologise, he did the same again. The Queen was not amused. All this and crossing there and back in a ferry over the river Pattack, which must have been in roaring spate, gave Albert a heavy cold. Some years later as luck would have it, a visit to Deeside was made in bright sunshine; all was *gemütlich* and so like dear Coburg. So Laggan missed becoming Royal!

Cluny's financial embarrassment was despite the fact that grazing rents must have been at their highest and sheep numbers at their highest also. We hear of 10,000 wether sheep in Ardverikie and Ben Alder. However in 1870 just before wool and frozen mutton began to come in from Australia and elsewhere and the great agricultural depression came, Cluny managed to part with the land between Loch Ericht and Loch Laggan to Sir John Ramsden.

Cluny died in 1885 and received a Chief's funeral. So passed Old Euan with all his Highland pride and self-importance, and with his passing came the end of an era and the beginning of another. Cluny was succeeded by a Mr Albert MacPherson, and chieftainship then became vested in someone in New South Wales. From then on the estate diminished bit by bit until just after the last war the last part of it, two tenanted farms, half a dozen 'small tenants', the Castle and policies and some abutting mountains passed into the hands of strangers.

Sir John Ramsden, who came of an ancient and distinguished Yorkshire family, later acquired Aberarder. Later still he purchased a vast area stretching from East of Laggan Bridge, round the top of the Corrieyarrick, past the headwaters of the Spey and the Roy, far down Glen Roy, thence to Moy at the West end of Loch Laggan and in the East Strathmashie and an enclave adjoining Dalwhinnie. He was a gentleman of great energy, ability, perspicacity and foresight. Not only did he build the present Ludwig of Bavaria style mansion at Ardverikie, the old 'Shooting Box' having burnt down in 1870, he also built seven large shooting lodges, replete with walled gardens and splendid houses for the employees. He put the sheep off Ben Alder, Ardverikie, Aberarder and most of Brae Roy, though retaining a large stock on easier grazings on the Upper Spey. He introduced female red deer from elsewhere to increase the low deer numbers and English park stags to improve the quality. In giving evidence to the Crofting Commissioners in 1886 he suggested large scale reafforestation not only to replace the forests so recklessly plundered in recent decades but also to give steady work to crofters in winter. He himself planted extensively. In fact he took every advantage of the coming immense boom in Highland sport. Sir John was well liked and highly respected by his very many employees. Indeed it may be said that he kept a great area of the country going economically for several decades; as also did his son, another Sir John, who was also well liked. Gradually, however, the estate shrank and, while the family continues to take a lively interest in Ardverikie, which was the original acquisition, that and a hill farm on Brae Laggan is all that remains.

This era of sport gave employment to some, seasonal employment to many others, and proved a goldmine to local tradesmen. Its general effect on the gradually shrinking population may be more questionable. Thus matters continued until the outbreak of the Second World War. Between the wars hill farming was at a low ebb. Farmhouses, cottages, steadings, and all fixed equipment were in a deplorable state and sport reigned supreme. The dreadful and disproportionate losses of young men during the Great War, as in every Highland parish, exacted a toll on population numbers never to be made up.

Losses in the Second World War, though tragic, were slight, due partly to possibly a two-thirds loss in population since 1914, and partly to the majority of men being agricultural workers and so exempt from military call-up. During the Second War several hundred Newfoundlanders were imported for timber felling. Some married local girls – one of these, Peigi Og MacPherson, was a daughter of the last occupier of a house in the abandoned crofting township of Crathie. After the war hill farming improved, much helped by the passing of the Hill Farming 1945 Act which provided grants for improvements and headage subsidies for breeding cows and ewes.

By now the North British Aluminium Company had acquired the area of the headwaters of the Spey, had dammed the river at Crathie, drawn water off by pipe to Loch Laggan, thence to another dam at Roughburn in Glen Spean and piped thence again to the factory at Fort William. The Company carried on the large sheep enterprise successfully, tree-planted sensibly, including many shelter belts, and were good employers and good neighbours. Regrettably it allowed General Wade's old officers' quarters at Garvamore to go to ruin. This had been built about 1735, and was occupied as recently as thirty years ago, still complete with officers' box beds. In today's climate of opinion it is extremely unlikely that this would happen.

The Third Statistical Account was compiled in the 1950's by the Minister, the Rev. M. Johnstone Titterington, and the writer notes, *inter alia*, the excellence of the husbandry and apparently immense increase of the red deer population, and while many a stag from the hill was brought home on the quiet, the brutal commercial deer poaching by carlight had not yet started.

By now the number of humans had shrunk to 320 compared with the 1,200 noted in the previous 1838 Account. Adult sheep population was around 10,000. There were two primary schools in the parish, the larger at Laggan Bridge, the other at Kinloch Laggan. Until recently there had been a third at Glenshero, West of Crathie. Gaelic speaking had of course declined although most of the older people used it to each other; some were splendid story tellers. I well remember Archie MacDonald, the Gardener, acting as precentor with a tuning fork and leading the praise in the psalms at our evening Gaelic Sunday services in the parish church. About 100 people took communion regularly in the parish. Roman Catholics were, by now, a much smaller proportion than the one in six in Scotland, although in Glen Spean and Glen Roy in the adjacent parish of Kilmonivaig they were in a considerable majority. There was a lively community spirit and much home-made entertainment. The high day of sport had passed and the letting of the big shooting lodges was becoming rare and foreign paying guests commoner. The landowners, during their autumn residence, were on the whole helpful and generous, though now (with one MacPherson exception) absentees as regards their principal homes. Macdonald was easily the most common name, followed by MacIntosh with a good scattering of Camerons, Campbells, Gillies, Grants, Macleans, and MacRaes. MacPhersons and Cattanachs were by now sadly scarce. There were few other than native Highlanders as all-the-year-round residents.

Since the Account was written the fortunes of the parish have taken a turn for the worse. There are more incomers and fewer natives; Gaelic speaking is said to have died out. Four well established working farmers carry on with modest success. Aberarder, with its aboriginal birch woods, fine alpine flora and Highland wildlife, has now been bought by the Nature Conservancy Council and the Royal Society for the Protection of Birds, at heavy cost from a commercial forestry group. Large scale mechanised afforestation operated by gang labour from without the parish has been of minimal help. Yet gallant efforts continue against the odds to hold the community together.

To end on a bizarre note, at the time of writing a person of Maltese domicile is said to own the ancient MacPherson 'domus' of Dalchully. When in residence he has been reported to be accompanied by two gun-toting gentlemen − far different from the Chief's *tail*. He is reported in *The Times* as being at present a guest of Her Majesty awaiting deportation to the U.S.A. to face a Federal charge of fraud! *Sic transit gloria.*

With acknowledgements to Mrs Grant of Laggan's *Letters from the Mountains*, Thomas Sinton's *By Loch and River, County History of Inverness* by J. Cameron Lees, and *Victoria in the Highlands* by David Duff, and gleaned from the First and Second Statistical Accounts, Minutes of Laggan Kirk Session of the time, and local tradition during thirty years of residence in the parish of Laggan and in the County of Inverness.

NOTE

1. *Badenoch.* An administrative District of Inverness-shire embracing the upper strath of the River Spey.
2. The only previous body of soldiers raised in the Highlands during the 18th century was the 43rd Regiment, better known as the Black Watch. They were embodied in 1740 out of what were called the Independent Companies raised by the Government during the years after 1726 for police duties in the Highlands alone. When sent overseas against the terms of their engagement they had covered themselves with glory at the 'blood

bath' of Fontenoy in 1744 and had done so again at the disaster at Ticonderoga twelve years later in the New York wilderness where the regiment suffered heavily having 647 casualties. On returning from Flanders in 1745 the regiment was kept in the South of England during the rising, perhaps because the Government did not trust such formidable trained warriors, some with Jacobite leanings.

The various armed bodies of Highlanders raised by the Government and by Whig chiefs played an undistinguished role. Their effectiveness was probably as variable as their behaviour. We hear of Campbell militia succouring poor starving, homeless women and children in Glen Nevis; but also, as I have been told by a member of the Grant family, now dead, of the Macleod Militia turning Glen Moriston into a human desert with indiscriminate acts of brutality.

3.   *Clan Chattan.* A clan confederacy to which the MacPhersons belonged. Lady Anne MacIntosh, whose husband the chief was serving in the Black Watch, and who afterwards became a much petted Jacobite heroine, seems to have had difficulty in getting those 'of name' to join up, for in a list of killed, died, transported and pardoned, Smiths are nearly as numerous as the MacIntoshes.

4.   *Tacksmen.* A tacksman was a tenant of the chief, often a relation, and often a well educated and cultured gentleman. He paid his rent for the most part in kind and services. He in his turn let out parts of his tack to subtenants who paid him in like manner. The tacksmen were the cement which held the clan together. Without them it is more than doubtful whether the Prince could have raised an army: it was they who brought the people 'out', sometimes by cruel coercion.

5.   *Keppoch.* Chief of the Macdonalds in Glen Spean and Glen Roy.

6.   *Heritors.* Land owners with power of patronage to 'place' Parish Ministers and the responsibility for their stipends, i.e. pay gathered from 'teinds' (English tithes) calculated on the yearly outcome of cereal crops. They were also responsible for the provision and upkeep of Church property.

7.   This was related to me by a descendant.

8.   *Hereditary jurisdictions.* Abolished in breach of the Treaty of Union. Inherited justiciary powers exercised by some Scottish notables including a number of clan chiefs such as the Duke of Argyll, Grant, and Mackenzie of Seaforth. The abolition removed immense power from the hands of these chiefs.

9.   *The Horse Guards.* This was the equivalent of the modern War Office.

10.   *The Statistical Account.* Sir John Sinclair of Ulbster, who might be described as the first self-elevated Secretary of State, enlisted the help of the Parish Ministers in every parish in Scotland to compile the *First Statistical Account of* 1791. This and the Second of 1845 forms a vast compendium of information, often written in splendidly rolling periods sometimes with down-to-earth asides and wry humour.

11.   *Feudal superiority.* A feudal superior levied feu duty, broadly a land tax, and exercised control of land usage. It still exists today but is sparingly used in minor matters.

14

'THE STRONG COMMAND, THE WEAK OBEY ...'
by
Christopher Small

Christopher Small is of English birth and education, though of dilute Scottish extraction; resident in Scotland for two-thirds of 66 years, and believes that Scotland is, by reason, attachment, and the generosity of the Scots (to one of whom he is married), his proper home. By trade a journalist, he is now retired. He has lived mostly in the west, either in Glasgow or, whenever possible, on the island of Lismore. He has published books on Mary Shelley's *Frankenstein*, George Orwell, and the history of printing.

A MODERN WHIG historian used to declare his conviction that 'any further publication of narratives about the '45 . . . ought to be banned by statute under heavy penalties.' It was of course no more than a pleasantry, an urbane way of declaring an interest, or the want of it, in the whole matter.

But it is interesting to see the reason given, that concentration on the '45 – together with two other of Sir James Fergusson's *bêtes noires*, Mary Stewart and Burns – had distracted attention from 'other events and personages of Scottish history which really need it'. Anything more on these over-cultivated subjects was justified only if there were 'new aspects', 'unfamiliar fields' to examine and present; this was always possible, but had become increasingly unlikely with the multiplication of books and the passage of time. Such were the implications of Sir James's remarks, and to

most professional historians, to students, and even to the common un-
informed reader of history books they probably seem very reasonable.

What people call history, the past, is generally thought of as an actual
territory, laid out for inspection: the expressions used, 'fields', 'regions',
'beaten paths', and 'by-ways' of historical research show what is expected of
those who undertake it. The historian is a discoverer, and no one is interested
in twice-made discoveries; even though in discovering new detail the same
'ground' can be gone over profitably many times, it will eventually be used
up and historiography will have to move on. (Again, the metaphors used are
significant; if the purpose of historical study is often thought of as a kind of
cartography, and a means of establishing a permanent record, the method
sometimes appears more like slash and burn).

Such considerations have at least some weight nowadays for anybody
writing or reading about history. But they are not of course the only way of
thinking about the past; certainly they haven't always been so. Older
societies, deeply attached to whatever was known of former events, have not
wearied of hearing about them, over and over again, and often in exactly the
same form, or in forms which have changed only very slowly from one
generation to the next. History then was not an exterior object, capable of
being investigated and described by individuals for the interest of other
individuals, but a collective possession; as a part of society's actual, present
life it had no more need to be new than the common elements of daily diet.
As in the story of the shepherd who had porridge for breakfast, dinner, and
supper and who, when a solicitous inquirer wondered whether he didn't get
tired of it, replied 'A man doesnae get tired of his meat' – so, when the story
of the past affords real nourishment, posterity doesn't tire of telling and
hearing about it.

In that case it is called 'story' rather than history, and there is supposed
to be a great gulf fixed between. In practice the gulf is regularly crossed by
historians themselves, much more respectful nowadays of stories, 'popular
sources', even of old wives' tales, than they used to be. But they return with
their 'findings' to their own ground in a one-way traffic which few today
would question. It is much more questionable, even subversive, to propose
a movement in the opposite direction: that, equipped with modern historical
knowledge and critical method, an attempt should be made to regain the past
as tradition. That is to say, not as an object, of whatever great or little
interest, exterior to the experience of the society that 'comes after', but truly
as something handed on, which therefore constitutes a living connection
between past and present.

That some such connection is necessary for the health of society is,
perhaps, generally accepted – though usually in pretty vague terms, and not
permitted to be a very serious concern of those 'living in the present.' Nor
is it supposed to be the proper business of historians, who are meant to keep
their professional pursuits well separated from whatever may presently
engage their passions or partisanship. Perhaps again, those are principles
often happily ignored in practice. In any case, the enterprise represented in

this collection does seem to assume that there are connections between what once happened and is now happening, that they are important, and that they make demands on us. There is evidently a shared assumption that the '45 is still interesting in the full sense of the word, as touching our living interests, the matters that actually concern us, and that it hasn't in the least lost its interest by being much written about already; that, on the contrary, it has collected so much writing, talking, arguing, singing, playing, and romanticising about itself precisely because it is important for us in a way we no longer fully understand, if we ever did, and which therefore it is needful to inquire into.

If those who approach the subject in this way can be described as 'engaged', that need not imply partiality or abandoning the careful sifting of evidence. All can surely subscribe to the declaration of Bishop Forbes, the great exemplar in this entire business, who carried as heavy a bias as anyone but refused to let it push him away from the truth, however painful to himself or anyone else. There are truths of fact and truths of feeling, and one has just as much weight as the other, but they mustn't be weighed *against* each other. 'Truth', said Robert Forbes, 'tho' never so glaring, when it runs cross to the partial notions and inclinations of poor frail mortals, grates very hard and becomes a very uneasy and painful thing.' If we want to find out what we truly feel about what as far as possible we truly know, it is usually a painful business.

The '45 is notoriously a great rouser of passions even today, and why people feel as many do about the events of 240 years ago is a question as much worth asking as what these events actually were. For Robert Forbes, of course, it was not a problem. As he had a perfectly clear idea of the 'meaning', the moral import of the Rising and its failure, so his interest was straightforward and unmixed, and he was driven to collect as many facts in relation to it as possible. For the Honest Cause only honesty would do; there were for him no shades of difference in the meaning of the word. So *The Lyon in Mourning* is the extraordinary hold-all that it is, containing everything from eye-witness descriptions of massacre to the exact inventory of household goods pillaged – the china, silver, fire-irons, and 'vast quantity of Chesser cheese' – by the Hanoverian commander from the indignant Mrs Gordon of Aberdeen; from the demeanour of men on the scaffold to the zeal of redcoats searching for the Prince in the Citadel of Leith, from garret to garden, 'under the cabbages and gooseberry bushes not excepted'. So in this wonderful jumble nothing is too small or too trivial to be worth recording; but also nothing is so inconsiderable that it does not matter whether or not it is authentic.

For us, it is not so easy. 'True facts' continue to accumulate, and feelings remain, but we are now reluctant to bring them into contact with 'the facts', fearing that one will destroy the other; even as we get to know more about the '45 as history we are losing grasp of it as story.

It is all very well to propose the restoration of a felt connection with the past; and it can further be urged that if feelings themselves are to be 'true'

they must, as Bishop Forbes understood, be based on a true apprehension of
events and not upon falsehood. A purely fantastic account of the '45, though
exciting lively emotions, will be easily rejected. Yet it is unfortunately also
the case that emotions, and the desire to believe what is flattering, playing
upon 'the facts' of an historical event, will cause them to be distorted, mis-
represented, and so vitiated with fantasy that one is no longer clearly distinguishable from the other. And looking back over some 200 years of 'feeling'
about the '45, we can see that this is exactly what happened.

It would be rash to say when the process started – indeed it is obvious
that romantic mutations of history antedate by far the year 1745 – but it is
convenient to look at its most celebrated and influential point, with the
publication of *Waverley.* It is still instructive and even astonishing to study
this work, 'the first great historical novel', the maker (literally) of its author's
name, the prime source of fashions, not only literary, that swept Europe, and
to recognise in it, as through glass which at once distorts and walls off from
contact, events of an actual and then quite recent history. The most striking
thing, considering the extent of Scott's knowledge and the nearness of the
events he was describing – only 'sixty years since' when he began writing
the novel in 1805 – is the way he quite deliberately set about to make them
unreal. *Waverley* is 'vivid' enough, to be sure, full of colour, movement,
frequently violent action, picturesque touches which successfully 'bring it to
life', but it is the life of a dream, or a day-dream: the more 'authentic' the
incident, the more unreal in presentation it becomes. 'The most romantic
parts of this narrative', said Scott in his conclusion, 'are precisely those
which have a foundation in fact'; and it is he, of course, who chose them
precisely for that reason. Romance for Scott as for most of his contemporaries (though not the Romantics themselves) meant something agreeable
but untrue; to decide that an 'authentic' historical incident, even an entire
episode was worthy of inclusion in romance was wilfully to remove the
happening in question from the standards and judgments, the moral context,
of real life. *Waverley* should be a novel of conflict, but it is not, because the
conflicting elements have already been translated to a realm where genuine
interests, the stuff of genuine conflict, have become unmentionable. One of
the oddest things about the story (and other of Scott's stories) is the way that
gentlemen remain gentlemen whatever happens; athough, like Colonel
Talbot, they may be momentarily thrown off balance by 'a concurrence of
unpleasing events', their 'natural manner', manly, open, generous and so
forth, will always return and prevail not only in their own character but in
the events themselves. Unpleasing events may unhappily occur, but in the
society of gentlemen, whatever their political or other differences, they will
not dominate the scene. In a properly ordered world history may be relied
upon to show good breeding.

Scott's own class feeling (in practical politics, as we know, his strongest
motive) was doubtless perfectly sincere. But he was far too intelligent a man
not to understand that the power and wealth with which he threw in his lot
was in process of destroying much that he was interested in and attached to.

Like the pastor of Cairnvreckan, he allowed himself to be attracted by 'wild visions of chivalry and imaginary loyalty', but he knew that real life, the life of money, law, and property, was different.

The desire to reconcile the 'old stories', old times, and old loyalties with the new times which had displaced them could be realised only in fantasy: the combination of incongruities solidified, so to speak, in gaslit Abbotsford, or sublimed in the person of Edward Waverley himself. Waverley obviously is not Scott, but in him, as in any hero of fiction, can be seen a playing-out of some of his author's difficulties. He is a curiously inert hero, carried helplessly through the transformation scenes of the plot by other people – rustic Lowlanders, wild Highlanders, dragoons, beautiful and mysterious women – and the long arm of coincidence. He doesn't make things happen but things happen to him, as to Candide; unlike Candide, he doesn't learn anything from them, being protected from any too painful effects of experience. Indulgence in make-believe is from time to time conscious and explicit: there is no more revealing passage in the cosmetic treatment of history than the scene in which Waverely, having for the time being opted for active Jacobitism, puts on 'the garb of Old Gaul' and sees himself in the mirror, tartaned, bonneted, blue-eyed and becomingly bashful, as 'a very handsome young fellow'. Here, if not before – for the whole narrative is often like a tour of a costume-museum – Scott's '45 becomes, not a subject of historical research, however learned, not even an assembly of anecdotes and objects collected by an antiquarian, but a fancy-dress charade.

A direct line of descent could be traced from this elegant tableau to the grotesque apparition of George IV, Cumberland's nephew, fitted up (again with Scott as impressario) in philabeg, eagle-bonnet, and pink tights to keep out the Edinburgh cold; to the tartan inventions of the 'Sobieski Stuarts' and to the furnishings, decor, and holiday-wear of Balmoral; and through an entire range of nineteenth century fiction and adventure story to the present day. The contemporary end of the line is graphically shown in the engaging tartan-clad children's comic cartoon, created with loving care and in great unhistorical detail by the Englishman who contributed, in this and in the parallel cartoon-histories of the Broons and Oor Wullie, so much to the self-image of generations of modern Scots. A hundred years of poetry and prose fiction, with a large body of pictorial art and a complete sub-division of sartorial fantasy, combined to synthesise a 'tradition' of which the cartoon story of 'Wild Young Dirky' is, though lacking the erudition of *Waverley* and the stylistic sophistication of Stevenson, perhaps the most perfect production.

It presents a series of escapades set roughly in the years 1745-46, in which the boy-hero, with his slightly less heroic but equally amiable and picturesque comrades, and by variously ingenious but invariably successful stratagems and ruses, outwits and puts to flight crowds of wicked Whigs and whole detachments of redcoats. The ambivalences of Scott, who can be seen 'sixty years since' still undecided between the romantic appeal of Jacobitism and the solid advantages offered by adherence to the House of Hanover, have by now quite disappeared. Young Dirky (his by-name as a knife-thrower, more unerringly skilful than ever performed in a circus) is on the side of right, or we are unequivocally on his; the White Cockade is the only badge of honour, his heart knows no doubts, his strength is as the strength of ten and his aim is also true.

Cruelties and oppressions are prevented or requited, but not by cruel means. The lonely straths and wild heather-clad hills are permanently invaded and occupied by the enemy and permanently being liberated. Culloden, though sometimes mentioned, is somewhere else. No one is actually killed, and Wild Young Dirky, unchanging Super-Boy in a kilt, is ageless as Peter Pan. Such are the privileges of art.

The comic strip is for juveniles, but has doubtless been followed with pleasure by many older readers. In any case its spirit is derivative, not too far removed from loftier romantic originals and in a sense perfecting them. A cluster of assumptions about the world, pleasing to our self-esteem, are inbuilt there: in general, that bravery is rewarded with success (or Who Dares Wins), and that heroic exploits, especially those against odds, can count on a kind of secret underwriting by Providence; in particular, that 'the Highlander' is a special creation, of extraordinary physical and moral qualities, who is not or was not like other members of the human species. The same attitude which made it easy for real men and women in the actual Highlands to be treated as animals, or worse, survived to make it easy to forget about such things. Walter Scott, dwelling in theatrical and admiring detail on the proud nobility of Fergus MacIvor almost to the last, shrinks from the horrible facts of hanging, drawing, and quartering. For Dudley D. Watkins, drawing out the adventures of Wild Young Dirky for Scottish children of the late twentieth century, they are unthinkable and, we will say, quite right too. No one will wish the '45, at this or any other level, to be made the material of a horror-comic. But if its treatment ends here, in a flattering and endless fairy-tale – endless in the sense that, like the soap-operas of TV, its situations are forever repeated, and never have real consequences – then maybe the whole subject really ought to be dropped. It is not good for people – so it may be said – to indulge in unrestrained illusion about the past, especially when, as in this case, it is so clearly an anodyne for present ills and disabilities. People, it is said, should rather brace themselves to accept the stark truth, or, acknowledging their weakness, turn their backs on what can't be faced in the past and think only of the present and whatever may be agreeable in the future.

But what is the stark truth? It is, we know, hanging and quartering, slaughter, burning, robbery, starvation, pride, folly, cruelty, weakness. It is expected to be unpleasant; consequently those who don't mind being described as cynics claim to have the key to it. Sentimentalists, in this respect more modest, don't aspire to anything more than what they would *like* to believe, whether true or not. But their views in practice support one another, and the most violent cynics are often, intermittently, the most sentimental. Sentimentality is the tribute that cynicism pays to true feelings. If the stark truth is what the cynic believes, then it is unbearable, and relief must be found in some less horrible aspect of affairs, even though it is not consistent with 'the facts'. So cynics, in their sentimental turn, believe what they know not to be true. It is surely not accidental that the era of unmitigated utilitarianism and its applications, from the Poor Law to the Clearances, was also the time when, among other sentimentalisms, the sugar-coated version of the '45 took over. That it did so was not much help to the victims, those who had gone under in the struggle and its social and economic consequences, but it was of great benefit to the victors who, being by this time incontestably on top and in possession of the varied material spoils, could add to these the flattering conviction of presiding over a pleasing and romantic landscape. This was the time when Highland scenery came into its own, to be valued on its own; people were of less importance, but properly disposed and adjusted, made a suitable contribution to the whole composition.

Sentimentality and utility joined hands in what was perhaps the greatest benefit reaped by the victors from the defeat of the Rising, the addition to their disposable armed force of the very people who had been defeated and crushed. Nothing is stranger (though not without precedent in the history of warfare and conquest) than the swiftness and ease with which the victorious power, soon with other and bloodier wars on its hands, was able to draw upon the resources of manhood and to command the loyalty of the society it had conquered and was in process of destroying – the haemorrhage of Highland blood in America, Europe, and Asia furthering and accelerating the work of destruction.

It was not the first or the last time that 'savages' were discovered to be a 'hardy and intrepid race of men' who could be relied on to serve their masters with fidelity and conquer for them 'in every part of the world', but the speed and manner in which it happened have still, it seems, to be understood and digested.

The psychological processes and economic pressures by which the transference was brought about and continued; the part played by the clan chiefs, both former Jacobite and anti-Jacobite; the combined effects on their followers of opportunity, flattery, and desperation – these make too large and complex a subject to be unravelled here. What may be remarked upon is the effect on received ideas of history and nationhood. The raising of the Highland regiments, their service through nearly 200 years, make a stirring and heroic record – or one at least well furnished with authentic incidents of heroism – and it is, of course, one cherished by posterity with traditional pride. But it must be said (and, I hope, without offence where there is a large emotional investment to this day) that the story of 'the Scottish soldier' is a bitter commentary on the glamour of warfare and the uses to which it can be put by power. And it is precisely those with a glamourised view of the '45 who have found it easiest, making a scarcely perceptible change of step, to be consoled and fortified by the receding spectacle of kilted Highlanders marching away to death on successive battlefields from Ticonderoga to the Somme. The story of the Highland regiments is, to be sure, no more than part of

British military history in the past two centuries, and has no more, perhaps, than its share of the pathos, as well as the horror with which such history is filled. But because of its origins, in Scotland at least it lends itself with peculiar readiness to the emotional slide from the perception of a hard and painful truth into tempting consolation.

Indeed it may well seem that in any genuinely traditional history – the history that belongs in memories as well as books – the long and paradoxical military aftermath of the '45, as Highlanders became the first of the 'martial races' pressed into the service of empire, has got in the way of understanding the event itself. At least until recently much of the sense of nationhood, or of national identity, has been associated with it. A parallel may be assumed between the growth of identity in a nation and in a maturing individual; common experience as well as psychological theory suggests that in both cases the truth and completeness of what is acknowledged is crucial to the kind of identity achieved. Individuals, it is notorious, can cherish a 'false identity' based on a false idea of the same individual's past; the great task of such a person (at any rate according to the prescription of classic psycho-analysis) is to recollect, face, and fully acknowledge as much as possible of his or her 'history', from childhood up. Especially is it important that in this process of recollection painful, repugnant, shameful, and 'unacceptable' memories should be brought to light and given acceptance.

The life through time of a group or nation cannot, it is true, have so neat a beginning and end as an individual's, but in its spiritual growth a closely analogous process can be seen; and the same importance can be attached to discovering matters not so much unknown as overlaid and distorted by forgetfulness and self-deception. It is possible to think of the historian's commitment to 'truth' and to finding out 'what really happened' as the same, even if the aim is not directly therapeutic, as the psychoanalyst's. A people which forgets or ignores its past will have as much difficulty as has a single mortal, deprived of memory, in retaining any sense of identity. But a people sustained by *false* ideas of the past, by illusions of glory or projections of blame, is not in a healthy state either.

The trauma of the '45 doesn't seem as yet to have been (to take use of the jargon a step further) 'worked through'. But perhaps we are a little nearer to the place where this labour can at least begin. It has to be seen not simply as study of what happened then, but of its meaning now: in other words its context is not only supplied by the general history of the mid-eighteenth century, but by the modern world. The catastrophic events of the twentieth century, and especially of the past 50 years, have conditioned our understanding of a slightly more distant past. In the midst of extremes of violence in 'our own' times, conscious both of human inter-dependence and the chronic instability of human institutions, we may find it surprising that, not very long ago, such an episode as the '45 could be removed from any sense of moral participation or given the distant and soothing form of a work of art. Just because we have been overwhelmed by the monstrousness of current events, we can see that enormity doesn't depend upon scale. 'Larger' happenings have made 'smaller' ones more, not less significant: place-names like Auschwitz, Lidice, Katyn, Hiroshima, bring Culloden nearer. It is not any longer possible to think of the Rising and it suppression as aberrations: rebellion, massacre, and deliberate destruction of a society appear to be the norm.

It is just this question which forces itself upon us, whether indeed such acts, which we cannot pretend are not regularly recurrent, obey anything that can be called a rule: whether what appears to be normal can be considered in any way normative. For today not only are we forced to recognise that human beings very commonly behave in these ways, but we respond to the fact with theories of behaviour which seek to subsume it under the heading of *'Natural Law'*. This in turn is one way of imposing a pattern upon history.

It is true that reasoning of this kind is not in itself new. It was expressed with classic succinctness when the social theorists of Athens told the men of Melos that *power over others will always be exercised to the full,* and that there is *no exception to the rule that the strong command and the weak obey.* This formula, it will be recalled, was disputed by the Melians, but was put into practice by the Athenians with the slaughter of all grown males of the island and the sale of the women and children into slavery. General statements of this sort are usually followed by murder.

Because murder is a human act (beasts kill one another but we don't call it murder) it must receive a specifically human justification: elsewhere we note that when the unnamed 'Captain' is instructed to kill the captive Lear and Cordelia, who have lost the battle, he agrees *because* he is a man – 'I cannot draw a cart nor eat dried oats; if it be man's work, I'll do't'. Just so, perhaps, may the redcoats have reassured themselves as they obeyed Cumberland's orders.

All this has been well understood for a long time, and has the traditional instances and proverbial gloss to sustain it. Today our ideas have moved a stage further, to the point where distinctions between mankind and other species are harder to maintain. Sociology and 'socio-biology' can point to behaviour among other animals which, when found in men, is called atrocious or benevolent as the case may be, and is in either case no more than reaction to circumstances. We'll say the accusation of murder must be, dropped. We'll say that a section of the past under the heading of 'the '45' may be accounted for as part of a general system or mechanism in which groups of people, their inter-relationships and means of existence, with all the complexities of language, custom, and modes of property, are interlocked and in motion together under the same common impulse of survival, and to differentiate morally between kinds of behaviour is futile. We'll say it is only necessary to describe how one kind of society, already pushed to the edge of West European history, came into violent contact with another, of rapidly growing power, and was rapidly transformed. The rapidity was such that it involved large-scale robbery, starvation, slaughter, the enforced removal of populations and suppression of custom and the means of group identity, including dress and in due course language. But we'll say that details, incidental to the speed of the process, are in a sense irrelevant to such an account, just as are the accidents of dynastic rivalry which precipitated it.

The assumption is that 'it' – the accelerated destruction of clan society in Scotland, and the slightly more prolonged disintegration of its culture – would 'have happened anyway', which has been a great source of comfort not only for posterity but for some at least at the time. For it was certainly believed by some of the participants, and not all of them on one side, though most obviously among the strong and victorious. When the Duke of Cumberland saw the ragged and famished condition of the men who had dared to oppose a regular and civilised army he knew that his cause was just and his triumph doubly assured; and most of the society at his back agreed with him. A little later Scott's assumption is the same, that what happened was bound to happen, and ought to have happened, in the spread of civilisation and the dominance of wealth and power.

It is a strong position, possession of the actual ground being as in other matters nine points of the law. Those who wish it had not happened as it did, or had not happened at all, are driven to the desperate expedient of imagining other 'possible' outcomes, a diversion which, regrettably, historians of the '45 are especially prone to. What if the march on London had continued? What if the choice of ground on Drummossie Moor had been different, or a pitched battle avoided altogether? It is easy to see and sympathise with the motive for such speculations, but they do nothing to further understanding. As Leo Tolstoy remarked, ridiculing those who try in this way to turn history into a game of chance, 'one cannot invent for a plant new growths, new seeds or flowers which shall be the counterpart of those it already produces.' There is no answer, if one wonders whether this or that might have fallen out otherwise, to the voice which says, Yes, perhaps it might, but it didn't.

Tolstoy (in his Epilogue to *War and Peace)* is a useful cautioner for those who look for meaning or pattern in historical processes. The 'cause of historical events', he tells us, is 'power', but what is power? If it is the will of men exercised on other men, it also has causes, which have other causes, which extend 'to the circle of infinity', beyond the grasp of any human intellect, a historian's or anyone else's.

So for those living consciously through historical events, what strikes them most is accident, pure randomness; most of all in the midst of a battle, where human power over humans seems to be exercised to the full, but makes itself felt as utter chaos. People, as Tolstoy said, become mere molecules, the more so as we get near to them. When we look as closely as distance allows at distinguishable individuals, the known and named actors in the '45, their actions are apparently nothing but automatic jostling and rebounding: the hunting of the Prince in the heather, the misunderstandings, mistakes, mistrusts, the blind-man's-buff of pursuers and pursued, seem as near, perhaps, as human activities can get to pure Brownian movement.

What distinguishes the deeds of human individuals as we get close to them is that they demonstrate, not the existence of meaning in history, but the longing for it. The actors have longed for it, as we continue to long. Any meaning or purpose imposed on events from without is by definition beyond the grasp of those immersed in them. But the desire for it can be recorded, and is put to the test by events themselves.

The strong command and the weak obey, but they are remembered differently. Though many people, obviously, did well out of the defeat of the Highland army and the break-up of clan life, theirs is not the side that meaning-seekers fasten upon. Culloden has its place on the maps and in our minds not as a victory but as a defeat. This is the point to which both 'history' and 'story' persistently return us, and if we want to take bearings from it, its nature cannot be forgotten. If national pride and identity are to be fostered by contemplation of it, in what way? However defined, even explicitly as 'moral', victory is not just; rather justice is 'fugitive from the camp of victory'. After his famous and noisily acclaimed victory, justice unquestionably fled from Cumberland's camp, whether or not she be supposed to have had a lodging there before. But where did she go?

Is it possible to adopt Pilsudski's motto, "To be defeated and not to surrender, that is victory."? Certainly, it seems forcibly to express the spirit of another nation, Poland, preserved through disasters which multiply appallingly the worst of Scottish experience. But victory is a word to be used warily, even in such a paradoxical way, (and we remember that the man who so used it sought victory, and sometimes gained it, by orthodox methods whenever he could.)

There were possibly more among the Prince's followers than in the government army who were there because they truly believed their cause was just: it was a proof of their sincerity that many like Lord George Murray ('the just man', the Highlanders called him) were engaged although they never expected it to succeed. Lord Pitsligo brought his followers on an enterprise he knew was doomed simply because, as he said, 'Oh Lord, thou knowest our cause is just. Gentlemen, march!' If he and others allowed themselves occasionally to be sustained by hope, some may also have recalled the continuation of the Melian Dialogue, and the retort of the Athenians that 'hope is an expensive commodity, and those who are risking their all at one cast find out what it means only when they are already ruined.' Like the Melians, however, they went on.

And it is this readiness to take part in a struggle known to be hopeless that most attracts us to the Jacobites of 1745: whether it was through attachment to a 'rightful king', or a particular idea of monarchy or church government, or simply for the sake of 'honour' (all of which could certainly be matched by some on the other side), it is because the best who were so moved rightly reckoned the odds against them, and persisted, that they are admirable. But in defeat what happens? The 'cause', just or not, is broken past mending; justice, driven from the field, is now with the defeated, not on account of the cause for which they fought, but simply because they are defeated. As the strong command and the weak obey they can no longer hope to command justly, nor can they expect justice to be done to them by the victors. They possess nothing which should persuade the strong – nothing but their lives, which may so easily be taken from them. They have become suppliants. That is why they continue to trouble us.

They join the innumerable throng of victims of injustice who hold out their hands beseechingly to posterity, a crowd so huge that individuals are at first difficult to distinguish, but become visible as we pay close attention to them. It is because the defeated of the '45 are one small group, of one small nation, that their supplication can become real to us, and can in a sense be answered. It is answered partly by the very enterprise of historical inquiry, to put the record as straight as possible and, as Hamlet asked of Horatio, report their cause aright. But this 'justice at the bar of history', always provisional, is not all that the suppliants ask. It isn't simply that they beg to be remembered, and remembered as they would wish (not always compatibly with justice). It is that they should be taken into our lives.

"History to the defeated
Can say Alas, but cannot help nor pardon", said Auden.

I do not think it is true, or if it is true, then it shows clearly what is inadequate about the idea of 'History.' It depends on the notion (mentioned at the outset of these remarks) that the past is a self-contained and separate region, static and unalterable: those who inhabit it are and must be untouched by whatever we do or say. What has happened has happened, we tell ourselves, even God can't alter that. But to say so, whether of an individual life or the life of a community, ignores the continuity of time. A life, or a collectivity of lives, is continually changing, and can only be described as 'unalterable' when it is 'complete'. And when will 'History' be complete? And until that unimaginable moment, as part of a process not yet finished, the present can and does modify the past all the time. God who (as we assume) sees the whole as mortals cannot, is shaping it as men and women pass, through their free and alterable lives.

Such an admission of continuity, which takes for granted the organic connection between past and present, forefathers and posterity, is natural in a 'traditional' society. In essence it is because history is not regarded as a series of external events but belongs to the family, in which time itself is measured in family terms, in our fathers' time or being 'before our grandfathers' time'. It is reinforced by custom and ritual, by the repetition of legend and recitation of genealogies. But this deep 'respect for tradition', which looks like inertia, is in origin no more than due acknowledgment of responsibility. We speak much today of 'responsibility to the future', and it is obviously true that, since we are in the position to abort any possible future, we had better act responsibly. But our responsibility is first of all to the past: it is only by taking that seriously, and by acknowledging the debt that is owed, that any real value can be assigned to the future so precariously in our hands. If we think of those whose appeal is made to us simply out of their oppression and suffering, it will not be so easy, perhaps, to throw away all that they suffered for.

The appeal is for and on behalf of justice, the advocate of the injured and oppressed. Does that mean we should take sides in the old quarrel – that writing and re-writing the history of the '45 must be as partisan as were the contenders of the time? Something different is needed, and the best model is perhaps not historiography at all. The *Iliad* is not precisely a history-book, but in it can be distinguished, it seems, what most of all we should require of historians and of ourselves as we read about 'history'. In the Iliad (said Simone Weil):

> 'Justice and love, for which there can hardly be a place in this picture of extremes and unjust violence, yet shed their light over the whole without ever being discerned otherwise than by the accent. Nothing precious is despised, whether or not destined to perish. The destitution and misery of all men is shown without dissimulation or disdain, no man is held either above or below the common level of all men, and whatever is destroyed is regretted. The victors and vanquished are shown equally near to us, in an equal perspective, and seem, by that token, to be the fellows as well of the poet as of the auditors.'

Not that we expect, or even wish historians to be Homers; but it is in that spirit that, contemplating the '45 – another war of not numerous peoples, quite a long time ago – we want it to be written about, and will not complain that it has been written about a great deal already.

The nature of the debt, and the evident fact that it cannot be paid in partisanship, are well illustrated in one of the traditional stories about Culloden – not 'historical', indeed historically impossible in some of its details, but true surely to the Homeric spirit. It tells of the murderous aftermath of the battle: a dispute, it is said, arose between 'General Campbell' (who wasn't actually there; maybe it was his son, Colonel Jack Campbell) and Cumberland himself concerning the comparative martial virtues of the defeated, starved and ragged Highlanders and the victorious Redcoats. Cumberland, contemputous of the vanquished, boasted that 'one Englishman is better than three of them', and Campbell, nettled, made a wager by which one of a batch of prisoners should be matched against a select champion of the Red Army.'There are but 15 young lads together, and although they are as tired as they are, I could choose one out of these who would fight anyone that you could choose from any regiment under your command.' If Cumberland won the bet, the lives of all 15 would be forfeit; if he lost, they would go free. A swordsman 'as good as they thought was to be found in the English army' was sent for, the prisoners chose a representative from among themselves, and the ordeal-duel began, with the Highlander giving ground and merely defending himself, until he was reminded that death and life depended on him –

'The Highlander closed up with the Englishman then, and it

was but a short time until he struck him with the sword and killed him. When General Campbell saw that the Englishman had fallen, he went where the Highlander was, clapped him on the shoulder, and said to him, ''Go home now and thank your mother, because she gave you such good milk.'

The immediate result, according to the tale, was disastrous. The 15 prisoners went free, but Cumberland was so enraged 'because the Englishman whom he thought to be the bravest in the whole English army was killed by a little Highlander' that he gave orders forthwith for the slaughter of the wounded and the hanging of prisoners 'without mercy.' Thus the story 'explains', in the common manner of folk-lore, what history has recorded. The explanation may well be thought unnecessary, since the behaviour of Cumberland is so far from unique in British or any other national record that it could be called normal, in the sense already referred to. But the interesting thing is that it was *not* considered normal; that it actually did rouse indignation at the time and has continued to do so, demanding, among other reactions, some such explanatory account as the tale supplies.

But the implications of the tale do not end there, and reveal themselves only by degrees; for whether it is wholly apocryphal or not, the more one contemplates it the more it has to say. Courage is there, enhanced by showing in the defeated, and by the contrast between silent resolution and vainglorious boasting; there is also the generosity of the Campbell commander (whoever he was) who, as a fellow-Highlander, is able to recognise the human worth of his enemies. The indifference of warfare, in which men's lives may be carelessly bartered for trifles, and the humanity which endeavours to mitigate it, are both within the story's frame; as Simone Weil found in the *Iliad*, 'nothing precious is despised'. So on the whole it is an encouraging and consoling story, the kind that people cherish to salve the hurt of atrocious wounds. The heart of it is in the proverbial pay-off line, 'thank your mother, because she gave you such good milk.'

A whole culture is accommodated in these words, with assumptions about family custom and the rearing of children as it were built in; we remember the importance of bonds between those who shared milk from the same breast, whether of mother or foster-mother. We see the whole of clan society, the fraternal society of children, held together by the 'natural' obligations of kinship. Behind this patrilineal relationship we can glimpse the truly mythological relation to mothers, including the Earth herself, who nourishes heroes, and receives them.

The scope of the story also includes human cruelty and revengefulness, and the reactions of a society which *doesn't* recognise natural bonds, nor any bonds at all between men and women save those of force and obedience to force, either nakedly revealed in armed might or transmitted by the power of money. Whether or not the story 'explains' it, the defeated *were* butchered, their homes plundered, their mutual cohesion, tenacious though it was, worn down and broken. Clan society, with all its human failings and human virtues, was destroyed; other destructive processes, set in motion by the '45 or accelerated by its violent impact, have followed down to this day. We are left with a debt, and an obligation, The debt is simply that of grief: nature may suggest that grief passes, but grievous events do not really become less so with passage of time. I do not believe it is sentimentality or hypocrisy to say that if we want to understand the historical reality − the particularity − of the '45, we must share the painful emotions of *The Lyon in Mourning* and Smollett's *Tears of Scotland.*

The obligation of gratitude has to be paid in a different way. There are plenty of things to be grateful for in the history of the '45, as of other historical catastrophes. We are grateful that it was an occasion not only for much evil but also for good − good which stands the test because it showed in acts, on both sides, performed not simply without reward but in ordinary terms uselessly. The whole enterprise may well be described as useless, a reckless adventure fired by dynastic intrigue and power-politics, forcibly wished upon the participants without regard for consequences. Weighed against the consequences, the 'cause' is as absurdly inadequate as Helen's beauty and Menelaus's cuckoldry. If the triviality is outweighed by reason, it is in inverse proportion to the 'greatness' of the actor, from top to bottom. At the top the generosity and chivalry of the Young Pretender, attractive though they be, seem cheap enough, paid for as they were chiefly in the sufferings of others. The hyperbole of MacPherson of Breakachie, called away to assist the fugitive Prince and replying to his reproachful wife − she 'having so many children and being then also big with child' − that 'I put no value upon you or your bairns unless you can bring me forth immediately thirty thousand men in arms ready to serve my master' − is nowadays more revolting than endearing.

But at the bottom the loyalty of unnumbered and mostly unnamed men and women, who refused bribery and defied threats and took the consequences on themselves, shines as brightly as ever, and the more clearly for being manifestly in a 'lost' or useless cause. From a cloud of unknown witnesses particular examples stand out, poignantly invidivual and also pointing beyond themselves; named and unnamed officers of Cumberland's forces who risked much to help prisoners or wounded and who in some cases succeeded in saving them; the resourceful and undaunted Anne MacKay who also helped fugitives after Culloden, and when seized herself used every means, from feigned stupidity to plain stark endurance, to resist the torments and guile of her questioners; the messenger Ewan MacVie, lashed and beaten to death for his silence, who answered those who were urging him to save his life by giving information 'that his life signified nothing in comparison to those his confession might betray'.

The extraordinary nobility of this reply brings us up standing − even in an age which, disastrous as it is, is plentifully furnished with occasions for like constancy. It is truly a gift, of as great value now as then, and even more as it is detached in our eyes from its immediate 'cause'. Not the fervour of Jacobitism, nor devotion to the Prince as Prince, nor even clan loyalty draws us now but a quality which perhaps was clothed in these reasons at the time but survives them as they fall away and shows naked and pure in a new context.

In this present context, provided by our own lives and times, we are bound to say that the loyalty and strength nurtured by mother's milk, still needful, are not enough. That moral obligations are not circumscribed by kinship was obvious before as now – the story of Breakachie's wife underlines it – and the conflicts thereby produced were not less painful. But nowadays we distrust any attempt to resolve these by devising a hierarchy of obligation, in which observance of the 'higher' absolves a breach of the 'lower'. We are not to be tempted by the greater good of class, group, or country, certainly not by the greatest good of the greatest number; we are especially suspicious of the transcendent good which demands, as means, evil to be enacted upon others. Conscious as we are how far zeal of this kind may go, from the general who ordered the destruction of a village in order to save it, to plans for immolating whole populations in the name of popular government, we want to say that no cause on earth can justly demand the sacrifice of others. The very word sacrifice, we'll say, is thereby misused: no offering that is not voluntary can be sanctified or can express relationship between responsible creatures and the divine. We simply will not swallow the story of Abraham and Isaac except as one of the delusion from which, happily, the Lord awakened Abraham in the nick of time.

Mother's milk, the nurture of nature, gives the sanction of natural law. By their mothers' milk infant boys grow into young men strong and brave enough to fight and save their friends, and even on occasion – for it is after all the milk of human kindness – to be merciful to their enemies. The question is whether, so nourished, men and women can go beyond the law of nature, and so change it: for human nature is the changeable part of natural law.

That surely is where the study of history, and especially where it is as closely as possible 'our' history, can be of use. If we are to wake from our delusions this time, we must look closely, and feelingly, at grief and loss, the willingness to suffer and the endurance of suffering. Everything in our lives, said Simone Weil, is subject to 'gravity', the ineluctable force of circumstance and the way one thing follows another. We continually try to overcome gravity by force, lifting ourselves by our bootstraps: every attempt to 'make history' partakes in greater or lesser degree from such wilfulness, whether in efforts to 'push history forward', or hold it up, or even (as in the case of the '45 Rising) to turn it back. And in all such cases, it seems, human will is not absolutely impotent, but powerless to direct events; if events have a line of direction it is beyond human understanding. By a violent concentration of will a man may effect a small shift of balance, as someone dislodges a pebble on a mountainside: of the landslip which follows, and which carries him and others away, he has neither foreknowledge nor control. In the landslides of history the strong and the weak are swept away together, but the weak are naturally underneath, where the force of historical gravity is most crushing. They cannot resist it. They can try, and most do, to deflect it upon other bodies. But they can, in rare cases, accept it and receive its full force in themselves.

Those who do so are not history-makers nor history-avoiders. They have been in the thick of it, and speak to those who remain in the thick. Because of their extraordinary moral attraction they make the connection between then and now real and personal, not simply a chain of cause and effect. We won't say that they show 'the meaning of history'. But they reassure us that meanings can be found, in which we may share. Meaning is so slippery a word that it requires always to be nailed down, to a particular time, a place, a person, these particular actions and passions.

That the strong command and the weak obey can still be an overall description of historical events; but overall meanings are no use to us. On closer inspection, it is not true. In detail, the strong *think* that they command, but their commands pass out of their control. The weak may obey as best they can, but not always. They may choose to obey something other than the commands of the strong, and in doing so, and in willingness to suffer the consequences, they have both discovered meaning and proved its particular, personal truth. That is all we have any right, or need to ask, and it is what holds us, as it brings history and story together.

'THAINIG AN SAOR
by
James Fraser of Inverinate

THIS STORY was told to me by my grandmother, Morag Mackenzie of Polbain, Coigach. Morag had a very good memory and a fund of interesting stories.

A joiner from Coigach who lived above Dornie Mor joined the Prince's army in 1745. He was captured and imprisoned in the hulks in London and from there taken to the West Indies with other Scots. He worked there for some time and would probably have spent many years there if he had not been discovered to be a joiner. One day he was asked to carry out some work in the Governor of the Island's house. The Governor was one of the Mackenzies of Tarbert and discovered that the joiner was from Coigach. Coigach had been part of the Cromartie Estates and the Governor took pity upon one of the family tenants and arranged for a passage home by ship to Southampton. The joiner walked from Southampton to Coigach, a difficult and dangerous journey. When he reached home he cut across the hills from the township of Achnahaird and descended behind his house. He reached his house and opening the door greeted his wife with the words:

"A' Chairistiona Dhonn, thainig an saor".
(Brown-haired Christina, the joiner has come.)

My grandmother always ended the story by commenting that he was lucky that his wife had not married in the meantime, as many women in her position had given up their husbands as dead.

KINLOCHMOIDART'S WELCOME
by
Elizabeth Blackburn

DURING THE OCCUPATION OF Carlisle by the Jacobite army, a message came to some of Clanranald's regiment who were billeted in a house, asking them to be quieter as the woman of the house was about to give birth. After the baby had been born Donald MacDonald of Kinlochmoidart, an A.D.C. to the Prince, asked to see the child, and taking her wrapped her in a plaid, declaring that if ever she or hers came to Moidart they would be made welcome.

MacDonald of Kinlochmoidart was later captured and executed in October 1746; his four brothers, one of whom was a doctor, were all captains and lieutenants in Clanranald's regiment, but survived the rising.

The baby born at Carlisle was the great-grandmother of my great-grandmother, who with her husband did come north and settled at Roshven on the neighbouring peninsular to Moidart. The family have lived there ever since.

Two very old plaids were handed down in the family: one a woollen one, which wore out, and one of silk which was made into a baby's dress. This I discovered recently to be of Murray of Atholl tartan.

Elizabeth Blackburn or Grey
of Roshven and Garrygualach.